Lupus Novice

Lupus
Novice

TOWARD SELF-HEALING

Laura Chester

Foreword by Jesse Stoff, M.D.

STATION HILL

BARRYTOWN, LTD.

Published under the Station Hill Openings imprint of Barrytown, Ltd., Barrytown, New York, 12507, as a project of The Institute for Publishing Arts, Inc., a not-for-profit, federally tax exempt, educational organization.

Grateful acknowledgement is due to the New York State Council on the Arts for partial financial support of the publishing program of The Institute for Publishing Arts.

Online catalogue and purchasing: http://www.stationhill.org
E-mail: publishers@stationhill.org
E-mail address of Laura Chester: word@laurachester.com

Cover and Design by Susan Quasha
Cover photograph by Sabine Vollmer von Falken

Acknowledgements:

Selections of this work were first published in*: 19 New American Poets of the Golden Gate,* edited by Philip Dow, Harcourt Brace, 1984.

The author offers special thanks to:

Dr. Jonathan Ellman, Carol Callopy, Dr. William Seaman, Dr. Lionel Sorenson, Dr. Denny Tuffanelli, Veronica Reif, Dr. Roger Iliff, Dr. Roberet Gorter, Saskia Van As, Michelle Young, Dr. Philip Incao, Elizabeth Schlieben, Penelope Young, Dr. Philip Volastro, and Zoee Esty.

The publisher gratefully acknowledges permission to quote from the following texts:

Paul Tillich, *The Meaning of Health: The Relation of Religion and Health,* North Atlantic Books, Berkeley, English translation Copyright, 1981, all rights reserved. Thomas Merton, *The Dark Path,* Copyright held by The Estate of Thomas Merton and New Directions Publishing, Inc., all rights reserved.

Library of Congress Cataloging-in-Publication Data
Chester, Laura.
     Lupus novice : toward self-healing / Laura Chester : foreword by Jesse Stoff.
       p. cm.
     Includes bibliographical references (p.).
     ISBN 1-58177-020-0 (alk. paper)
     1. Chester, Laura—Health. 2. Systemic lupus erythematosus—Patients—United States—Biography. 3. Authors, American—Biography. I. Title.
RC924.5.L85C48   1999
362.1'9677—dc21
   [b]   99-11490
                                         CIP

Manufactured in the United States of America.

to my sister
Cia Chester McKoy

Contents

Foreword

JESSE A. STOFF, M.D.

Friendly Fire:
Transforming the Challenge of Autoimmune Disease

Lupus is one member of the family of "incurable" autoimmune diseases that also include juvenile diabetes, rheumatoid arthritis, multiple sclerosis, and myasthenia, to name a few. These are diseases which primarily involve a major dysfunction of the immune system. Currently, conventional therapeutic strategies center around the use of anti-inflammatory drugs to quench the fires of internal immolation. As the destruction progresses, stronger drugs may be used to counter-attack, stop, and destroy the immune system. Immuno-suppressive drugs like prednisone and methotrexate are often used, but in many or most cases, the short and long term side effects may be permanent and worse than the disease itself. This direction of therapy is aimed at the proximal cause of the symptoms (immune system dysfunction) and is hoped to offer immediate, albeit short term, relief that can, in fact, be life-saving but is not curative and is far from healing, as it does nothing to address the deeper causes of the disease and thus offers no hope for permanent cure.

The immune system is one of the fundamental systems of the human body, the first elements of which come to us as a gift from our mother through the placenta. It is a system which is enmeshed and highly integrated throughout our being. It is one of our unconscious senses, constantly "tasting" our blood as it searches for foreign infiltrators and, once identified, liquidates them without a second thought.

Normally, when we are threatened by disease, the immune system responds protectively with hungry macrophages and an army of trained white blood cells (lymphocytes) which function like independent units of the special forces. They are armed with pitch-forked antibodies and special enzymes, and are programmed to relentlessly seek out and destroy the intruders. The intricate web of defense and communication usually works magnificently well against viruses, bacteria and other trespassers. The armada of lymphocytes floating through our circulatory system and all other spaces of the body, is capable of quickly recognizing an intruder, telegraphing the alarm to the rest of the defense corps, and then zeroing in and destroying it with the precision of a laser-guided Tomahawk missile; yet, in growing numbers of people (predominantly women) the battle orders are garbled and chaos follows. Our legions of lymphocytes then become destroying angels, delivering destruction and even death in a consuming rain of "friendly fire"—the terrible phenomenon of getting shot by soldiers fighting on your own side.

On a biochemical level, the immune system responds to and is affected by our internal and external environment. For some people viruses and spirochetes (like those responsible for Lyme disease) can attack and systematically alter and dismantle the immune system from within. For others, toxins and metals can be ingested or absorbed from our environment and poison us by damaging our free-floating friends. Radiation can nuke and destroy our immune system from the outside. We are, however, more than the sum of our biochemical reactions. Research in this area has begun to show how psychological influences impact our immune system. This has given birth to an entirely new area of medical understanding called "psychoneuroimmunology." This level of psycho-immunological function has been shown to have a direct impact on the rate of healing that can be achieved.

Autoimmune diseases, like the one affecting Laura, will ride the crest of the next wave of human afflictions. Already their occurrence is rapidly rising to "epidemic proportions, affecting 8 million Americans"—so laments the Lupus Foundation in its recent literature and appeals for increased research funding.

Autoimmune disease: self against self, brother against brother, civil war.... The theme is an old one, probably as old as homo-sapiens itself, but now the war is different: it is within. The battles are infinitesimally small, yet to you, their host, the outcome can be overwhelmingly devastating, debilitating and deadly. Any of your organs can be attacked, resulting in inflammation, dysfunction, and destruction by the very elements of your being, your immune system, which is charged with the duty of protecting you. Suddenly, you are in a state of crisis.

Since the beginning of recorded time, a state of crisis has always preceded an evolutionary step. The bigger the crisis, the greater the subsequent evolutionary leap. For example, if we study the fossil record, we find gaps between species, as if the evolutionary streams were punctuated, giving time for consolidation and renewal. The same process is operative in our lives. If you reflect back through the chapters of your life, you may find a chapter of abuse, alcoholism, depression, bulimia,

CFS; or perhaps you will discover something more subtle like a longing in your soul to be an artist, or you may find yourself on a quest for the meaning of life. Then, usually when things are at their worst and most chaotic, you suddenly wake up one day and open your eyes, as if for the first time, and realize that today is the first day of the rest of your life. You *can* take responsibility for yourself to make your life your own.

The duty of our immune system is to distinguish self from non-self and to respond accordingly; however, when the self is in crisis, when we have wandered off of our life's path, the boundary between self and non-self becomes as fuzzy and impermanent as shifting political borders. Without clear boundaries and a well-defined sense of purpose, the battle plan for the legions of immune cells becomes confused, the wrong target is attacked and self destroys self. In the throes of a rampant autoimmune disease, sheets of skin may fall away like the hide of a molting snake, bones may become gnarled, organ functions may falter and death may result.

In spite of all this, healing can occur, damage can be reversed, you can live through it and then happily ever after. But it takes more than pills, powders and potions—it takes a commitment to yourself and your healing. You must become consciously engaged in the battle and actively seek to reduce your level of stress and reconnect to your path and purpose just as Laura did.

Your path in life is influenced by many different factors: where you were born, your parents, the pollution in your environment, the metals in your mouth, your beliefs about religion, politics and ... yourself. Inlaid within the tides of our time is the ongoing process of your own evolution. So too do you evolve emotionally, as evidenced by your own changing political views, changes in hobbies and interests, or your relationships. Personal evolution is normal, healthy and tension-relieving; it dissolves crisis.

The world is in crisis: the environment is so polluted that, in some areas, it cannot support human life anymore. Societies are in crisis everywhere. To an individual with an autoimmune disease, the problem is no less overwhelming. A crisis has occurred and is "tolerated" within the immune system. Regardless of the specific autoimmune disease, part of the immune system has become an aggressor that attacks components of the self. The behavior is "tolerated" by a failure of other segments of the immune system to recognize and terminate the unwanted aggressive activity. Thus, the immune system has produced and now permits the rogue behavior to manifest in a myriad of associated diseases. You must find ways to get out of the way of your body's natural tendency to heal.

Through Laura's example and courage to face the crisis you will see that personal growth and development is not only possible psychodynamically and spiritually, but is critical for the re-establishment and maintenance of health. Through each chapter in one's life, from the healthy extroverted exuberance of youth, to the ideal penitent wisdom of the elders, existential questions come to the fore, either consciously or unconsciously, and must be reconciled in order to peacefully continue along one's path in life.

If questions or issues are buried and not answered, then tension develops and a crisis ensues which slows the healing process. The questions are as old as man himself. Religions, families, societal customs, cults and governments have, in the past, served as a source for the answers. But now, *"the times, they are a-changin'"*; human consciousness is evolving faster. You must now gather the courage, through prayer and meditation, to look within yourself for most of the answers. Many of you will find that it is your relationship to the "authority structure," be it a family dynamic or the expectations of a male dominated society, that has prematurely stopped or encumbered your path of personal evolution. So be it—but deal with it ... NOW!!!!

Through examples of consciously addressing the natural process of personal evolution, this wonderful and enlightening book offers help, hope, and guidance to those who suffer from the Lupus.

Tucson, AZ
December 17, 1998

Introduction

On my thirty-third birthday, towards the end of my first flare-up with
s.l.e., I received a letter from a woman writer whose encouragement of
my literary work made me regret that I'd ignored that part of my life
during the previous two years. As she entreated me to face my present
condition, I felt the urgency to begin this book. She wrote:

> Now you are very sick with this strange disease, about
> which no one knows much, and I wonder why you. There
> must be some reason; disasters cannot be so randomly
> dealt. And I think it's because you of all people, will write
> about this. With all the energy left you, I know you will
> make sense of what is happening to you and so many other
> women.

So I began to confront both the old and new self, the estranged writer,
as well as this strange invalid self, a true novice in the world of disease.
But I realized, as I began, that if I could give back a reflection, to those
who weren't able to express such painful places, seeing them clearly
before they slipped past, then perhaps this work would diminish the
state of aloneness one enters when a disease such as lupus is named.

Much of the existing literature on this auto-immune disease,
seemed to stress how Systemic Lupus Erythematosus was best known
for its confusing, illusive symptoms. No two cases appeared to be the
same. One felt even further isolated within the disease itself. But I still
hold to the belief that we have much in common, a lot worth talking
about.

I wanted to transform that polite, embarrassed, solitary silence into a
greater social awareness. I hoped that a degree of identification would
lessen the negative aspects of encountering any serious illness, helping to alleviate fear, making room for a heightened response to the
challenge.

This book illustrates some of the healing alternatives, as well as
methods of traditional care, not as a guide on How-To-Get-Well, not
as a proposal of a particular plan, but as an example of one anxious, yet
hopeful search, a conscious effort to explore available realms, with a
certainty that demanded I do all that I could in the face of the word—
"Incurable."

I personally don't believe that any disease is truly incurable. I think
that label leads many patients to make a similar search, going from

doctor to doctor, in hopes that some answer will be found, "out there." I did find this journey to be illuminating, and I did receive much reassuring care, but again and again, I found that I was being redirected back to my own self. I had to look inward, rather than solely attempting to escape the situation by searching outwardly for some cure or solution.

All along I think I realized that I had to confront more than just the physical realm, my sick body, and though this was a big struggle for me, it eventually lent me strength. My leaning toward the healing alternatives, and in particular, an anthroposophical approach to illness, stemmed from this desire to be well on a deeper level.

I abstained from cortisone drugs for so long, because of the dangerous side-effects, and because I was aware that cortisone was no ultimate cure, that it merely suppressed symptoms, and postponed the confrontation. But finally, when I did take prednisone, I was extremely grateful for its existence. It helped stop the debilitating pain and allowed me to continue. As I regained strength, I returned to alternative methods, and found that I could even begin taking a regular regimen of homeopathic medicine while easing off my allopathic drugs. Perhaps that overlapping helped me to achieve this present remission.

There are no absolutes in the world of disease. Each person finds her own way. I would only encourage doctors and family to be supportive and nonjudgmental. I also hope that the articulation of my particular journey will help others involved with chronic disease, for we are all faced with similar emotional and spiritual problems, when the physical body undergoes attack. Disease only heightens the process we all inevitably face. Lupus, like all threatening diseases, brings up that primal fear of the unknown, which is the future, and which includes our faith and death and all we love. But even fears can be transformed. So too, this book began to chronicle, one step at a time, the unknown as it became known to me.

I

Naming It

The Beach

August, 1980, La Jolla, California

Queen palms provide no shade in Southern California. No escape, no hiding. Sidewalk, stucco, sand and surf all multiply the brightness, and those Spanish walls at blue noon, seem made for a wealth of bougainvillea. Bare feet. Hot ramps. Table tops of glass. "The beach is best in August." So there we were at La Jolla Shores, Clovis becoming so large and daring for his six years, learning how to catch a wave on his new styrofoam bellyboard, while ten month old Ayler and I basked, crawled and patty caked in the sand. Ayler wore a huge bonnet and long-sleeved shirt to protect his delicate skin, but I was enjoying the roast, exposure, the smell of cocoa butter, keeping one eye forever on the waves.

Though the afternoon was still intense, we headed home, sand weary. Back at the house, long damp towels, buckets and bags came spilling out. Off to the tub for a cleansing splash and a rinse of swimming trunks. Clovis peeled off the t-shirt he'd been wearing and his belly was streaked a shocking red. I panicked—*blood poisoning*. We rushed everyone back into the black Fiat with its scorching seats, flying up the hill to Scripps Emergency.

When the dermatologist arrived, he took a quick but careful look at Clovis' chest, and said that it wasn't serious, probably just a contact reaction from his bellyboard. Of course we were greatly relieved. But then, just as the doctor was leaving, I caught his attention again, asking, "Do you have any idea what this is?" I pointed out the crusty lesion on my left cheek. "It seems like it's been there for months." He looked closely at the small dry red area on my face, and then I also showed him the itchy scabby scales I'd been scratching on my upper arms since spring. The dermatologist squinted in close, as if he were taking a microscopic look.

"I think this might be discoid lupus," he said quietly. "It could be very serious. Where are you from, Berkeley? You should have this looked into immediately when you get home."

The tests were complicated, he said, and I should have my own doctor. It might be serious. It looked like *lupus*. I felt named. Almost a different person. Stunned by the light.

But discoid lupus was different, wasn't it? I'd heard one gruesome story about a girl with lupus. It had made a horror newsprint impression on my mind. *This* was certainly something else, yet I was vague, still on vacation, only beginning to sense the tension of possibility.

My sister-in-law, Michele, sent me off to the local health food store to buy a jar of Paba Cream for sun protection. Standing on the corner of the busy boulevard, ready to cross over towards the ocean, I unscrewed the small white jar and dabbed some tentatively on my cheeks. It didn't seem wrong that this was happening to me, but expected, as if an anticipated phase of my life had begun. Shadows on high. I was aware of myself with an almost adolescent self-consciousness—So *this* is my body my face my soul. I always knew I had something in store.

Walking the two blocks to the surf, past the tiny immaculate front gardens, pinched into shape, I kicked along in the sand with the rhythm of the rollers, picking my path along the fresh wet edge toward Marine Street, vaguely nauseous and vulnerable in the sun. I admired my own tan arms, how gold my ring looked, how white my nails. The Last Sun Tan. There could be worse things, right? Yet still my emotional shadow slunk back like a shunted kid, kicked out of parental radiance, not allowed to play outside with the others for a while.

Back to Berkeley

September, Berkeley

As soon as we returned home, I made an appointment with a dermatologist at Kaiser, a large health maintenance organization. After a few weeks wait, I went in to see Dr. Neigh, and told him what the doctor had said at Scripps, in La Jolla.

"Yes," he corroborated, rolling his chair back, "you do have discoid lupus." He was looking at me with a certain smugness, from four feet away in a rather dim office, and I wondered if he'd have diagnosed me so easily if I hadn't helped him out.

"Don't you want to do some tests, to make sure? I thought it might be complicated."

"We'll do some tests," he nodded, opening a huge tome, glancing back up at me as if I were the cause for his bored aggravation. Then suddenly he switched into lecture gear. "You know there are two kinds of lupus, discoid lupus and systemic lupus erythematosus. SLE, the more serious form of the disease, is fatal."

Fatal?

He went on to describe SLE as a disease with no cure, no hope, and then shaking his head gravely, "The medicines are even worse than the disease."

Worse than fatal?

"But you only have discoid lupus," he assured me. "And yet you have to be careful, because if you aggravate the discoid form, you can end up with systemic lupus. So... now, do you have any children?"

I was numb. I felt a prickle of animosity marching up my spine, urging me to react. "Yes, I have two boys."

"Well that's all. No more children. Two is enough."

I was flabbergasted. We'd just been talking about a girl.

"And what's most important, is that you don't go outside during daylight hours."

"What do you mean?" Incredulous, I almost laughed in his face.

"I mean you stay inside. Period. You have two children. You have a reason to live."

This was too much. Was he just trying to scare me? He hadn't even taken a blood test. What if I didn't have discoid lupus. What if I *did* have SLE? "Before staying out of the sun for the rest of my life," I blurted, "I guess I want to be sure about what I have."

"We'll make sure. You can come back, just make an appointment," he waved towards the door, "and we'll do a biopsy."

"How do you do that?"

"Just a little cut, this big," he measured with his fingernail, a tiny hunk, and then tapped his cheek, meaning, *my* cheek. He proceeded to write out an order for blood tests. "We should find out about these in ten days or so."

"Thanks," I inhaled, keeping my breath tight in my chest, screwed way back up and in there, battling with the gush that wanted to exhale out in a gale of grievance.

I held it back until I pulled into our driveway. My good friend, Summer, was standing there in obvious concern, while Geoff sat on the steps, not looking up, reading a letter. I got out of the car, took one look at both of them and broke into tears.

Geoff thought I was being hysterical. But that word fatal kept working on my inner ear. Why should the doctor set that kind of worry on my shoulders, and why wasn't my husband worrying a little more for me. He refused to believe it, refused to baby my agonies during the next two weeks of waiting. My girl friends were more serious and sympathetic. When Gloria called, Geoff told her, "They've given Laura three months." She was horrified by his joking.

I think this was the first time in my life that my mood had turned morbid. I had discovered a black calla growing too close to home. I was no longer in my twenties, where I could just mosey along, happily contaminating my body, thinking it would last forever. Mine wouldn't. I was now in my thirties. Magnolias turned brown in my mind. Ferns withered into fetal curls, burnt dry and brittle. I found myself crying, scared and angry, curled up in bed, trying to retreat back into a place of safety. *Life Between Death and Rebirth,* by Rudolf Steiner, lay open on my bedside table. The bed lay open also, as I burrowed into it. Far away as I could.

Dermatological
October, San Francisco

Finally, after two weeks of waiting, my blood tests came back and I cleared, no SLE. Still, I wanted to see a lupus specialist, and found the name of a very reputable dermatologist through a geneticist at UCB.

Summer accompanied me to San Francisco for my first office visit. Nice to have her moral support. She was now big and pregnant, and having her with me made it feel like an outing. It also helped to have another ear, to compare what was said afterwards.

Together we nearly filled up Dr. Tuffanelli's tiny office, but as soon as we sat down, he put me at ease. Of course I needn't worry about this fatality business. I told him I would prefer it if he could do the biopsy. Rather than scarring and disfiguring my face, he decided to take a sample from my upper arm, which also had the discoid lesions. He used a simple device that resembled a hole punch to pop out a crater of skin.

He felt that I should have several more specific blood tests to make sure that SLE wasn't a factor. "Patients with extensive skin lesions are more likely to have internal manifestations of SLE," the Merck Manual read. "Though the disease is limited to the skin in 90% of patients with typical Discoid Lupus, approximately 10% eventually develop varying degrees of systemic manifestations; approximately 5% develop SLE even when an initial study does not suggest systemic disease. Since the cutaneous lesions of DLE and SLE may be identical, a patient presenting with typical discoid lesions must be evaluated to determine whether systemic involvement is present. Skin biopsy will not differentiate these two types." Because of the expense involved in the additional blood tests, he suggested that Kaiser do the lab work for me.

When I asked him about having another child, he said that it certainly was possible to have another child if I wanted one, that I might aggravate the latent disease, but then again, I might get hit by a truck tomorrow. He was so matter of fact, I could hardly worry. He even added that there were women with active SLE who managed to have successful pregnancies. He encouraged me about the drugs now used, and said that it certainly wasn't considered a hopeless condition anymore. In his fatherly way he restored my wrenched confidence.

Putting a very bright light up close to my face, he looked again at the larger lesion on my cheek, and then the smaller one on my right. I was given several quick shots of cortisone directly into the lesions. Needle pricks of blood. Summer's face read—Mild shock. He offered me several tubes of a topical cortisone cream, assuring me that it would have no systemic effect. He believed that the shots and cream together would help clear up my face, indicating that if another spot appeared, I could just come back for another poke. It all seemed pretty dermatological.

Summer was surprised that he had gone ahead and given me the shots before asking or explaining himself, but I was so relieved to be in the hands of a decent doctor, I didn't quite care. He had certainly also been generous, loading me down with *Eclipse 15*, a sun block cream. He suggested that I use it on any exposed part of my skin, even my hands, and a nice big hat would help. But of course I could go outside, and lead a "normal" life.

I never dreamed that I would have more trouble with that Kaiser doctor again, but when I returned to have the additional blood work done, he refused to authorize a lab slip. "All of these fancy tests are a waste of money. They just drive the cost of Kaiser up for everyone. This isn't necessary. I can tell just by looking at you." The test that Dr. Tuffanelli had requested only related to 5% of all discoid lupus patients. There was only one chance in twenty that the blood tests would show the possibility of SLE.

I wasn't going to argue, and turned it back on him, professionally, saying that I had seen a lupus specialist, that he had specifically requested these tests, and that if there was a difference of opinion, then he should give Dr. Tuffanelli a call and discuss it. I offered him the phone number and sat back, heart pounding, and he took the challenge, dialing, quite disgruntled. Amazingly enough, he got through on the first try. They argued and talked and disagreed, talked some more, and when he finally hung up, he refused to even look at me as he furiously wrote out the lab slip, pushing it across the desk. He mumbled on about the waste of money, not worried about the waste of lives.

Beyond Tentative:
AN INTERLUDE
October, Milwaukee, Wisconsin

The walls were forest colored. An oval of green glass lay beneath the center chalice, steaming with split potatoes, candles on all sides, and Cia, my sister, was there as a young girl, leaning towards the chalice as if about to kneel. The rest of the round dark room was filled with the muffled disturbance of family, chatting and eating, as everybody was there.

The hostess left no time in describing exactly how the food for this ordeal had been processed. There was a white chrome truck, a food truck, parked outside, and inside the truck were rows and rows of knives, that slid back and forth to mince the meat. These sets of knives were operated by basset hounds, but now there seemed to be no hounds to operate the food machine. I was on my back in the truck, and my hand went up into the knives which started to move—I had to pull against the blades as if out of something's jaws.

At the table I grew more disturbed, and questioned my hostess again. She turned on me then and announced that she had lupus. This shocked me, for I knew this to be an auto-immune disease which I myself had. I knew that this meant that my body was attacking itself, rejecting its own cells in a kind of confusion. My sister was also ill, and in a panic I could see why we were placed together at this table. But the hostess went on, snarling and dog-faced, and her words came at me—"Lupus," she said, "not only means that one attacks oneself, but one's closest too!"

And so I approached the darkening of Advent. There were no windows filled with glittering light to open on the way. I was merely beginning my pilgrimmage, with my great aunt's breath beneath my book. I knew that the spiral would lead me on, through all four kingdoms, past the minerals, towards the dried moss bog before the jungle, up to the realm of the animals, mewing and howling, to man.

My own dog was a chow, of the lupus strain, as was the dog of my Great Aunt Isabelle. I found a stuffed replica in her bureau drawer. I found every-thing just as little-gramma had left it. Nothing had changed in the house during Auntie's lifetime, and now she had died in the bed she was born in, ninety-two years before.

A letter lay on her dresser from 1949. The journal opened onto her account of Europe as a young girl, and my grandmother's words beside hers spoke as a child of nine, and yet I could hear their voices plainly. My great grandfather, the lawyer, was there beside little-gramma, who always appeared to be smil-ing in these pages, just as he appeared to be riled, sick or disgusted. Time ticked back louder as the rings of the spiral grew larger, curving away. It was the voice of my genetic stream, the whirlpool I had dropped into, that pool where I had made my ungentle dip down.

My great-aunt's funeral took place on the most Wisconsin of autumn days, the golden leaves against the blue, fell unattended over the grey headstones. Cold pumped from below, sun struck from above, and no one but my brother, the lawyer, knew what our aunt's real name was. He had seen it in her bible, though I hardly think of her with a bible, and now it was a surprise on her tomb. Her name began with Laura, as did every other name in this family plot—Laura Greenwood, Laura Bowker, Laura Chapman, Laura Isabella, though we'd always known her as Isabelle, and her grave began a new row.

My mother was hosting the party after the funeral. Everyone was there, all of my cousins, their parents, the babies, husbands and wives, all come to ease her passing, to help her go on, to carry her casket. There were too many in the room to hear or speak to anyone, and the air was dry on the twenty-third floor, but from the balcony you could see the orange stone Victorian, where Auntie had once been born. It was three blocks away, with a green copper roof, and a basement from another century.

My sister and I left the funeral party, and drove the three windy blocks to Auntie's house, which was warm still on entering. I saw her pink eyeglasses on the dining room table. They too felt warm and slightly oiled. Delicate as she was, with her certain toughness of mind. I collected her personal articles from the table, her black coin purse, containing three pennies. She hadn't married and was a very private person. She never let anyone into her room, and now we were to go brazenly in there.

It is strange that my father's battery-run watch had stopped the night my great-aunt died, and that no one discovered her for a good while the following day, because she rarely came down before noon, and then the police had to break the door down, as she always bolted the door from the inside.

I was afraid that the death had not been peaceful, but actually very bloody, that she had gone into the catering truck, but my great-aunt's room seemed perfectly normal. I rested on her bed, and apologized to her privately for being there. It didn't seem that she minded. I felt very much at home. I understood that she knew that I cared, that I would try to save what had been saved. Soon the entire house would be torn down for another one of those buildings, and my life as a grandchild was over.

I was given a candle to see into the darkness. I had taken all of the letters out of all of the drawers, an excuse to see into what was inside and behind our common name, repeated for generations, the pages of poetry, all of the "thank yous" delivered by boat to Broad Oaks in the country, grocery lists, postcards from everywhere, correspondence dating back to 1854, the writing there so fine and stylized and faint, one could only read it, concentrating from three inches away . . . the note from little Isabelle at the age of seven, apologizing to her father for not practicing the piano, colored pictures made by my Gramma, aged four, recipes for scones and silver cake, charlotte russe, preserved citron, the pages falling out of time, drifting into butter, the smears of passage, glancing backwards, which was where I wanted to go.

I felt driven to uncover all that I could, and I took my sister's hand as we approached the attic. I wasn't planning on taking anything, except the little stuffed dog. I just wanted to see. My sister wanted to get out of there. She wasn't curious or greedy, and perhaps she'd seen enough. But I made her stay with me as I began to open trunks. I found a small girl's dress, red and white stripes, covered with tiny bells, green silk slippers with matching stockings, a tablecloth woven heavy with gold, a silk embroidered kimona, a crumbling cardboard box, where a lifesize doll lay doll-like. The hair was a dusty yellow, and the lids were shut. When I lifted the doll the eyelids opened, but there were no eyes on the balls that rolled.

We left the house for the last time, and returned to the apartment of my parents nearby. Everyone had left or was asleep as it was dark now. We sat up into the night together in our nightgowns. The lights on the water of Lake Michigan were strung out just so far on the landfill. The little rock island was there, just as it had always been throughout my childhood, mysterious to me, though my brother, the lawyer, had just told me that morning, that our great-grandfather, the lawyer (they also shared a common name) was behind the construction of this island out there in the water's distance, this odd little manmade rock.

There was a long tunnel that led underwater from the filtration plant to this spot, and our Great Aunt Isabelle had walked all the way out there through this tunnel when she was a young girl, with her father, our great-grandfather, whom we had never known . . . I know there is much more I do not know, that will never be told me, there is much I have yet to believe, about this journey underwater, and my preparation for it, in the darkness, through the tunnel, to the rock.

I look to my sister in the dark of the modern apartment. The white of her nightgown glows in the darkness. I curl up on the sofa, way beyond midnight, and tell her that I am afraid. She comes and places her hands on me. Her hands are warm, a comfort. I close my eyes, when she begins to pray, plainly and openly aloud.

From the Inside Out
November, Berkeley

There was no clinical or serological evidence that I had anything other than cutaneous lupus erythematosus, for my lab studies, including an ANA, CBC, c3 and anti-DNA, all proved negative or normal. The biopsy confirmed the fact that I had discoid lupus, and then there was also my supporting history of false positive serology. I had received false-positives to my syphillus test when I was twenty and getting married, when I was twenty-five and pregnant, when I was thirty, "with child" again, and now. This test indicated possible collagen disease activity.

I wasn't totally convinced that I simply had a "cosmetic problem," as Tuffanelli had described it. I wondered if I couldn't get to the root of the problem, get rid of this discoid lupus altogether. Would I always have to stay out of the sun? The plaques that had been injected with intralesional triamcinolone had clearly diminished, and then with the additional corticosteroid cream, *Flurone*, they disappeared. Nice to see an unmarked complexion after so many months of poking, scratching and wondering.

But now there was a strange depression in my right cheek, where I had received the shot, as if a little bit of my face had collapsed. After several months, the dent did return to normal. *Normal*, I thought, would I ever be normal again? Or was there such a thing.

Richard Grossinger had recently brought by a copy of his new book, *Planet Medicine, from stone age shamanism to post-industrial healing,* and I was particularly impressed by the study of homeopathic medicine. He described how conventional (allopathic) medicine, generally supported by the A.M.A., usually attempts to suppress symptoms, while the homeopathic remedy aims to stimulate the body's own healing processes, in order to cure from the inside-out, rather than driving the outward symptoms inward, where they could eventually manifest in a more hazardous, internal form. The skin, being the furthest away from any vital metabolic organ, was the least dangerous place of expression. In general, homeopaths regard the suppression of superficial skin symptoms as a big mistake.

After reading *Planet Medicine,* I decided to go to the Hering Family Health Clinic in Berkeley and to take a homeopathic remedy for discoid lupus. During a long preliminary talk, Steve Cummings asked me pages and pages of questions—everything from my particular food likes and dislikes, to my reaction to heat and cold, sleep patterns, sexual life, moods and energy level...so that he could get a clear picture of my over-all "type." Homeopathic doctors don't use the same remedy for everyone with the same problem. You are treated according to your various symptoms and your specific type.

Once the symptom pattern is clear, the homeopath then uses the Law of Similars, which basically means, "like cures like," in an attempt to match the symptom pattern with the substance that would reproduce the same symptoms in a healthy person. In order to do this, he must consult large volumes of "provings" which homeopaths have compiled over the years. I was also interested to learn that when working with a chronic disease, the appearance of skin eruptions following treatment of an internal problem is considered a sign of healing, that it is literally—Working itself out.

When Samuel Hahnemann, the founder of modern homeopathic practice, experimented with reducing the dosages of his remedies, he found out that they actually became more potent. This Law of Infinitesimals is a bit hard to grasp. When the medicines are prepared in a specific way, so as to make their intrinsic energy available therapeutically, the greater the dilution of a remedy, the more effective it is in stimulating the body's own healing forces. Some homeopathic remedies are diluted to such a degree that none of the original substance can be perceived. Yet these dilutions are the most powerful. It leads one to believe that this form of cure doesn't just work on the material plane. While the remedies *are* materially verifiable, the reason for giving a specific remedy is philosophically/spiritually based. Of course this is difficult for many patients and conventional doctors to swallow.

Steve Cummings decided to give me a sulphur remedy. I was to take the whole little package of tiny white granules all at once, and not to eat or drink or smoke anything for a while. I was also to avoid caffeine and camphor related substances, both of which can antidote the remedies.

Within a few days, a slight itching on my upper arms returned, as did the old eruptions on my left cheek. There I was, back where I started, but now I assumed that this skin condition, moving outward, rather than inward, might be for the best. Certainly a disease manifesting on the surface of the body is less serious than one which appears inside, on the systemic level. I considered myself lucky.

Planet Medicine had warned against swinging from allopathic to homeopathic methods, but it was a see-saw course I would continue to follow for quite a while, slung as I was between my own contradictions, in a continuous oscillation of opposites. The polarities of disease and true inner health, of material vs. spiritual well being, would continue to pull me in conflicting directions as I took from both worlds of medicine.

The Mistaken Mastermind
Winter & Spring, 1981

As the weather warmed up that spring, a more severe rash developed on my upper arms, and now I had a little triptych of discoid lesions, one on each cheek and one on my forehead. A trinity of symmetry.

But I really had no time to worry about my cosmetic problem, with a toddler and his wild escapades, plus the constant pressure of school business. Being a board member of a new Waldorf school in Berkeley, and having one of the oldest children in the kindergarten, I wanted to make sure that the school would expand into the grades the following year, as promised. I was in charge of the site-search, in a town so glutted with groups and activities there was hardly an inch of space to spare. But I was optimistic.

As Ayler ran about the house taking things apart, I was constantly on the phone. Then both of us were up and out to the car, off on intuitive searches, walking into church after church, unannounced, talking to ministers, getting little leads, then off to the xerox, jotting down realtors' numbers, discussing our plight, our needs and our problems, money, arguing over regulations, the fire marshall, the congregation, Codes & Inspection, writing up proposals, getting our school board excited about a fabulous new site, which was given away, first this site, then that, each one slipped on by. Finally we located one small room in the basement of *Friend's Meeting*, and went through all the busy-work for a public hearing. At last, mid-summer, I unloaded my exhausted lap, my over-stuffed file folder and my towering stack of index cards. As I left for Wisconsin, I was emotionally and physically drained. I didn't blame it on the school but on myself, for not knowing my own limits, not asking for help a bit sooner, thinking that I alone was the mastermind who would see the problem through to a solution. I functioned like an obsessive, and the coffee and cigarettes drove me further and faster. I was still simmering along on unhealthy energy as I returned home, the last reserve of some jittery stuff.

Unlocking The Last Room
Summer, Wisconsin

When my Great Aunt Isabelle died, I had collected ten big bags of letters from the family home. They had never thrown anything away. Now I read through it all, editing out the best for a family album. Indeed I was engrossed by this accumulation of past, dating back to the days of my great-great grandparents, but it was too much to absorb so fast, these histories, tangible in print. And now all of the clothes that my relatives had worn and all of the treasures they had lived with were finally being disclosed as each closet door was opened and all the trunks brought downstairs.

I had had my peek, but now I would have a mouth-watering look. All of the supposedly valuable items in the house were numbered and appraised. The four families were all going to get together and select from these things later in the summer, while the other, unmarked items were considered unimportant, trivia, up for grabs, and suddenly like a crazed two year old on Christmas morning, I tore into it all, abandoning restraint.

My good friend, Jill, was visiting me from Massachusetts, and she accompanied me on that first dig, up there on the third floor, at the height of summer's heat, black smears of soot across our faces. The two of us felt like we'd stumbled onto buried treasure, as if we'd unlocked a lost tomb. We dragged down those immense trunks from the attic, and unpacked them in the ballroom, pulling out drawer layers of gowns, each costume with its own history—*Alice wore the white tulle with pink buttons at graduation, Rosemary Hall.* Little Gramma's wedding dress weighed a ton. I slipped on the beaded headdress and kept digging. We were hanging up these costumes for all the girl cousins to look at and try on, but I put a few aside for myself, a heavy red velvet skirt with tiny velvet covered dangling beads, a silk matador's jacket with skirt, and a white dressing gown with angelic lace sleeves and a big blue ribbon at the throat. I knew it was unfair for me to have the first pick of all this, but my father said that I could take what I wanted. Given permission, a mounting greed quickly hooked its claws in me. I was the first to tear into the neat brown paper wrappings, little instants of awe before pressing onward, closet after closet, breaking string, hauling out dainty parasols (women protected themselves from the sun in those days), a banjo falling from its decaying case, five foot feather pillows, embroidered linen and glass doodads, a vest like a powder puff, mother of pearl fans and opera glasses, a box of rare lace, gilt frames, miniscule ivory dominoes, a pink tea set robed in dust, a child's pop-up book from 1894, Indian baskets and rolled up rugs, a huge camel's hair blanket marked "carriage robe," a pink satin table-cloth with voluminous napkins, a quilt topped stool, but my favorite was the rectangular box of baby clothes, long long white, with *Laura* stitched in cursive.

Yes, I had gorged on curiosity, but was still not satisfied. I was exhausted from all the discoveries and yet energized, frantic at the same time. I had taken a car load of treasures, but still wanted to go back. I had inherited the given name, but what else did I inherit. What more did I deserve.

Within a week, I remarked that my fingers felt slightly stiff, as if I'd just ridden a powerful, difficult horse, and was experiencing rein fatigue. But my horse was so easy, I knew I hadn't struggled with his mouth. Then I began to notice a slight bone ache throughout my body as I sat in the saddle, and the sensation in my hands remained day after day, increasing very gradually, until by late August, I thought of it as a condition.

> I dreamt that I found a completely new room in my great aunt's house, as if I had unlocked the last door to my heredity. And what did I find there—in the ruins? (the contents glistened like candy-preserved antique toys) Greed, for material possession, which must be the top layer over some other layer of need. But there in the icing of the dreamwork, I spied the perfect arthritic bicycle, made entirely of wood, every curve, each spoke—I knew it would collapse if I touched it.

> My father did give me permission to ransack the past. Might I even say he encouraged me? But it was my move flicked the cellular switch, self-repulsion on the structural level, collapsing the castle, setting the bones on fire, exhausted under the noiseless hum. I tightened up the reins on life itself, until my hands ached as if from a horse ride. But we know the fingers were just too eager to take, that conscience doesn't want you to cheat one bit, that life is constant in its demand for you to give, and that you cannot control The World.

I knew that arthritis was often a first symptom of systemic lupus erythematosus, SLE, but supposedly only a very small percentage of discoid lupus patients ever developed the more serious involvement. Maybe I'd been misdiagnosed, or maybe my condition was changing.

Panic Includes No Time
September, Berkeley

By September, I was concerned enough to return to Dr. Tuffanelli's office for more blood tests. Summer came with me again, but now she brought her nursing baby, my god daughter, Joanna. How time does fly, I smiled, holding out my arm, once more, for the unpleasant prick of the syringe.

I had been rather nonchalant about the possibility of SLE, but now as I waited for the results, I realized I was shaken. We had dropped our Kaiser insurance and switched to Blue Cross, but with the stipulation that they would not cover SLE for five years. At the time I'd switched, I thought this would be no problem. Had they outguessed us all?

Finally Dr. Tuffanelli called and explained that my blood tests had changed during the year. He thought that both my husband and I should come in together, so that he could explain a few things about the disease. It was as if the edge had just been reached— so *this* was the waterfall we'd been hearing all along that easy river. Panic includes no time.

As we waited in the anteroom for our appointment, an attractive woman with slick dark hair came out to the receptionist's desk, crying, wiping away her tears. She glanced at me, as if to say, *You too? Or am I alone in this world.* How was her life, my life, going to be ruined. I clutched Geoff's hand as my name was called.

Actually my pronouncement wasn't that horrible to hear. He said that my "C 3 Complement" test was abnormally low, and he thought that I had a very mild case of SLE, so mild at this point that there was nothing to do. Just wonder and wait. He didn't say that this was just the beginning of something worse. There was no way to make an absolute diagnosis. Most women weren't diagnosed until they were extremely sick, and perhaps having an early warning would give me some advantage.

Hatcheting the Habit

September, New York City

I knew there was something I could do. For one, I could give up coffee and cigarettes, and give my body a better chance. This was no easy task. My identity was wrapped up in the pattern of those addictions. My resolution to quit took a few weeks to sink in, but finally, when the perfect moment presented itself, I plunged.

I had spent a long weekend in NYC, celebrating my brother David's wedding. Jill had come down from the Berkshires to be with me, and all my cousins and siblings were there too. Though one dazzling event followed another, the city pressures, noise and social bustle, all felt extreme, and reverberated in my own shakiness. I knew I didn't look well—thin, tired, poor color, with those discoid blotches on my cheekbones, and when family told me how "wonderful" I looked at the rehearsal dinner, it was an embarrassment. Each cigarette I smoked, I took in lingeringly, knowing it was one of the last.

Jill had brought me a copy of *The Will to Live*, and though I had to laugh a little, I figured it might make good jet-time reading. She pointed out that the lupus had first surfaced when I decided to put my writing aside the year before. I had felt used up and dreaded the idea of a forced, empty production. I also had a new baby, and didn't want to push him away due to my own personal demands. Shifting from an isolated, inward involvement with art, to a more social commitment, I had worked to strengthen a new Waldorf school in Berkeley. I wasn't about to agree to any nifty correlations: Stop Writing/Get Sick, but I'm not one to instantly discredit anything either. Maybe poetry, for me, was a constant purging, and when the words no longer flowed... stagnation.

While sitting on the sidewalk beside the on-going street fair, having just polished off some decent Chinese food, I had a smoke, and Jill said, "I guess you're going to have to give that up." I could take it from her. She was always nudging me in the right direction, and I had to admit that I probably would, someday.

Someday came that week. In the La Guardia lounge, waiting for takeoff, I opened the book Jill had given me and lit up. Did I want to die? Did I secretly want to die young, my half-buried, romantic notion. No. I placed the pack and lighter on the chair beside mine, just so, like a neat and thoughtful camper, leaving a goody for the next sorry wanderer. I had asked for the non-smoking section. They announced my flight. I walked away, and walked on.

Defense Turned Mutiny

October, Marin, California

A Chapter of The American Lupus Society was meeting regularly at Marin General Hospital, and Dr. Juneau Pallen, a leading immunologist, was going to be speaking about new approaches in lupus research. Apparently there were promising new areas regarding treatment, and Geoff encouraged me to go by offering to accompany me.

I was also intrigued to see and meet other women with lupus. What would we find there, in the auditorium, I wondered. I pictured a room full of women with a variety of handicaps—wheelchairs, crutches, severe rashes. I thought I'd see my future in that room. But when we arrived, an energetic young woman welcomed us into a small conference trailer, where there were a few other normal looking human beings. I had imagined a crowd, like the hopeful at *Lourdes*, but by the time the lecture began, there were perhaps fifteen people, and I was the only one with any sign of a rash on her cheekbones, my telltale splotches.

Dr. Pallen appeared very relaxed and confident as he began. He was not going to talk down to this group, who already seemed to have a good grasp on the machinations of SLE, but he did want to cover some of the basics, to ground his discussion.

"As you know, in SLE, " he began, "the immune system, which normally reacts with foreign matter, such as bacteria, viruses or tumors, instead begins to react against the body itself. Now there are two major parts to the immune system: cellular immunity, where cells can kill or alter the function of other cells, and humoral immunity, the production of antibodies. Antibodies are molecules that recognize and help to remove foreign materials or, in the case of SLE, self material.

"Both immune cells and antibodies are highly specific in recognizing their targets," he continued. "Anything that they recognize and which stimulates the immune system to react against itself is called an antigen." He drew a picture of this on the board, with many little antibodies darting the bigger antigen. "In some patients with SLE, red cells become antigens, because there is production of antibody against the red cells, and this increases their destruction."

I could tell that this was going to be a lot to take in, and my brain was stretching to absorb the language. Here was a whole microscopic world unfolding, weird shapes building on the blackboard, a few cells magnified to a strategic plan. Natural defense turned mutiny.

"In SLE, most of the clinical problems are the end result of antibody production against self-antigens. In the case of red cells or white cells, the antibodies help to destroy these normal cells. In addition, antibodies appear that react with DNA, genetic coding. Small amounts of DNA are released from cells and when these react with antibody, they clump together. The aggregates of DNA and antibodies to DNA damage blood vessels and the kidneys."

One young woman in the room, who had had a kidney transplant, spoke out and said how sick and tired she was of all the testing. She felt like a stuck guinea pig, some sort of curious specimen, but Dr. Pallen stood right up for what doctors were trying to do for patients with serious renal disease. One could sympathize with both sides. I looked around the room, and almost everyone was drinking coffee, eating cheap, assorted cookies. The woman next to me had brought her own bag of herb tea, and later she told me, "You know caffeine and sugar aren't good for prednisone ladies."

Dr. Pallen erased what he'd drawn on the blackboard and continued. He seemed to do all of this so naturally, and I wondered where he got his stamina. "Although the problem in lupus is mostly due to antibodies, it appears that the production of antibodies is regulated by the other part of the immune system, cellular immunity. The cells of this system are called "T cells" because they mature in the thymus. The cells that actually produce antibodies are called "B cells.""

I was glad Geoff was taking notes too, for I was afraid that this scientific stream of talk, heard for the first time, was flowing well above my head, reminiscent of high school algebra, where I always understood what was being explained on the board before me, but ten minutes later and time for recall—*nada*.

Still, I found it terribly interesting to picture this activity of the body on such a microscopic level. I had the feeling that the more closely one examined the infinitesimal in physical life, the more mystery and awe one received.

Someone raised a hand and wanted to know, "What actually unmasks lupus? What sets it off." And Dr. Pallen explained that researchers were trying to figure out what caused an auto-immune response, but there still was no conclusive answer. Possibly genetic, environmental, viral and hormonal factors were involved.

"It's not clear what goes wrong in SLE. There is some evidence that the B cells escape regulation by T cells, and thus begin to react against self-antigens. Other evidence suggests that the defect is in the T cells themselves, which fail to suppress abnormal immune responses.

"We have been trying to improve the selectivity of therapy by turning the immune system against itself—by making antibodies that react only with T cells, and using these to selectively deplete the target cells. In one mouse model for SLE, we've shown that treatment with these antibodies reduces T cells and improves auto-immunity, renal disease and survival of the mice.

"The antibodies that we use are so-called monoclonal antibodies. That is, all of the antibody is of the same specificity. These are made by immunizing a rat to make antibodies against mouse cells." He drew a large, rather decent looking rat on the board, and I imagined the cages and cages full of those little white creatures which repelled me in a truly irrational way. I wasn't one to worry about their ultimate sacrifice. Rubbing my eyes, I knew I was fading, but I tried to stick with it.

"The rat makes hundreds of different antibodies, each produced by different B cells. These B cells are then made to individually fuse with a tumor, so that the two cells become one, and when this happens, the hybridoma, or the fused product of two cells, can grow like a tumor and make the antibody that the B cell is making. By selecting among the thousands of hybridomas that are made, it is possible to select hybridomas that are making antibody that is selective for mouse T cells. These hybridomas are then allowed to grow and produce large amounts of the antibody, which we then use to inject into the mice." He smiled. Whew, what an incredible task.

Instead of being worn out by this whole discussion, Dr. Pallen seemed to be even more awake, and quite willing to go on, but we all elected to take a short break.

Geoff asked Dr. Pallen some more specific questions, while I talked to several of the women there, trying to find out what it felt like to have an established case of lupus. One woman told me, "You *know* when you have it. You're too tired to even walk up those stairs." There were no stairs in that room, but there were in her memory. Another woman, who had been clutching her husband's hand throughout the meeting, told me about a workshop Carl Simontin was offering. Simontin, an M.D. from Texas, had become well known for his innovative work with cancer patients, using visualization.

Most of the women in the room seemed to be enjoying themselves, even if there was a continual effort for humor, insider's humor, slightly forced and over loud. I sensed a certain nervousness coming from the women on prednisone, almost an intensity buzzing deep inside them, which had the weave of anxiety, trouble and fear, almost imperceptible—like the distant hum heard inside that house filled with honeycomb, but what was going on here wasn't so sweet, no panels of honey hidden in the walls. Something was working overtime inside these women, I thought. An alien hum imposed on the lulling rhythms of the blood.

Physically Disturbed
October, Berkeley

I hadn't had a complete physical exam for years, so I decided to go to a general practitioner for a thorough check-up. I felt that something serious was going wrong with me and feared that the lupus might be affecting some part of me, possibly even my kidneys, as I was extremely sensitive in that area and exhaustion seemed to locate there.

When I went to see Dr. Ulrich, I described what Tuffanelli had said about my mild case of SLE and told him about the arthritic feeling in my hands. He counteracted by saying that he too often felt arthritic, that it wasn't unusual as one grew older. Then he proceeded to ask me a hundred quick questions, concerning possible problems from head to toe, and admittedly, I simply answered, "No," to almost all of them. I felt silly. Think of all the awful things that could be wrong with me. Maybe I was simply upset or worried. I knew I was on edge.

My mother had just been in town, and it had been a particularly painful visit, laden with continual, unpleasant, critical comments— "Berkeley is such a slum! Doesn't anyone ever pick up their yard, or take care of their home here? That school for Clovis is ridiculous. He's never going to catch up. Why don't you try to look more attractive, get your hair cut, lightened." On and on and ON.

Walking down Milvia Street towards University Avenue, on our way to dinner, my mother kept up the comments with that tone of disgust, pointing out a toilet parked in someone's driveway, and I snapped, "Keep it to yourself, ok?" She clammed right up and refused to speak during dinner, which was just as well, since the restaurant was noisy and the food poor. It was enough to experience it, without having to *hear* about it. I had just given up smoking and couldn't gracefully ignore remarks like the good duck I used to be. I was as ready to fight as I was angry to smoke, and I had just about had it. Enough water had rolled off my back for ten lives.

Luckily we went to see a charming French film, and we could sit in the dark and not have to try and converse, but afterwards, I thought I should try and make up. As she got out of the car at her hotel, I got out too to say goodnight, and with a great effort I asked her, "Will you be coming over for breakfast tomorrow morning?"

Stiffly, she walked away, "I don't think so, Laura."

And I just blew, screaming at her on the sidewalk—"Don't push me too far God Damn it!"

Horrified, she backed away, while Geoff pulled me into the car, where I continued to kick and fume at him.

They all probably thought that the lupus was getting to my brain. That wasn't exactly the case, but it was affecting me emotionally, that is, my physical state was unsettling me to the point of emotional upset, and that made my physical stability even creakier. The barely detectable first phase of illness was throwing me off balance, though it's hard to draw lines between the physical and emotional at this point, or to be sure which came first, the diseased chicken or the rotten egg. Perhaps it was some psychological pattern, some syndrome of criticism and repression that was finally exploding and expressing itself now.

It was in the midst of this dark, disturbed mood that I saw Dr. Ulrich. Finding nothing to pinpoint in the physical realm (other than perhaps this hint of lupus) he turned to questioning me about my emotional life. When he asked me about Geoff, I said that things were fine, but that Geoff wouldn't acknowledge that something was going wrong with me. He had to ignore it, probably because his father had just died of cancer, and his mother had too, years before, and he couldn't face anything else going wrong with someone close to him, but that added a burden onto me, not having his comfort or support, when I was on this borderline. I gave a big sigh. I rubbed my forehead.

Then Dr. Ulrich asked about my relationship to my parents, my mother. I tried to talk, but then I looked up at him and burst into tears. It startled me as much as it startled him. I don't do this sort of thing with strangers. So there I sat, sobbing, trying to tell him, why, I was still so upset, and he came and stood behind me, rubbed the back of my neck, trying to calm me down. It seemed like such a kind gesture, to stand there comforting me. I needed that moment of contact. And yet there I was, suffering from something physical, and it was having emotional repercussions, and my doctor didn't suspect that there was anything seriously wrong with me. No wonder I was confused.

He asked me if I'd ever considered seeing a therapist, that he knew of some very good people.

Oh God, is that what I need?

He thought perhaps Geoff would like to come back with me for the follow-up exam. We could all talk. I felt reluctant, embarrassed. My head was still spinning from the upset as I left the building, and I never did return to his office. Maybe I was afraid to see a therapist. Maybe I didn't want to have to face what I might find out. I was surprised when Summer agreed that it might be good to talk to some objective person, outside of my own personal realm. But my emotional problems seemed fairly well shovelled out in the open. I had simply wanted a physical exam, and now, holding the receipt in my hands, I read— Diagnosis: Discoid Lupus. But I knew there was something bigger going on, something more than a cosmetic problem.

Mistletoe Kiss
October

In late October, I went to a series of lectures given by Dr. Robert Gorter, an anthroposophical doctor visiting from Holland. The Waldorf School, in which I was involved, was the educational expression of Rudolf Steiner's findings, just as this form of medicine was derived from his discoveries concerning man and health. There were very few anthroposophical doctors in the states, partly because one had to first become a regular M.D. and then go on to do additional years of study and training.

I liked Dr. Gorter a great deal. He was a thin, small man with tremendous vitality and had that European sense of impeccable taste. He was almost whimsical, light in his blond appearance and sense of humor, but he could be serious and sensitive in his concern.

During one of his evening lectures, he described the three main systems of man: the nerve-sense, rhythmic, and metabolic systems. *What Can The Art of Healing Gain Through Spiritual Science,* by Steiner, says that, "the metabolic-limb system is the polar antithesis of the system of nerves and senses, while the rhythmic system is the mediator between the two. Each of these three systems is permeated by the four members of man's being—physical body, etheric body, astral body and Ego-organization. . . .

"Life consists of two tendencies or streams. . . . Our life is incessantly going to pieces . . . the blossoming life is always giving place to the decaying life. We are actually dying by degrees and at every moment something falls to ruin in us, and every time we build it up again. But whereas matter is being destroyed, it leaves room wherein what is of the soul and spirit can enter and become active in us.

"Within the physical body lives the etheric or life-body, which contains the forces of growth and of nourishment, something which we can gain a conception of when we behold the growing and blossoming plant kingdom, for the plants as well as human beings have an etheric life-body. In so far as man is a sentient being, he bears within himself the next member, the astral body, the mediator of sensation, the bearer of the inner life of feeling. The astral body contains the unbuilding forces of destruction. Just as the etheric body makes the being of man bud and sprout, so all these processes of budding are continually being disintegrated again by the astral body. But man excells all other kingdoms of nature because he possesses the Ego-organization."

Hahnemann's form of homeopathy and Steiner's vary on many different levels. The medicines are prepared differently and prescribed for different reasons. Homeopathic medicines are given after looking at the collective symptomatic picture of the individual, holistically, while anthroposophical medicine is given with insights into the overall stage of development of that person. Anthroposophical remedies are also designed to work through the etheric level—up to the astral or down to the physical. While both forms of medicine help work problems outward, rather than suppressing symptoms, homeopathy doesn't take into account the Ego-development of the individual, which is the focus of anthroposophical medicine. Steiner's indications always took into account the body, soul and spirit of man.

Dr. Gorter went on to explain the threefoldness of the plant kingdom, where the roots correlate to our nerve system, including the brain (gray, immobile, symmetrical); and the green rhythmically occuring leaves, which also "breathe" during photosynthesis, relate to our rhythmic heart & lung area; while the flower (which follows the light of the sun), relates to the metabolic system. "The plant is fixed with its roots in the earth, but man sends his roots into the cosmos and is free."

In anthroposophical medicine remedies are used which stimulate the human organism to combat the illness, ideally yielding health and future protection. The plants used in these remedies correspond to the part of the body affected with that part of the plant, so camomile flowers might be used for a woman with (metabolic) cramps; digitalis (leaves) for the heart muscle; or a root derivative for a nerve problem, ex. Valerian.

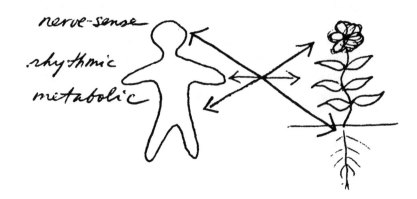

As Goethe observed in nature, whenever something moves against something which is in a state of rest (wind on water, bow on string) you have a rhythm, and this is also true in man, where the middle rhythmic system is the meeting ground. Health can be seen as a balanced rhythm, a balance between the life and death forces always in process—the continual breaking down, destruction of the body during wakefulness, and the building up, restoration during sleep.

With innoculations and antibiotics, and with fewer fever diseases, there has been (in our "head oriented" culture) an increase in the hardening diseases, including arthritis, rheumatism, mental illness, and cancer, where the body, or part of the body, as in a tumor, becomes head-like, hard and cold, immobile. Inflammation is a reaction of the body attempting to heal the mineralizations.

Later, when I met Dr. Gorter at a friend's house, we sat in the study and I explained what I knew about my lupus. He asked me if I felt cold at my extremeties, and I thought so, yes. My feet and hands had always felt unnaturally cold.

"What about your buttocks," he asked.

Yes, they too were very cold, though I had never even noticed that before.

"When I first saw you, I thought you would benefit by taking Iscador," he smiled, twinkly and warm.

Here in the United States, Iscador is called *Viscum alb.* I had heard about Iscador in relationship to cancer in Europe, where anthroposophical hospitals were having great success in curing cancer patients, but I was a bit shocked that he was suggesting something so radical for me. He didn't think of *Viscum alb.* in that way. He assured me that he recommended it for a variety of problems, that he'd taken it himself, and that he'd never seen any ill side effects.

Viscum alb. is a remedy derived from the mistletoe plant, a very curious plant indeed, the poisonous, Christmas, kissing plant, which doesn't adapt itself to earth, but rests above, as a globe, attaching itself to a tree for sustenance, forming no true roots, showing no geo-tropism, no vertical growth tendencies.

The two white boxes of *Viscum alb.* which he dug out of his bag, had labels from the *Institut Hiscia* in Arlesheim, Switzerland. I was to self-administer four series of seven shots, twenty-eight shots in all. Their strength increased during the seven shot cycle. You could see through the small glass ampules how the shades went from a clear liquid, to a honey yellow color. The ampules were lined with beeswax for addi-tional protection. I was to file the top of the ampule, snap it away and then draw up the medicine with a subcutaneous type needle.

Because my younger sister was a diabetic, I had seen her tap needles since she was ten years old, and the idea of shots seemed almost acceptable to me, though I'd always cringed and looked away when Cia gave herself a morning shot of insulin. But if my baby sister could do it, so could I, right? Dr. Gorter was very casual about it, saying that many patients in Europe administered their own shots. It was nothing. But it certainly wasn't common practice here. I felt optimistic about the remedy, eager to begin.

Dr. Gorter also instructed me to take one or two very hot baths a day, as hot as I could take them, and then afterwards I was to dress warmly in cotton and wool, to help retain the heat. I needed to stoke my furnace. He also wanted me to begin curative eurythmy with Veronica Reif, who lived in Berkeley. This form of curative movement was a Steiner based therapy as well.

Since Veronica was also a nurse, I let her administer my first shot, but then we both felt that the mixing of medicine and movement was too much at once. I wanted to be in control of the process myself, so I asked Carolyn, a friend who was also a nurse, to show me how I should proceed.

It was difficult getting the protective hat off the end of the needle without bending or touching it, but after accomplishing that, step by step, slowly and carefully, Carolyn reassured me that I could give myself a shot, that I wouldn't die from an air bubble. I wiped my thigh with an alcohol swab, and then squeezed the skin up before darting the needle in. Mildly shocking, almost like deliberately cutting oneself with a razor. I pushed the liquid in very slowly. Immediately the redness began to rise and itch like a mosquito bite.

I had a very strong reaction to the shot, the initial bite flaring out to a 9″ red pancake, swelling my entire thigh. The following morning I felt fluish, down all day, while the heat continued to radiate and throb. It worried me. But Dr. Gorter thought that my reaction was good. It showed that the *Viscum alb.* was taking effect and that I needed it.

When I went back to see him, he put his hand on the still hard swelling, acknowledging the heat, calming my upset with his sureness. I was worried that this inflammatory remedy might provoke my lupus, but he reassured me, saying that I would be fine. I could apply a mixture of green clay and liquid arnica onto the area of the shot, and it would help. It did. But because of my reactions, he thought I should only take one shot a week, rather than two.

I continued throughout the fall, giving myself a weekly shot of *Viscum alb.*, usually on Saturday morning, so that I felt a bit sick and slow on Sunday and could rest. My reactions became less marked as I continued the series, but I did notice a subtle change in my energy. I felt revved up in a good way, stimulated, flushed, turned on. My whole body felt warmer, as if it were hard at work, trying to keep me healthy and alive.

Iscador

Mistletoe kiss me sting—a waspish. To embrace the poisoned leaf, white berry bloodless. Poke that fire, started somehow on sheer ice. What melt can do, what flame say. Snow, well ... even covers. Into the long white dwelling cave we dug our blue. Little bears with noses (sniff) so bright our inner heat shone through. Yet don't forget those freezing tips—even cool bath water burns it.

Hearth can't wait another year. Need ignition, symbol roaring, right here. Else in cool we work a bend, to pillar of the past, look back, to stone. So much gather, sticks fall. Leaves let go. My room separates from the house, a crack of sky. Now is time to knock things back, air tight. Copper plate-back firelight for Mood Woman. Call me (wall me) what you will. Shhh, he touches, nuff now. Precious heat against such cave. Conch-song-echo, wing, waves, roll back to suck the living. Someone younger comes to wonder, watch and poke and feed the fire.

Saw and snap of small glass ampule, pushing in the lookless sting. Makes a ring of red in you, a swollen nest, a nauseous knot. You can not clearly—Come, Wake up. Days remaindered for a dime. Better sue the cream off that.

See thick nails quick up our lean. Tight and squeezed like fancy knees. By Summit Pass. The height and squeal of car appeal. We drove into another climb—circling up round shiver lake. It made us safe inside, in close, where wool and wheel and cloth slipped. Fires blazed along the road. A's framed the freeze to come, but yellow and red roar now instead. Hot and cold here meet their net, their duel, their test. From root to skull, from flower to flow. Harden, soften, freeze or flame. They set a fire in my name.

Lightness & Levity
November

Eurythmy is an art form and a science, where the choreographic movements of the body show the "formative" power that lies in speech. Vowels and consonants are actually made visible by using the characteristic movements inherent in each sound. In curative eurythmy, each patient is given a specific set of exercises, suited to her particular problem or disease, a unique prescription of vowels and consonants, in the hope that the processes of the human anatomy and physiology will become harmonized.

Veronica Reif was a large boned, dark haired, dramatic lady with an excessive love for puns. I liked her. She seemed to live for the musical expression of language. When she showed me the movement for a particular sound, she would intone that sound with a resonance that was as pure as her gestures, carved through the air. She was cheerful, forceful, with meaning and control embedded in each gesture.

We usually began our morning session with some conversation, each of us sitting in a chair placed in the far corner of her empty living room, which also functioned as the movement space. Sharing our concern for the Waldorf School, we often spoke about that, and then she would go on to ask about my physical health, and if there was anything bothering me. I found it easy to talk with her, but especially enjoyed that moment when we leapt from the verbal realm, into the world of sound and movement.

I stood facing her in her 50's-modern living room with its grey wall-to-wall. It was always a relief to come here, so peacefully empty, no toys, no clutter, the quiet, meditative moments, losing myself in form, the forming of sounds that both entered my ear and body. I mirrored her movements as she intoned, trying to imitate her grace and care, though often I was sloppy, bumbling. She pushed me to perform with integrity, encouraging and approving whenever she could, and I was hungry for approval.

Veronica was intent on keeping my body in motion. She could see that my body wanted to harden up, to stiffen and stop, withdraw, close down, and the gestures she had me perform were opening ones, lifting ones, lightening. Sometimes the movements felt grand, and sometimes small, when a mere movement of each finger did the job. I always felt warmed up and energized after those sessions, never exhausted. It was as if my very blood were grateful. It took me far from my every day mundane moves, and let me unfocus and concentrate at the same time, suspended, yet attentive in space.

The sound we seemed to return to the most was "L." We would make big L's, and medium size L's and little butter leaf lettuce l's. It seemed like such a feminine gesture, this lifting of my hands to make a circle, a caressing of space—the world, myself. I resisted this gesture at first. It felt so delicate, too open, but soon I came to like it. I loved the letter "E." It made me feel my own power, strength, as if I were ready to sail, to glide, soar, stride on, centered, right arm rising firmly up at an angle, left arm lowering, so that my arms made a steady diagonal, leaving me somewhere between heaven and earth, secure between the forces of both worlds.

In a Motion

The dangers of drifting while driving, in a daze—Loosening the reins that last ride on Eagle. I had the premonitions that day, galloping alongside Old Farm Road, newly spread gravel hid the edge of asphalt, my horse nicked—Sliding, weight of horse flesh—Thrown, into a splash of view, as if I were the landscape, skid-hot palms, even liking that later, the wakeful, stinging, unexpected smasheroo. It all felt familiar, as if I'd read that page, somewhere, or someday, like "The End" plucked out of the saddle, oddly marvellous and shocking, like birth, but not squeezed, rather—Freed from the tiddlywinks of shape.

To summon inside —The brave shining warrior, glittering hero of the skies with flaming sword, astride a horse so white, you know you are ready, to meet and overpower the dreadful. I've got my firm together now, my word drawn up, to hold and to swing into warning. Big "L's" begin lifting, for lightness and levity, raising the sediments Up in the body. L is for lucia, I said with my slipper, for all of the liquid that rises forever and falls into falls, to further the flowing, to keep us in motion.

Now each yellow girl on the bright red background of my new knit vest, reaches up to catch a heart above her head, while the boys down below around the border are running and flexing—They all warm my chest. They are not your modern children, who expect to be questioned, throwing up the hooves to their little lamb costumes. To resist what this culture insists on, strikes a light that cuts fad image into doubles, until a million brooms sweep wild water in a panic, and yet, this is such a tiny world with a placemat of maniacs, so why not try to set it right. How to walk the white steed, each step lifting, and carrying, and placing to stand. The electrical smell falls in a ring at your ankles. You are the shining rain. You draw a Number 1, in a motion, to the sun —The globe itself hovers there before you. Yes, you can touch it, give it a little "L—" That's what it's come back for, to set you on your way, gladly, with a hum —An approval.

I didn't know if it was the Iscador or the eurythmy, or both together, but within a month, I no longer felt the achy, arthritic symptoms in my hands or body, which had been steadily on the increase all fall. Perhaps together they had released the hardening through motion and heat. It was gone. Temporarily gone.

Disaster, Called a Vacation

December, Tahoe City

Two weeks before Christmas, I decided to take a break in my eurythmy sessions. I had so much to do getting ready for our vacation in the Sierras—cooking food to freeze, cookies, chicken pot pies and spinach lasagne, mailing of last minute packages, preparing our own family gifts, which would all be dragged along, not to mention the clothes and equipment.

It was raining dreadfully as I pulled out of the driveway in my old orange VW van, Summer and I up front, Ayler and Joanna secure in their car seats, Felix and Clovis crammed into the way back, and the floor packed three feet thick with our things. The car climbed very slowly, as if stunned by the weight and the constant downpour.

In Nevada City, we all got out for lunch and a stretch and got soaked. Inevitable. By the time we reached the summit, Ayler awoke from his nap and was very cranky, crying all the way into Tahoe while I tried to drive and comfort him. It seemed more than tiredness or car weariness. I thought it was the altitude, for he was strangely upset.

That evening, installed in our little cabin in the tall wet woods, all unpacked and almost exhausted from the maneuvering of children and things, choosing bedrooms, unloading suitcases and cases of food, getting dinner ready for hungry impatient ones, soggy and slightly uncomfortable, but relieved to be there, my back still aching from the eight hours of driving all by myself, and yet finally happy and relaxed with a fire lit and the kids asleep, Summer and I sank back to have a quiet chat, when something startled me—that horrible hack-sucking sound—Croup.

Summer said she saw the mother tigress in my eyes as I heard Ayler make that sound. I leapt for the stairs. Something in me, always ready to over-react, my natural tendency accentuated by the disease. It was croup all right. Summer volunteered to go out into the night in search of a humidifier. She had a very dark tour of our neighborhood and came back, bless her, with a nice big humidifier from some folks four houses down. There was no phone in the cabin. I didn't know where a hospital might be. What if I'd been more isolated, or alone, the only adult, snowed in. What if we hadn't turned the hot water on, and there had been no steam from the shower. I was panicking a mile a minute, as if my steering wheel had just given out, going downhill on ice and heading toward finality.

My older brother had almost died of croup as a baby. Clovis used to get croup that sounded like he'd swallowed a chicken bone, but one steam shower always did the trick for him. It only helped Ayler for a while, and then it would begin again. He'd wake with a gasp, sit up, breathless, trying to breathe and cry at once, waving his arms in desperation. I tried to sleep in the same bed with him, and when he started, I too would jerk awake, and take him down for another steam room treatment, six or seven times in one evening, cleansing my own pores, hot cold, Hot Cold, HOT COLD, all night, until I hated the sight of that bathroom mirror.

I was surprised to read later, in *The Body Against Itself*, by Blau and Schultz, that the croup virus might set off a lupus flare. There I was, night after half-slept night, emergency weary, with my sick baby. The doctor I called upset me further. When I asked him, "What do I do if his larynx swells so much that he can't get air," he responded—"A child can last a long time without breathing." I was really ready to go home, but I was stuck. Stuck in those dreary rain-soaked woods.

I lay back on the long couch by the long picture window and watched the boring rain, until right there, right before my eyes, it turned to the palest of flurries. I jumped up, yelling—SNOW! The first snow I'd seen in years. I wanted to cry for the love of snow. Felix and Clovis went berzerk. Even Ayler and Jojo clapped and romped. It didn't stop for fourteen hours, and when we awoke the next morning, it all seemed worth it, to witness this whiteness, so delicately piled, layering each branch and every surface, six inches of softness on the rail.

I cross-country skied down the road to call Geoff from a pay phone. He would be arriving that evening, and before dinner, he and Stephen pulled in after a speedy drive. Our Christmas tree was up, strung with lights from home, and the reflection on the window strung the little pine outside with identical reflected colors.

Geoff's coming certainly relieved me. The next morning, Summer and I left the men with our little ones, and made a dash for the mountains. While Felix and Clovis skied downhill, we managed to cross-country ski, creating our own trails in the deep, falling and laughing beneath the clear blue sky. I had forgotten to put on sun block, and the sun tripled its intensity off the fresh white, high altitude mounds.

That night I could feel a cellular shimmy, similar to what one feels at times of great exhaustion, like a coffee overdose. I felt like something in me was being undermined, as if an army of unseen ants was carrying away the sand beneath my feet, my support system shifting imperceptibly. I had given up coffee last fall, but now I was allowing myself one good strong cup a day. It tasted great and felt invigorating up there in the cold country, but the aftereffects left me unsettled, disturbed. Might I be allergic to caffeine? I ignored the signals, wanting the rush it gave. It would take a long time before I began to realize a few things about the old rush-rush.

As night approached, I became more tense, apprehensive about the inevitable evening croup. I needed to take a ten day jaccuzi. *Relax,* I said, but I could not. Geoff got angry when I wanted to change bedrooms with Summer. Her downstairs room was right next to the shower and the ceiling was much lower. It would help hold in the humidity, but Geoff thought I was nuts. Then when I tried to bring the baby crib down into the small bedroom, he blew up, yelling irrational insults. His verbal attack entered like a physical stab.

Summer, Stephen, Felix and Joanna, all left the next day, as planned, and the mood relaxed with only our foursome. Geoff said that he would sleep with Ayler, while I tried to regain some sleep by crashing on the living room couch, but even that didn't help, as I was strung so tight, aware of Ayler's every sound. I kept getting back up, going to check on him, giving him steam treatments when he coughed, as Geoff remained sound asleep. Probably ignoring more of the sounds would have been best, but I was over-reacting because of my own unidentified problem.

We had made little bows out of white homespun wool for the Christmas tree, and it was a cheerful Christmas morning, singing and opening presents, eating sweetrolls and fruit. We decided to take Clovis' new sling-shot bird out to the lake shore beyond Tahoe City. Having a nice family walk on the ice and snow, taking turns making the bird fly and swoop and dive, it seemed like the mood of the trip had changed, but then on the ride back to the cabin, I mentioned something about the timing for the lamb for our Christmas dinner and Geoff just blew— "God! Why do you have to *control* every aspect of this goddamn vacation! Wouldn't it be nice if we could just *let* things happen, maybe eat at a restaurant? Why do you have to be such a fucking control artist."

How I would have loved to dump the weight of accumulated plans and preparations on him at that moment. Mr. Instant wins the prize for hanging loose. Reprimanded for having organized this drastic event called a vacation, I was ready to let all three of them eat at Taco Bell for the rest of my life. We were to leave Tahoe the next morning, and I was silent and hostile until we were well off the mountain.

Disaster seemed to decrease with elevation, but it wasn't until we hit sea level and the Sacramento Valley, with its pure green flat wet stretch of land that I took a deep breath and felt friendly. "You know what I'd really like to do," I said. "I'd love to live in Great Barrington for a year, next year." The idea hit Geoff as a pleasant surprise. He seemed to like the idea, a year in the country, Massachusetts, with the rhythm of seasons, peace, isolation, close to New York City for him, less organizational school pressures for me, fewer social and teaching pressures, time to work on our own writing, break the Berkeley pattern, eight years of frenetic activity. I couldn't believe that he thought it was a good idea, but he said that he agreed. Maybe he was just trying to make up. And yet it did seem possible. Anything was possible.

I made him take me out for lunch (with a smile) on that drive back. No sandwiches were packed, that's for sure.

Theater of One's Body
January 1982, Berkeley

The very next day after returning home, our friends, Philip and Susan Pahner, arrived for a five day visit. It was all part of the on-going, over-extended, holiday rush, and though it was a good visit, the constant socializing, food preparation, and party organizing, didn't come at a very opportune time for me.

That same arthritic stiffness had entered my hands again. I was extremely sensitive to coffee and would get exhausted tremors, not that I paid much attention to them. I felt physically claustrophobic at times, as one does in the late months of pregnancy, as if there weren't enough air to breathe in the theater of my body. Cell suffocation, more easily irritated, crankier than usual.

The night we ate out with John and Gloria at *Turning Japanese*, I felt extreme physical claustrophobia and thought it was brought on partly by the soy and the fish. Restless, trapped in my skin and close to tears, I found it difficult to make conversation. The flashing neon and new wave music made me feel nauseous. Not myself.

By the middle of January, the stiffness was spreading to other joints as well. A general achiness accompanied every movement. It hurt to sit down on the toilet seat, but I truly believed it would soon go away, like it did last time with the help of Iscador and eurythmy.

Now the eurythmy felt uncomfortable, difficult. Maybe the disease was too strong for the medicine. I ached in so many different places, the points of pain roamed so fast from day to day, I almost disbelieved my memory. Veronica said that this continual movement of pains was similar to rheumatoid arthritis, and her face looked serious, concerned. I felt like I was rapidly going downhill, on a terrible ride I couldn't stop. As I attempted to do the movements, it felt as if there were weights inside each limb. I rested, then stood up again, a lead figure. I tried, but in the middle of the verse exercise, I broke down— "I'm falling apart, I can't do it," I sobbed, retreating to the chair in the corner.

Meeting My Rheumatologist
January

A researcher at UCB, Claudine Torfs, contacted me about a study she was working on, concerning siblings who had lupus and childhood onset of diabetes. She wanted to get blood samples from both my sister and myself, and we were both eager to participate. While talking to Claudine, she recommended that I go to a lupus lecture at Merritt Hospital. She said that there would be two excellent rheumatologists there, and so I went.

One of the doctors was a black woman who practiced in Oakland. She was extremely articulate and sharp. A greater ratio of black women get lupus, and almost 90% of all lupus patients are women. I asked her if she felt that flare-ups were stress related.

"Personally," she qualified, "I think so, for stress can certainly affect one's resistance and ultimate health."

The more taciturn of the two doctors practiced in Berkeley, and I liked his steady, relaxed manner right away. Dr. Ellman was also young and handsome which didn't hurt, and he seemed accustomed to Berkeley's odd ways and alternatives. I thought at the time—If I ever need to see a rheumatologist, I'll call him.

Now, months later, in this new phase of achiness, I found his number and gave him a ring. I was a bit startled by his telephone voice, quick and matter of fact. After I briefly described my present condition, he asked me, "What insurance do you carry?"

"Actually, I don't have any insurance for lupus," I explained. "I dropped out of Kaiser, and then Blue Cross said that they wouldn't cover SLE for the first five years, four and a half more years now."

"Well what are you going to do if you have to be hospitalized?"

I was dumbfounded. "I don't know." I had never thought I'd have to go into the hospital. Not yet. "I guess I'd go in, if I had to. I do want to take care of myself." What a dummy I was, sick with no coverage. We agreed that I should have some lab work done, and that he'd call in an order to the Pathology Institute.

When I went there to have my blood drawn, I couldn't help noticing the sign for dialysis on the open door to this large room, where patients lay watching individual t.v.'s, each person hooked up to a huge mechanical device, which takes out the blood, cleans it and replaces it, a process necessary when your kidneys dysfunction, renal involvement being the most serious aspect of lupus.

One older, black woman lay there, making this awful, uninhibited moaning sound. It sounded as if she were in agony, and I was aghast, but the receptionist just shook her head, "Oh that woman, she's such a nuisance. She always makes such a scene."

o

The aching wasn't getting any better, though the pains continued to roam from day to day, so that it was difficult to remember where my complaints were located.

I was sitting on the edge of the chair in the waiting room, when Dr. Ellman swung open the door, chart in hand, giving me a warm and friendly welcome, "And how are you. This way," he pointed to a room on the right. "This isn't my office, but we can use if for now."

"Must be like cooking in someone else's kitchen," I said, looking around, and he chuckled. I sat down on the rigid built-in seat and had to screw around sideways to face the doctor. I liked him immediately. I even liked the fact that he was sucking on a mint to hide the smell of his last cigarette. This was the first time I'd visited a doctor who seemed to be of my generation. He was casual, and yet well dressed, hip, while still retaining a certain authority of manner with his dark clipped beard and strong forehead. He smiled as he tapped my records together on the desk. "You know your lab work looks extremely good."

I hopped right up to look over his shoulder at the list of abbreviations and corresponding numbers, all of it a maze to me. He took the time to point out a few of the particular tests, what they measured and how. Most of my rates fit right into the normal range, no problem. I sat back down, concerned, pleased in a way, and yet worried—Why did I feel like this if I was healthy.

I showed him the lab results from Dr. Tuffanelli's office, which indicated that my C3 test had been low, but it was normal now. Dr. Ellman thought the low recording was most likely a mistake of the machine, but I wondered if the change wasn't due to the success of the

Iscador and eurythmy. My sedimentation rate also looked normal. Everything, on paper, looked fine.

He asked me about my past history, and I told him about my discoid lupus and treatment. I was still using sunblock. I described how my hands had begun to feel arthritic last summer, and how I was afraid I might be developing SLE, but I'd never had a flare-up, so I didn't know what to expect, exactly. "I'm taking Iscador, a mistletoe derivative," I said, but didn't want to get too deeply involved in that discussion when the word "homeopathic" brought a quizzical look to his face.

"Just another way of looking at things," he admitted, with a learned amount of tolerance.

"I've had a history of false-positives to syphilis tests. And when I was seventeen I had a detached retina operation."

"Any other operations?"

"Just on my toe," I said.

"Was it a hammertoe?"

"Why yes. I think it was." And then there were my recurring swollen glands as a child, those undiagnosable swollen knees in high school, which came and went. Did any of this relate to lupus? Was medicine a game of detection, putting the far-fetched clues together, unmasking the mystery malaise?

I was startled to find out that this visit included a physical exam. It was time to move into the next room, and when he handed me the white examination gown he mentioned, "Just keep on your underwear," and left me to change.

I had been following Dr. Gorter's recommendations rather enthusiastically, dressing in multi-layers. I didn't feel comfortable these winter days unless I was good and warm. So now off came a homespun vest, then a green wool turtleneck and a long sleeved cotton pullover, and finally a thermal undershirt, my appearance shifting from hefty to thin. I left on the long red underwear, slipped on the skimpy drape and sat down on the examination table feeling a bit chilled.

When he returned, he stood at the foot of the table and looked down at the tops of my hands. "I used to crack my knuckles as a kid," I told him. "That's why they're so big."

"That's not why," he answered kindly. His hands looked refined compared to mine.

"You mean they *lied* to me?" I laughed.

"Not exactly," he smiled. "They just didn't know any better."

They told me I was nervous. I shouldn't crack my knuckles or chew on my yellow pencils. Missy Renny knew enough to call me, "Knobby Knees," as I got on the yellow school bus, my big unshapely knees above my dark blue knee socks, beneath the hem of my polo coat. Knobby knees, two words, shattered my unself-consciousness. I was no longer simply me, but two awkward humps of bone, unlike the rounded caps of smaller girls. I was tall and lanky, a knobby kid with big clanky parts, but I had always been strong, always the fastest runner. Was my body going to give out on me so soon?

He gently checked each joint, each finger, elbow, this way and that. I looked down at the on-going action as if it were an intricate and interesting set of tools he was inspecting. No point was actually painful on contact—the aches were more illusive than that.

"What are these? he asked, tugging gently on the long red underwear. "Do they come up?"

"You said to keep on my underwear, and these were all I had on."

His face made a little jump of shock. And I was embarrassed. I realized he had to take a look at my knees. The long underwear were tight pulled up over my calves. I had to try and ignore myself. I wasn't a woman, just knuckles and muscles and joints and bones.

I lay back on the table so that he could listen to my chest. No organs were swollen or painful to the touch. My blood pressure was normal, lungs clear, no atrophy. Everything seemed o.k. I got dressed and we talked again.

"Well maybe these aches aren't from lupus," I suggested, "but some other arthritic condition."

"Perhaps," he agreed. He wasn't going to jump to a diagnosis. I simply wasn't obvious enough. There was no physical proof.

"If you do get extremely uncomfortable, you might start taking some aspirin, two to three aspirin, four times a day."

"I'd rather not have to do that," I said, as I generally didn't take aspirin at all. "I'd like to avoid taking any medication if possible."

"Well you probably won't have to. I think you'll probably feel better soon." Dr. Ellman had a gift for optimism, sometimes confusing to the patient who proceeded to get worse, but it was uplifting to look forward to the best. I suppose if one heard the list of all possible symptoms, the patient might begin to manifest them, or dwell on their possibility and get depressed.

He went on to suggest that I reapply to Kaiser for coverage. Despite my previous experiences there in dermatology, he said that Kaiser had one of the best rheumatologists in the area. "You could still see me if you wanted to, but just having your lab expense covered would be a great savings. And you know Alta Bates Hospital won't even check patients in unless they have coverage. Besides, none of us could afford $500 a day. None of us. Kaiser can actually be quite good for people who are very sick. They just don't pamper the worried but well."

Did he put me in that category? Did he think I was a hypochondriac? I agreed that I would reapply to Kaiser, and did, but it was too late. They didn't want me any more than I wanted them.

Because I didn't have any coverage for SLE, he reduced my initial check-up fee, so I felt justified in treating myself to lunch at *Le Picnique*, but I stupidly finished off the meal with two cups of coffee, which sent me into a caffeine dash all around town, doing errands, shopping for Geoff's birthday, and though I knew I was over-extending myself, I was still exuberant on returning home, just fine fine fine, but soon I ran out of fuel, and went down down down.

Was I trying to prove Ellman wrong? During the following few days, I started to come down radically. The pains became more intense, still striking different locations daily. My hands, the muscles on the back of my hands, which connected to my wrists, were most often painful. My knuckles became swollen, until it was difficult to bend my fingers. It was hard to get a shirt off, hard to hold the steering wheel, cut an orange, brush my hair. It was hard to function.

II

The Disease
Takes Hold

One Step at a Time

February 1982

Now that I was getting sick, I worried about my weekly shots of Iscador. Was I doing the right thing? Was I making myself worse? Dr. Gorter was back in Amsterdam now, and he hadn't responded to my last letter. I knew that my friend Jill went to a highly reputable anthroposophical doctor in Harlemville, New York, and this Dr. Incao was also a friend of Veronica Reif's. She encouraged me to call him. I was becoming increasingly nervous about my condition as it worsened, and I'm sure some of that anxiety was in my voice as I talked to him long distance.

I asked him if he thought I should continue taking shots of Iscador, considering my condition, and he thought that I could safely keep on, unless I developed renal involvement. He also thought that I might begin taking some raw adrenal concentrate to help my adrenal glands do their job. He seemed sympathetic and reassuring, but still I felt like I should be under a doctor's close supervision if I were to continue giving myself these shots. I felt that a homeopathic approach would be best for me in the long run, but I also worried that the Iscador might encourage the inflammation. I didn't know. I didn't know enough and had no one who could give me confirming support about my condition and this medication. I was frightened. My body was attacking itself.

The pains roamed from neck joint to knees to the soles of my feet, and my shoulders ached too, especially when I tried to sleep on my side. So painful to sleep now, moaning and turning. I began to wear only slipper socks, and came down the stairs one step at a time, painfully descending. It was time to start taking those aspirin. I took eight aspirin a day for a while, but still kept getting worse, so I tried twelve aspirin, and felt a slight improvement, but also experienced ringing in my ears, heartburn, and nausea.

After a week of this aspirin therapy, I came down with the flu, and it dropped me for three solid days. I just slept, hardly moving. I stopped eating, stopped taking the aspirin, stopped the Iscador. I didn't want to put anything more *in* me. I wanted to sleep the magical sleep. But when I awoke, I cried so easily, full of self-pity. A horrible sore throat. Drugged on sleep but still exhausted.

I could hardly read. After a few paragraphs my eyes would close. My knuckles looked bruised, shiny, as if they'd been rubbed with lead pencil. I was dreadfully sore between my shoulder blades, and also in my chest, as if I were getting punched here and then there. I was sore on both sides of my spine, just above the hip bones, and I worried about my kidneys, though the tests had shown no involvement there. How could I trust those tests! The tests said I was normal.

By February 9th, Geoff's birthday, I was worse off than ever. Geoff had to push me up in bed that morning, and then pull me to a standing position. It was hard to move at all. Each morning he helped me get into a steaming hot tub, holding me under the arms, lowering me in as I carefully moved into the water, rigid as a Barbie Doll. Once in, I could move my limbs a bit better, pushing back and forth like a child making the water swell and splash. I'd sit there until I felt soggy, while he got the children fed, and Clovis ready for school. Then I'd call for him to help me out too. It was extremely odd, as if my brain couldn't remember how I had ever gotten out of a bathtub before. I tried to think, but couldn't fathom. I was astounded by how unconscious one is of simple movements, which now seemed extraordinarily difficult. I promised myself that I would be more aware in the future, that I would always move gracefully, with the dignity of an upright human. I sat at the large round dining room table and looked out the front window onto Cedar Street, watching all the young *and* old as they sauntered, strolled, ran and roamed, walking along with swinging gaits, with such pleasurable ease. I was envious.

We opened Geoff's presents, and then I too indulged in bacon and eggs, his once-a-year birthday special. I chased it with milk and three aspirin, still feeling queasy, quickly heading back to bed.

Usually by mid-afternoon I looked human, and was almost limber for a couple hours. Geoff drove me over to Dr. Ellman's for a brief drop-in visit. I didn't have an appointment, but wanted to try an aspirin substitute. He came over from the hospital to give me some Trilisate, and I apologized for the nuisance, but he didn't seem to mind. He suggested that I start by taking one pill in the morning, one at night, to see how my stomach handled it. Then I could go on and take two pills, both morning and night, until my symptoms disappeared. I thanked him profusely as he handed me samples and the prescription, confident that I had the cure in hand. Though I was exhausted from that short visit, I felt optimistic that the worst was over.

The next night I slept more easily, in bed by 8 P.M., but again in the morning, it was extremely hard to get out of bed. Sometimes I'd call Clovis in, ask him to hold me under the arms, and with a *one, two, three—Pull*—get me up into a standing position. The morning tub ritual had become so boring, but necessary. I'd never been so clean in my life, two tubs a day, the second one taken before retiring, when the stiffness became extreme again. My left knee made it particularly hard to move. Both knees were swollen, and my jaw was beginning to ache.

My throat also continued to be extremely sore, difficult to swallow. Sometimes in the late afternoon I felt flushed, warm, but I almost enjoyed that mild feverishness.

One day I was on an upswing, and the next, sent back, way back. Dull as that child's board game, *Chutes & Ladders*, with those slow slow climbs and easy slips. Easy to feel demoralized, defeated, when evening sleep doesn't roll in regular.

That afternoon the chills really shook me, and my regular afternoon fever climbed to 102°. Trying to sleep, I heard this noiseless hum. When I opened my eyes, fixed on the beam above, it stopped, but then as soon as I closed my eyes again, voices kept turning on, coming in and out, overlaid, overloud TV type reporters, mostly men with disturbing, bad news.

Far Away/Valentine's Day
February

The children seemed so far away, taken care of, surprising when I saw them. Nicole, Geoff's sister, came by often to help with Ayler and the house. Ay continued to go to his playgroup twice a week, but he began to seem more whiney, upset, and there was nothing I could do. I could no longer even dress him. It almost hurt to hold him. I couldn't pick him up. I protected my body from him.

I usually went straight back to bed after breakfast, though I was also determined to get in *some* movement, afraid that my body was going to atrophy. I did a slow motion pick-up, shuffling around our tiny bedroom. Feet no longer swollen, but now my back was worse, throat worse, sore butt, sorely tired of this immobility.

Dr. Ellman had gone to a conference the night Geoff called in, and so he talked to Dr. Weaver, who didn't think I was in very good shape. He thought I should probably be in the hospital, where they could keep a close eye on me, but that would only be an emergency option for us, without insurance. Being at home was so much more comfortable, preferable. (Though if I'd been a single mother, or lived alone, I would have felt helpless.) Staying home was the luxury of love.

Here it was, Valentine's Day. Geoff gave me a glorious, bright red blow dryer. And then after dinner, my sister-in-law, Michele, arrived from La Jolla. I cried in relief, with thankfulness to see her, giving her a big welcoming hug. Her mere presence was a healing balm. Her deep warm laugh carried with it a soothing, mothering wholeness.

I took my evening bath and then upstairs she gave me a massage, working slowly, gently, taking her time, talking to me with that lulling voice of hers. I almost drifted off to sleep, but then, as she slipped away, I was aware that the table light was still on, and then I became more awake and tense, wanting so badly to sleep! My evening flush and panic took hold, oh *no*, insomnia.

> *Insomnia is a bore. So what if I sleep all day. I want to sleep all night too! I want to respond like a human being, not a creature. I am waging war with the moon, that ovum. The moon seems to mock my sex and situation. Do you have to be so demure? So face-like? Do you have to teach me some unwanted lesson. Nearly invisible, you recede, up there in your matinee, while driving me crazy on your showy nights. Bothered by this cold brand of brightness, my bones stiffen under your influence. Even warm milk with honey won't help. Am I supposed to be serene, is that it? Am I supposed to give in to this changing? Drown myself all day and wash ashore in the evening? I try to outstare the moon, stretching my mouth wide open, wrapping my long white robe, tighter and tighter.*

Sleep. I used to treasure the luxury of at long last lying down at the end of an evening. But now it was an agony to endure, and hopefully, finally escape. I could only get comfortable under Geoff's arm, secure with my Valentine man, but he wasn't always ready to sleep when I was, and I was beginning to disturb him with my groaning and tossing and endless peeing. The Trilisate was clearly not helping. I decided to switch back to an aspirin routine, seeking relief.

The Gerson Diet
February

I was greeted that next morning by a tall glass of carrot juice, surprisingly delicious. Michele had brought her juicer with her, and she wanted me to start on a purification diet. She thought that the Gerson diet would work wonders. This was a no meat, no wheat, non-fat, no salt or sugar, non-milk product (except yogurt) diet. This ordeal of under-eating would last at least two weeks, with grains and fruits and vegetables permitted, only rye bread, lots and lots of juice.

It seemed that Michele and Geoff were constantly making juice. Geoff went out and bought a fifty pound bag of carrots, and I often had an orange ring around my mouth. Michele also had me begin taking some additional magnesium and zinc, along with vitamins B and C. We were following a modified version of the Gerson Diet, not making fresh calf's liver juice, but drinking a daily potassium soup made with vegetables and potatoes. A baked potato, yogurt and asparagus seemed like a satisfying meal.

Removing the toxicity from the body, rebuilding the body with fresh juices from raw, organic foods that have not been denatured, was essential to this diet. Gerson attempted to reverse body chemistry by getting rid of excess sodium, and by putting a great deal of potassium rich foods into the body, reactivating the digestive system and the body's ability to generate enzymes. The detoxification stimulates the healing mechanism that exists in each of us. Many chronic, "incurable diseases" including cancer, lupus, diabetes, M.S., heart and kidney disease, respond well to the Gerson therapy. The diet helps to reduce swelling and water retention, while cleansing and stimulating the liver.

Part of the regime is to take a morning and evening coffee enema. The enemas help cleanse the body of excess toxins, and the coffee is used because it also stimulates the liver. I wondered if we couldn't put the enemas off, but Michele just laughed and told me not to worry— "It'll make you feel wonderful."

She certainly was a brave coach. I hadn't been drinking coffee for a while, and so we made a pan full of CO-OP instant. It smelled quite foul. We had a brand new red bag for the occasion, but where and how would we perform this. It was so difficult for me to move, both up and down, and impossible for me to move quickly. We decided that the best spot would be for me to lean forward on the baby changing table in the small upstairs bathroom. Odd how illness or an altered physical state, makes one feel less modest. If I had been completely well, I don't think I would have been comfortable with this operation of vaselined plastic tube up buttocks. But now I was up for any attempt which might help turn this illness around and emptying the bowels did make sense. I had confidence in Michele.

She had some trouble getting me in position, with several pillows under my head, and then getting the bottle hung up to the right height for action, but once it began to drain, the shock hit my face as well as my bowels—panic/filling/excess/Stop. She cut the cord which cut the flow. My eyes widened. I could control the feeling. It almost felt good as it retreated. Ready? Right. Again, and once more, until the bag hung limply. To relief—load after load exploding. What a great feeling, to be totally unplugged, rid of all that excess, all those potential poisons when blocked up inside. I felt much lighter. But how on earth would I manage that feat alone? An unattractive coffee smell filled the room, and I wished that we were using some other substance, like chamomile tea.

I was taking well to the new simple diet, and I approached it each day with greater eagerness. It helped to think about what *was* allowed, rather than what was *not* allowed, putting it in a positive framework—all those vegetables I liked, and potatoes always were a favorite food. The home squeezed juices were delicious, but it was a bit much, trying to keep up with what they prescribed, almost a full-time job for someone, bringing a glass every hour on the hour. I managed about six or seven glasses a day, rather than the fourteen recommended. Michele still tried to convince me to go to the Gerson Therapy Center near Tijuana, Mexico. She even offered to accompany me, stay with me and go on the diet herself, but I was unwilling to budge from my little chalet-like room with the redwood rafters. I was most comfortable being uncomfortable at home.

By Light Alone
February

Saskia, A Dutch M.D. and acupuncturist, came to visit. She and Michele seemed to talk the same language, as if healing were a dialect.

They sat there at the foot of the bed, while I lay back, the patient. Saskia listened to a number of different pulses, and then they both looked me over, discussing this point and that. She thought I should see an osteopath about my lower back, and she felt trouble in my lower intestine. She agreed with Michele that a purification diet would help. She also thought that my kidneys weren't functioning properly, due to the swelling of my feet, the color of my tongue and one particular pulse.

Before using the short acupuncture needles she wanted to warm me up with a massage. Together, she and Michele, one on each foot, began. What a treat. It felt extremely comforting to receive. Many of my muscles were tense, probably from all those stiff-drops onto the bed, into chairs—up & down, no longer a graceful process. Saskia showed me some helpful relaxation exercises and got me to do some deeper breathing, for my breath was very shallow.

I found the acupuncture itself disconcerting, as if a thread were being drawn up through my leg inside a vein. It was extremely disturbing when she'd twirl a needle. One of the kidney points sent me wailing! Into a real crying jag, but together, they both soothed me with strong and calming rubs. Oh, that was awful. I lay on the bed, so tired, and then barely conscious as Saskia continued to work over me—she the expert baker, and I, the willing dough ball. She placed pressure on certain hip spots, shoulder spots, sliding in a pillow here and there to make me amazingly more comfortable. Her melodious accent also helped relieve the pain, at least temporarily. (But how quickly I forgot how to position those magic pillows! Maddening.) After a long, two hour visit, she kissed me goodbye on the cheek, told me to stay down, rest, that she'd be back in a few days.

I lay there, backwards on the bed, with my feet up on pillows, and watched the light come in, saw how it crept over the white cover of my comforter. Quick warm light slipping up on me. I pulled my hand aside, out of its reach, thinking—How strange, how strange to have to stay outside that luminous circle. Regard. Respect. Revere. By light alone we live and eat, by light alone, do we remain on this cold planet.

The isolation of illness did not seem to be a bad thing. Left alone enough to revive the inner seed, which had withered under the intensity of interaction. I had never before appreciated inactivity. I always had to be doing something, even if it were just knitting or reading— getting to that row in the pattern, or going as far as the next chapter.

Why was I so driven, compelled to attempt perfection, whether it was a poem, that needed rewriting eighteen times, or a dinner party, where every detail, flower and dish had to be set just right ahead of time, the lint picking of daily life; or in my site search for the school, feeling that I, personally, had to canvass the entire town, in control of the whole geography of possibility; or in creating a household atmosphere, trying to keep the plastic toys, TV junk food consciousness from entering, trying to keep my ideals as real as the cotton & wool on our backs; or when planning a vacation, having to have everything ordered, cooked, prepared, planned and controlled ahead of time... yes control, just as Geoff had said. Now I could see it was a factor to acknowledge. But mothering does demand a good degree of management. When you try to control the domestic realm (which almost defies control—you make dinner after dinner into dishes; you clean a house that's a mess within minutes) you can become more rigid in the attempt, for the home isn't a fixed environment, it's people within a living space, and organizing them, making a plan that suits all, can be tough. You have to be infinitely flexible, endlessly orderly and relaxed. Here was one female perfectionist who was at odds with herself.

I knew I had to nurture a looser harmony, let some things go, let dinner slide sometimes, accept the *schlock* if necessary, approach Geoff in a way that wouldn't set us both off—into, who can out babyscreech who? He was good at that, and I always leapt into the emotional froth when offered a splash, flailing my inarticulate outrage, seeing choleric red, instead of phlegmatic green. Purging myself with amplification was no solution. Anger left me rattled.

Perhaps in a disagreeable situation, it was best to simply not respond. Quietness was the killer, the loudest ax. But I would have to work on self-control and a few basic will exercises, before approaching that reasonable log.

But now this bed felt blissful, nothing. Nothing to do, nothing to say, nothing expected. I craved nothing at all. I wanted nothing. Pure of demands, free to be silent.

It was during these afternoons that I felt my soul opening and strengthening, like a muscle. I closed my eyes and imagined a large shaft of light coming down to me, warming the whole bed. I let it enter me, come into my heart and being. I would smile, and my eyes, closed as they were, would fill—so *glad*, as if I were taken back in again, accepted and loved. And I returned it. This feeling moved, both up and down, strong and solid, joining.

During these times I seemed to escape my physical state, but later in the evening, that restless, aching body made its presence felt. No way to lay me down. I wanted to sleep on deep water, a bed of whipped cream, ten layers of lamb's wool. My feet and hands were swelling, back tense and shoulders sore. Finally, I thought to double up our old feather puff, and slept on top of that, which eased the points of contact.

Arthritic Bouquet
February

I could admit it—I liked being pampered for a change. The word was out—"Laura is really sick." And the gifts began to arrive. There were always fresh flowers in the living room—bouquets from Mia and Marianna, Philip, and Jessica. One friend left a bunch of bright colored straw flowers on the doorstep, and their starched look helped me laugh at myself—"The perfect arthritic bouquet!"

When friends came to visit with their children, I could see those young eyes wondering—Why does she move like that? Why does it look so hard. Children are shy around illnes. And I was so easily tired.

And yet each little gift, each gesture took on a special meaning, as if it were part of a love potion meant to heal me...a jar of pears brought in from the country, the books and copper bracelets, casserole dishes, and soups that arrived at our door. I began to feel blessed by this kindness.

Geoff too, was softer, kinder, more considerate than I'd ever known him before. Had I simply overlooked these qualities? He was no longer my jouster, but my protector. I felt this swelling surge of thankfulness for him, and our love seemed to deepen, to mature, as if a history of details had burned down into an essence, a gleam.

I knew Geoff worried about me, not that he would show that. He had helped his mother die seven years before, and just this past summer, he'd also seen his father die of cancer. Sometimes my painfully slow shuffle reminded him. I did look weak and withered, but I never thought I was dying.

That morning Clovis was standing in the kitchen with Michele, while she cut a grapefruit for me, and then she turned to Clove saying—"Can you run this up to Gramma?"

I laughed over that later with her as she prepared to shampoo my hair. It had gotten uncomfortably dirty and snarled, but I didn't have the energy or inclination to take care of it. Hard, with an aching wrist and shoulder to reach behind and brush down. She slowly combed it out—that touch of hands on scalp and hair, making me quiet as a girl.

Michele could see that I had to have some help in keeping the household together. She had to return to her own family soon and Geoff couldn't do it all. Summer offered to get on the phone and locate someone to help us. I felt slightly resistant, but we hired the first and only women we interviewed, Elizabeth, an Iranian woman who seemed very eager. She began the next day.

Unfortunately, she was not effective when it came to cleaning. She took Ayler's woolen soakers, and mopped the bathroom floor, leaving a watery-waxy pool, stuffing the soaked soakers behind the toilet. I got the impression that she wasn't experienced and that cleaning work was beneath her. But her manner with Ayler was disconcerting as well. She was angular, impatient, and it hurt me to hear her urging him to do something, to go somewhere in that anxious, abrasive tone. I wasn't fit to intervene, wasn't able to take over the job, and yet I couldn't be comforted by the situation either. Finally, I managed to focus her activities in the kitchen, where she flourished, cooking up wonderful, exotic dishes that appealed to the whole family.

Jeanne, my high school Mother's Helper, agreed to come in and clean, taking care of the boys during those long afternoon-evenings when Geoff taught late. Her neat, pleasant gracefulness really saved me and the feeling tone of the household. She was always cheerful and calm, gently coaxing with the boys, and yet playful. They adored her, and I did too.

I had no tolerance for noise or upset now. The slightest irritations—a saw starting, a truck roaring up the street, Ayler crying in the backyard—exhausted me from a distance. I missed the children, but I had to shield so much out now, and I hated myself when I snapped at them like some old dry twig. When the children refused to go to bed, I felt myself getting hot with anger and immobility. "Jeanne!" I'd call into the kitchen, "Could you take these children upstairs!" And she'd whisk them calmly away with a true suppleness of spirit, and I'd cover my eyes, depressed, that I couldn't even mother anymore.

Here I was in my early 30's, and I was beginning to have the premature understanding of what the aging process could be like. When you become physically stiff, hardened and in pain, it's easy to be crotchety, unyielding and uptight, but I was determined to see the arc go the other way, soaring above the physical restraints and complaints. It was a struggle. Sometimes I felt like I was no more than a bust-up pile of kindling, left in preparation for some big bonfire.

Trying to Sleep
February

I usually woke after my awful nights feeling whimpery and weak. The nights, the nights. The miserable nights. It wasn't getting easier. I began to feel my optimism drag.

It was such a struggle getting positioned for the night. I was lucky if I could land just right on the edge of the bed—blowing my breath out as I released down, so that I wouldn't tense up on hitting the mattress. Then slowly, I would scoot inch by inch back and around, getting pillows somehow placed under knees, and then dragging the heavy puff over me, reaching for the heating pad, which was pressed to the most demanding spot, and then once I was positioned, if not in a raging sweat from this frustrating set of moves, I remained comfortable for a matter of minutes. Then it seemed excruciating to have to stay in that one position any longer. It was also agony to move. With a huge force, I would will myself over on my side. I could never have made it onto my stomach without help. I became almost frozen with arthritis at this time of night, and the rheumatic pains became worse, more intense. Perhaps the darkness concentrated the pain, no sound or sight to distract me.

But then, when I did manage to settle down, and felt like I might sleep—the hope for sleep a very fragile thread—when complete tiredness lay on top of me, then, I realized that I had to pee, urgently had to pee *now*. Hadn't I just relieved myself? Perhaps, but it was necessary again. Getting myself back up to the edge of the bed was a brutalizing feat, my feet aching as they touched the carpet. I was using a bread pan for a pee pot, slipping an old diaper beneath me in case I missed, and then pushing my buttocks a bit off the edge of the bed so that I didn't have to really get up.

One feels so reduced, subtracted, down to a kind of helplessness, dependency wed to despondency. Dependency can call up the best in the person depended upon. That seemed to be true with Geoff, and it made me think that perhaps in normal life, I hadn't been dependent upon him enough. I realized that he liked the fact that I needed him, needed his complete support. He hardly ever complained about my restless nights. So often I would call out to him, crying to please help push me over, to help me change position, and he would always come to my rescue.

And yet each night I grew more and more panicked about my insomnia, that seemingly self-produced torture. I'd whimper like a battered puppy in my sleepless state. Geoff asked Dr. Ellman if I couldn't have a prescription for sleeping pills, but he didn't want to give them to me. "They're too addictive," he said. "Insomnia is better than withdrawals."

Saskia recommended that I make use of this quiet, middle of the night time. "When I was pregnant," she told me, "I had a terrible time sleeping, and I'd get up and light a candle. I had my own comfortable little place in the living room, with pillows and pictures, flowers there waiting for me, and I'd sit down for a while and just meditate. Maybe you could try and read. It's all right if you don't sleep. Just don't get tense about it." But the mere thought of having to move, having to actually get up, find a book, and read, at this hour of rigor mortis, made me furious. This wasn't just a state of sleeplessness, but a state of wakeful pain.

Nothing Works
February

I never left the house now except for my weekly visit to Dr. Ellman, those traumatic treats. Going out made me feel more normal, but trying to feel more normal was exhausting. I truly felt like an invalid now. I needed help walking down the front stairs of the house, needed help to get into the Honda, help to get out, help to get up from the waiting room chair, help Help, HELP. But Dr. Ellman was always cheerful and kind, and managed to make me feel better. His concern only made me feel confident, rather than worried. I still wanted to avoid steroids, though the aspirin wasn't helping. My blood tests showed the possibility of hepatitis and he ordered a viral hepatitis panel.

Because it was difficult for me to climb up stairs now, the office nurse came down to take my blood, and as I shuffled into the other room, I looked out the window towards The International House of Pancakes, there on the corner of Derby and Telegraph. I couldn't resist pointing it out to Dr. Ellman—"You know that's where we first worked when we moved to Berkeley."

"You're kidding," he said, amazed or amused.

"Nope, the summer before we got married, I was a waitress and Geoff was a busboy." That was thirteen years ago, summer of People's

Park gas mask hysteria, and ReVoLuTion, while I, in a dreadful orange and white uniform served hot plates of short stacks to both sides. Not once during that summer of waitressing did I walk out of that garish building, and look over across the parking lot to this more sober, dark green stucco office building and wonder—What's going on in there. It's easy to look back on the past and smile, harder to grin at the future.

Dr. Ellman wanted me to stop taking aspirin, because of this indication of hepatitis. (We found out on the next round of tests, that I didn't have hepatitis, it was simply that twelve aspirin a day had been making my liver dysfunction.) After stopping the daily aspirin, my liver returned to normal. I was now taking Naprosyn instead, another aspirin substitute.

My urine and blood tests indicated no serious renal involvement, but during the past few years I'd felt a growing sensitivity surrounding the area of my kidneys. I simply couldn't bear to be tickled or squeezed around the waist. I didn't even like to be surprised there with a touch.

I wondered if I should avoid certain foods—salt, dairy, red meat? When I asked Dr. Ellman, he said that he thought that diet had nothing to do with arthritis. Nothing had been scientifically proven. He thought most diet/arthritis books were simply written for the money, and that disturbed him. Maybe one diet would work for 3% of all patients who tried it, but then maybe something else would have worked for them too.

There did seem to be this rift between naturopaths and allopathic doctors, and it was unfortunate that both sides didn't learn more from each other.

Sometimes, while trying to contemplate the "whole picture," I felt certain naturopaths were sincerely trying to help me while knowing next to nothing about lupus itself, and that made me mistrustful. But I also believed that there were good things to be gained from the alternatives, that how one lives, loves, eats and feels *does* make an impact on the progression of disease. More holistic knowledge and more research was necessary, and less snobbism, less suspicion, from *both* sides.

I had begun to ease off the Gerson diet, slowly, indulging in a bit of butter and then that touch of mayo or cheese. I felt so clean that all the food I had eliminated seemed to be unclean, tainted, and yet as soon as I brought them back into the realm of possibility, new cravings began. I decided to stay off of red meat, and I also wanted to limit my salt intake, but I do adore salt. Pretty soon I wouldn't even turn down a potato chip. Maybe if I'd stayed on the Gerson diet for months, instead of weeks, it would have had some affect on my arthritis, but my condition had only gotten worse. The weekly acupuncture treatments weren't helping either. Medical friends were encouraging me to take prednisone. But I wanted to hold out a bit longer.

A Loving Oven
February

I had just read in a lupus newsletter—"When life gives you lemons, make lemonade!" Pretty corny, *tra-la*, but I did want to know the flipside of sourness. I was sure some strength would come from this time of weakness. Laughter from tears.

One of Steiner's FIVE BASIC EXERCISES, entailed choosing any object (a candle, a pencil) and holding it in mind for five minutes, every day for a number of weeks, preferably at the same time each day. One could imagine the specific object in a variety of ways. The will task was to keep other ideas and mental ramblings from intercepting that concentration.

I chose the lemon to meditate upon, and as I lay there in bed thinking "lemon" I sang my own composed mantra—*the blossom the fruit the seed the tree*—until the images started juicing.

> From the thick skinned, bright yellow, nipple tipped green stamped fruit, to the sweeter softer lemons Ayler picks in the backyard at Joyce's. Summer tang clings to your fingers. Peeling the skin, then the white underwear, ways of slicing, in sections or circles—the wheel—then the seed, that slippery pip, containing potential for an entire tree, grandparent to an orchard. The mind multiplies the sun-scent of citrus. Cuteness in the form of bud, pushes out from the tip of branches, until smooth little leaves lip the air. A bright smell of flower lifts up, floats into the bedroom window. You regard the heavy fruit, a zeppelin of light, you give it just a gentle squeeze.

○

I humbled myself before the sun, remained—head bowed, before its forces. But I didn't think of the sun as my enemy. Even here, back in the shade, I still did partake, for everything is *of* the sun, everything that lives, all that we eat, part of the process of sunlight—*Oh sweet link to life.*

When I felt the warmth of the sun filling my room, saw it gliding into my window, I turned inward, and the light inside me flew upward, streaming in both directions, amidst the holding tone of stillness, the infinitely heavy made perfectly light, the slightest touch of angelic presence, left in an imprint of sunlight—I am filled with it. I am Filled. I am full. At peace with it, growing well, accepting of it, at one with it, belonging to it, open, turned over, surrendered to it. I am glad. I rest, asleep.

O

There is a girl with bare arms, in the summer sun, she has few clothes and the air is a comfort to her limbs. Her hair is gold while the grass is green and light-filled. Her heart is hunting for a small warm nest to rest in. She knows a place in the open field, and makes a bowl in the tall grass. Her skin smells warm like curved oats, but the little hole in the green grass shows only tremendous blue, with clouds shooting through it and the summer heat is a loving oven. Her blood is as warm and fresh as the green juice she sucks from a stalk. She loves this heat, the sun of summer, her bare limbs, this young life, without even naming or knowing it.

O

The ease of sleeping forever it seemed, not having to take care of everyone and everything, letting all that slide, away on some gradual downhill ride, away from this place where I rested.

Saskia encouraged me to visualize myself in my own large egg, a womb room place of protection. She said to fill the space with color, and I chose a golden rose, swirled together, letting me turn in its soft warm sac, keeping all the faces quietly, calmly out there, on the outside, where they would be well taken care of, and I was too, safely slung in the peaceful fluid of recovery. I let the warmth and color come in through my head as I breathed in, breathing deeply, and then all the way out, down through my feet, as I exhaled. The colorful light was flushing me clean, warming me also. Protected like this, I was at ease.

And when something negative came at me from the outside, with its inky spear, I lowered my light shield—*shoooump.* I would not let it, they, him, words or her, actions or phone calls upset me.

I am whole and the light is shining, blazing before me. Let it burn my eyes clean. Let it burn away sickness, hatred and evil. I feel this force behind me. I don't have to look behind me. I know it is there, like wings, and I'm going to walk on through.

Big Bad Wolf
February

The children were screaming, running and playing—Big Bad Wolf. It bothered me, this game. I didn't like to hear it. I didn't quite know why.

Ayler raced to the bed, jarring it, and he was terrified, as if something were truly on his heels, ready to devour him... Clovis crawled in slowly, growling, and he was as wild as the real wolf to Ayler's two year old imagination. Was Ay too young to be frightened? Or did he like this game of scare & chase, fear & rescue. When he looked at the card which pictured a wolf, he said viciously, "I'm gonna *cut* him up," making a slicing gesture. Just like the story. Too young for that story. But I was too young too, for any old wolf to swallow me up.

Geoff pointed out that they had been playing a lot more of this wolf game since my flare-up started, and maybe somehow, to them, it was literal, lupus being the big bad wolf. Was that a juvenile connection? Or was I as frightened too? But wouldn't admit it. I didn't like the game because I didn't want to have to think about the possibility—"I'm gonna getchyou, gonna eat you up." I never felt that close to mortality's edge, and yet I knew that this disease was full of surprises— Life itself, both giving and threatening, inhaling, exhaling, restoring, depleting. Hard to think of those rhythms stopping. Slowing perhaps, changed, but not over. Cycles. A world without end.

When Ayler thought he saw the monster by the bookcase in the morning light, pointing—"Big, bad, wolf," in his ultra-scary voice, all I could say was, "Blow on it, and it'll go away." I blew. "See, it's gone, all gone."

But was that an attempt to make nothing of his fear, which was real. Was it simply wishful thinking to imagine that my disease would also blow over, slip into remission, off into the woods, only to lie there waiting for me to step off the path again. My body had been so altered, it was as if *I* had swallowed the grandmother. (And who would be my huntsman.)

The wolf game led to monster talk. "There was a Monster driving on a tractor, and he said Stop and he was *mean* and he Eats you up!"

What were these shadows creeping forth, shadows without bodies. More monsters before bedtime, monsters in the dark. I tried to tell him that he was protected, that he had a guardian angel. That Clovis had an angel too who watched him while he slept. That I also had an angel, who was leading me and helping me.

"Mamma," he cried, in the middle of the night. "Mamma," and I came. "There's a big dog under my bed!" For a moment, I too, was afraid.

I could see how both children were upset by what was happening to me—the quiet talk, the inferences heard, the "Oh NO," reactions people had, Geoff worrying out loud on the phone. Clovis showed a child-like disgust when saying the name of the disease. Did they wonder—What *is* wrong with our mother. Will she leave us all alone? Why's she so tired.

I didn't think that they questioned my condition, or asked for an answer from the future, but my condition had upset the regular rhythm of their lives.

"You *sick* Mamma?" Ayler asked, with real concern anchoring his eyes. "You sick *this* much?" He measured.

I nod, smile. I lift my hand. He nods, then trots away.

Last Resort
March

Saskia thought that a lot of my muscle soreness was coming from tension and fear. That didn't seem accurate, but then again, maybe I wasn't admitting fears that were expressing themselves physically.

Sometimes, naturopaths seemed to put too much responsibility on the patient's mental state—it's all in your head—you can change your physical state with will power, positive thinking, or prayer. I believed in the will to live and a positive outlook. I believed in spiritual forces, but a physical state is also physical. No one tells a diabetic to visualize it away. Sometimes it's a lifetime's pattern that has built up towards the expression of an illness, the result of years of parental and environmental effects, years of food and bad habits, general wear and tear, hereditary factors coming forth, and then when it appears, it seems to be—Out of the Blue, an expression of the moment.

One book in particular became irritating to me, when it said that I didn't have to experience pain if I didn't want to. Sounds like those birth books, right? You don't have to be sick if you don't want to be sick. Baloney! It's all in your mind, your diseased soul. Believe me, it can be a relief to talk about one's physical state with a non-judgmental rheumatologist.

So what were we going to do about this physical state of things. The Naprosyn wasn't working. My fingers were so swollen, Dr. Ellman was concerned I might have to cut off my wedding ring. A waking, moving existence had become a continual pain. We would try one more week of another aspirin substitute, Clinoril, and then prednisone. I was softening in that regard, reaching the end of my endurance rope.

I called around and talked to other women with lupus, and prednisone seemed inevitable. One very friendly woman, Ann, mentioned that she got a big lump of fat on the back of her neck, like the lump of fat on a bull's neck. She said that she got sores on her scalp from the sun and reacted very easily from sunlight—even just driving home from work in the car. "I used to be so blond," she moaned. "My hair would almost get bleached white by the sun. I had to come to accept this new self-image. When we go out, I often have to just go lie down, and if people don't understand, too bad. It sure helps to have a supportive husband. My husband's been so patient. And I guess I've just gotten used to prednisone. It's part of my life now. I'm going to be weaning myself off again soon I guess." She seemed to be taking it all in stride.

Prednisone appeared to be something you came to accept, learning how to deal with side effects, finding your own way off.

But we had heard so many awful things about prednisone, Geoff was already calling it, "Dreadnisone." It seemed like the last resort, out there on the desert, pretending to be an oasis. I wanted to wait a little bit longer before taking that kind of vacation.

Permission
March

While I kept a cheerful expression for most of my friends, often when Summer came up to see me, I'd look at her and collapse into sobs. Her presence gave me permission. Maybe I had always leaned on that, for she soothed so well, not over-reacting, and yet not pulling away from emotion, not telling me—Don't cry, you'll get better—but acknowledging that I felt rotten, and that this was all so rotten and that she was upset too. I always felt so much better after letting those tears go, and surprised at myself too, for I hadn't realized how much I was holding in—always trying to be the happy sick girl.

When I cried first thing in the morning, making my feeble attempts to get out of bed, I knew the children were aware of my lamentations, and I tried to repress my tears. I felt guilty if they caught me crying, mainly because I thought it would only further confuse and upset them. It was all right for them to see me physically sick, but not emotionally weak. With Summer, I was relieved to be myself. *Sad.* It was enough to impress on a friend how miserable I felt. Then we could talk, and she would fill me in on the news from Out There, never making me feel dull for having no news to return.

When my father came to visit, I was so glad to see him, and almost pleased to impress upon him the seriousnes of my state. He and Mom had been on a cruise, and they had had no real idea of what I'd been suffering these past weeks. I had refrained from telling them about the flare-up before their trip, because I thought they would only worry, but now my condition was plainly visible, as I shuffled across the room, arms held up at waist level. I slowly lowered myself down onto the piano bench, which had been piled high with pillows, so that it wouldn't be such a painful drop down. I had to excuse myself from our banquet of take-out Chinese food. It was difficult to stay in one sitting position for long, achy all over. I let myself down into the armchair, and then after a little more talk, Dad helped me back up. One step, rest. One step, rest. Back up the stairs to bed.

My father, so often boisterous and ready to clap his hands together for some more fun, for the next activity, was rather solemn and quiet. I liked seeing him that way, liked making such an impression on him. I had the feeling, that he felt like he was talking to someone else, not his known daughter, but his orphan, met again after so many years, distant, different, strange.

Sitting there on the edge of my bed, he seemed even bigger than usual. He said that he wanted to help pay for some regular household help. He could see that we needed someone to come in more regularly, to do all the things I wasn't capable of doing. There could be no better gift. He had also splurged on an extravagant Pierre Deux bathrobe for me, and had brought gifts for the children. Aunt Marion and Uncle Verne had sent along a gorgeous Parisian, all cotton, designer dress that suited me to a T. It lifted my mood, to have a new outfit, as if I had somewhere to go.

I did. Back to Dr. Ellman. I felt incredibly shaky maneuvering into that outer world, as if its mere speed and complexity would topple me. But now it was time for medication. I was weary of the endless struggle. Everything about me seemed swollen and stiff and pained.

Dr. Ellman saw that my discomfort was severe as Geoff walked me into his office. Shuffling in, I joked, "This is the best part of my day!" He checked me over. My spleen was still not enlarged, which is often the case during a lupus flare, but my sedimentation rate was climbing steadily and we agreed that it was time to stop dreading the prednisone. I was even anxious to give it a go, to see if it would really yank me out of this pit.

He prescribed 60 mg of prednisone for that first night, and then during the next two weeks, I would reduce the dose by 5 mg a day, taking half of the dose in the morning, half in the evening, until off. He thought that this regime would knock it out of me. I was also going to begin taking 400 mg of Plaquenil, an anti-malarial drug, which would take effect over the long run, and I would continue taking 500 mg of Naprosyn in the morning and 500 again at night.

Geoff ran up to the Co-op Pharmacy and filled all of the prescriptions. After dinner that evening, taking six of those 10 mg pills of prednisone, I felt like I was throwing fate down the hatch.

Nothing happened. I didn't explode or disappear. So I went to bed, and woke up later, in the middle of the night in a pool of sweat. It was pouring out of me. The fever had broken, the heat was flowing, the aches were going as the waters were soaking. Even my fingertips were soggy as if I'd spent an hour in the tub. Completely awake, I felt like I'd just cruised out of the fog, into desert brightness. But this was also like a childbirth sweat, the only other time I'd ever heavily perspired, drenched from head to toe. I took a towel and wiped myself, but the covers were cold with wetness and the sheet was drenched through to the mattress. Geoff left for the hide-a-bed, giving me his side which was warm and dry. I turned the puff around and fell back into a deep sleep.

The sheets were stained yellow by morning. It was an amazing pouring out. Every night for a week the inflammation flowed. I thought perhaps that the sweating was due to the toxicity of the drug, that my body was trying to eliminate it, but Dr. Ellman looked surprised at my odd interpretation. He described the sweating as a flushing out, comparable to pneumonia when a fever breaks and the sweating begins.

I sat on the edge of the bed that first morning, weak and wobbly as a newborn colt, but just as eager. I wasn't in pain. I wasn't in pain! My knees felt full of softened cartilage and my bones bobbled as I tried to walk, loose and slippery as steamed chicken. My wrists and knees did click and pop with certain movements. Some of the achiness was still there, but it was amazing how much had disappeared overnight. I was astounded. I made a bow to modern medicine. All those muscle aches—Gone. So much for fear and tension.

Reversal
March

I was still extremely weak, and needed to sleep a great deal, but I was now on the road to recovering my strength. I stayed in bed almost constantly those first two weeks. No more insomnia, just blissful, grateful sleep, both day and night. As Flannery O'Connor said— "Sleep is the Mother of God," and I couldn't get enough of it.

> *Positioned with pillows, I would lie in the afternoon with my eyes closed, and the sun would flood in between worlds, redwood beams grasping the whiteness. Everything so still, it was a blessing that stillness. The plum tree full of flower, a gentle feeling as sleep came gratefully wrapped in soft swaddling.*

O

I was delivered from pain, but now I also had to deal with some of the other side effects of prednisone—a sudden transformation from having clean, clear skin, to having a spray of tiny adolescent looking pimples across my forehead, a Milkdud Milky Way. Also a proliferation of larger, less lovely "zits" appeared on my back, neck and face. My menstrual periods stopped, which was disconcerting. I no longer had a rhythm, just a regime.

I didn't mind the pills, though the Plaquenil tasted especially nasty. I learned how to fast-pop a couple on top of some tongue-coating raw milk. I was speedily decreasing my dose, and felt better and stronger every day. I was glad that I would only have to take such strong medicine for this short two week period. I was now down to 20 mg, then 15, 10 and 5. I felt decidedly uncomfortable on the 5 mg day, but ignored it. I was getting off. Then day zero—none—and I crashed.

The improvements which had been so radical, were now reversing themselves at an equally shocking pace. Twenty-four hours without prednisone, and I was a third of the way back to where I'd been— aching, shuffling, swelling, crying. *So,* the truth was out, I'd be dependent on this drug forever! Emotionally, I had hit bedrock. I spent most of the day breaking down into tears, hating what I saw in the mirror. Geoff was teaching all day at SFSU, and even had a course that evening. I cried over the phone as the weakness swept back over me, along with all those memories, of where I had been and how awful, memories washing up around the front door, wanting back in—*Go away go away.*

It had been a stream of fire, this illness, and it had only been piped underground, but now the pipe was broken, and so was the pipe dream—Health. I couldn't bear it. I crept back upstairs, while Jeanne took care of Ayler and the messy house. I lay back in bed, my afternoon fever returning, and just rocked and moaned and wept. I felt so utterly alone. Discouraged.

I really had believed that I could get off prednisone in two weeks. When I called Dr. Ellman, he wasn't in, and no one returned my call. I had an appointment to see him in two days, but hell if I was going to put up with a total regression. Finally I reached Dr. Weaver, another doctor in his office, and he suggested I go back to 10 mg that evening, which I did with relief, immediately. Happy as a satisfied addict.

Follow Up
March

It seemed like I was always knitting while I waited to see Dr. Ellman. Knitting seemed to be good therapy, keeping those fingers moving, even if I couldn't do it for very long stretches of time. I enjoyed the handwork, watching the colors progress.

Dr. Ellman opened the door with his usual smiling, friendly face, leaning forward into the waiting room to say hello—a nice way to welcome a patient, I thought, to appear there at the door yourself, rather than having an uninvolved nurse direct you to an empty room, where you could wait again. I always looked forward to seeing him, and as I got up, my pink ball of mohair rolled out twelve feet behind me. He snatched it up, teasing me about enacting some ancient myth.

"What are you making now?" he asked, and I showed him the extent of the big loose luxurious sweater I was making for myself out of pink mohair, with a pale tan border. I was using a laborious seed stitch, and had found some fantastic buttons that combined the color of both yarns, silky pinky creamy balls like giant jelly beans.

After we'd talked a bit about such things, he'd say, "Now tell me about your health," and I'd switch back into that mood. He agreed that I would have to get off the prednisone a bit slower. He prescribed 5 mg pills, which snapped in half. He thought I should try taking the medication only in the morning now, alternating 10 mg one day with 7.5 mg, until I felt good about the low dosage days, then I could stay on 7.5 mg for a week before alternating that with 5 mg.

At 7.5 mg and above, prednisone takes over the job of the adrenal glands, and the danger of stopping medication suddenly is that the non-functioning glands are called back into action before they've had a chance to warm up. No wonder mine were so cranky. Because I am a tall woman, 5' 10", the effects would be less than they would be on a smaller person. With 5 mg and less, there would be few side effects, I was told. I relaxed back into the fact of daily medication, knowing I did want to get off eventually.

The drug certainly seemed to affect my mood. It lifted me up—like the best part of a caffeine high. The world seemed splendid, promising, bright. Hard to hold oneself back. The old drive to go and *do do do* came rushing back, quicker than better. I felt that little over-excited hum of false energy. I wanted to consume. I began to gain weight. Luckily in my case, I needed a little weight, having lost quite a few pounds during those five weeks in bed, being underweight in general. The added pounds seemed to be a good thing, at first, grounding me, bringing me back to earth. But then my pants wouldn't fit. I thought maybe I'd better start controlling myself. I didn't need to make dessert every night. I didn't need to finish everyone's leftovers. It was an oral urge that drove me, more than hunger. I felt so energetic, and yet I was actually too weak to do much. Eating doesn't take much exercise, plus it's gratifying on a sexual level. There too, after weeks of abstinence, I suddenly wanted to gorge myself.

When I had been sick and immobile, my soul had felt stronger, brighter, but now, as I physically began to gain strength, old bad habits started to seem appealing. I even indulged in a few cigarettes before checking that impulse. But why not drink coffee? Why not black tea? Because I felt good, I wanted to be bad, the mischievous, recklessness of spring, the full moon affecting my soul life, the illusion of physical strength.

Flannery's Fiction
April

My friend, Jill, had been avidly reading Flannery O'Connor's letters, and she urged me to get them from the library. Summer picked up the book for me, along with the collected short stories and novels. I was now well enough for sustained reading, and I began to read through all her work, without stop. She was a curious and yet comforting writer to come to, as she too was a lupus victim, though let's scratch that word, "victim," right here. I don't think it would fit with Flannery's notion of the disease, or her life. She had lupus. She lived with lupus. She didn't literally write about lupus, but she wrote from within the consciousness of the chronically ill, and perhaps her disease helped propel her, giving her that urgency. Perhaps that lonely place of illness, "where no one else can follow," gave her writing that edge, insight, fervor.

In the 1940's and 50's, when she faced the disease, so much less was known about lupus and cortisone drugs. She always seemed so courageous in her letters, with her steady severe bouts of the disease, matched by determined comebacks. Her wry sense of humor rose above all, despite the debilitation, crutches, operations, and medications.

When I told my sister, Cia, that I was deep into O'Connor's Southern rural writing, she sent me a paper she had written for a college class, describing Flannery O'Connor's view of Love. Cia wrote me— "The other students thought O'Connor was just morbid, sick and bitter, because of her lupus, but I disagreed!"

Cia and Flannery's orientation was biblical, and without that background it could be a perplexing work to understand, and yet I think the biblical focus brings up something primal, just as being sick also brings similar religious needs to the surface. In facing one's mortality, one grapples. One can not remain self-satisfied, unquestioning. You see things differently. I saw the healing goodness of inactivity, silence, and how the pace of the modern human is so driven— unbalanced. No matter how the spiritual is met or rejected, it suddenly seems to rise up as a route, the golden road out of illness, away from the physical body, or a way to meet the deepest part of the body, the untouchable source.

"It always amazes me," Cia wrote, "how suffering seems such a necessary part of God's training ground. I mean everyone has something to deal with, but sometimes it seems the Lord allows special trials for those who long to know more of Him. I continue to be amazed at how different the Lord's value system is from our own."

Flannery O'Connor's value system was also quite different from that of her age. Then what was the appeal? Something here rang true. She was able to see what was most fallen and corrupt in mankind, possibly because of her position as a double outsider—as a woman writer, and as a person with a chronic disease. She was also an outsider because she was not a materialist in a materialistic age, but a person with spiritual convictions, a Catholic, in the heavily Methodist, Southern Baptist south. "She was an unwelcome prophet to a world that was self-consciously churched, but spiritually dead or self-righteous," wrote my sister.

Being an "outsider" herself, gave her greater compassion for her often grotesque characters. She truly loved them even in their ugliness, with all their human imperfections, while portraying their obvious need for redemption. Her characters are often jolted out of their complacency by some extreme circumstance—just as someone is jolted out of ordinary life when they find out they have a serious disease. The present tense demands acknowledgment. Life comes up close and its meaning shines. The colors of the natural world are filled with light and portent.

My sister wrote—"For O'Connor, God's love is most often manifest as an instrument, not unlike the new electro-shocking cattle prods, compelling the spiritually blind to wake up to their true situation in relation to God, and the state of their neglected souls."

In the midst of disease, one confronts both body and soul, and wonders what has been neglected, what has been pushed too far. What is the way back to wholeness. What was I meant to do here on earth, in order to feel God's pleasure.

Another Skein
April

I decided that I wanted to get off prednisone by my birthday. I made a little chart and began to decrease, but when I told Dr. Ellman, he didn't like it one bit. He didn't want me making false deadlines for myself. "You can only take it one day at a time. See how it feels, and then decide, OK?" OK. He was right. I wasn't ready by my birthday. It would take me longer than I'd hoped.

I had decreased from 10 mg to 5 mg, but when I went down to 2.5 mg I was not comfortable. Dr. Ellman suggested that I just stay on 5 mg for a while, but I asked if he couldn't prescribe 1 mg pills, so that I could reduce even more gradually, from 4 mg to 3 mg, on out. He thought that was a good idea, and so I began my gradual descent. Going back down the mountain's always harder.

At 3 mg I felt withdrawal crankiness again, short tempered, less lubricated in the joints. After two months of medicine, most of my strength had been regained, and I was used to feeling good, so even the slightest arthritic symptom creeping back into hands, shoulders or knees was disgruntling. I could either go back up to 5 mg or get used to 3. I thought I had just better stay there and see. Soon, my adrenal glands seemed to accept the extra load, and all was even again.

It was springtime, and in Berkeley the sun was intense. I found it hard to protect myself. At a school picnic, I wore my visor, which left the top of my head exposed, and I came home flushed, cheeks blotchy. I was slightly disoriented, with a nervous jittery cellular shake. I was reminded of Christmas—too much too fast and on the edge. I had to take the time to conscientiously protect myself. The world was not organized around people who had to avoid midday sunlight. But I didn't have to sit out in the middle of the lawn either. Why didn't I sit in the shade? Because I already felt slightly out-of-it, because everyone knew I'd been sick, and I had withdrawn from school activities, withdrawn from the world, out of touch. I now wanted to enter back in again, while carefully guarding my schedule, not getting over booked. Hard to stay withdrawn enough to suit the needs of the body, while also fulfilling the social self.

We were withdrawing in another way too, away from the West coast to thoughts of the East, away from our struggling urban Waldorf school, to that established Waldorf school in the country. Our dream for a year in the Berkshires was coming true, though sometimes I wondered—what if this becomes another vacation disaster. Will the plans and packing pull me under. Will we be able to rent our house to good people. Will peace and quiet turn into loneliness and despair.

I felt slightly guilty, asking Jill to race around the countryside, looking for the ideal nest for us. There she was, pregnant, fielding all the answers to our ad, but then she found us the perfect dream farm, an old Victorian with a porch running around two sides (shade!) with an apple orchard and a big red barn, on top of a hill with a 360° view, two miles from school, close to Jill's house, a barn full of ponies close by, and good neighbors with children, a bedroom for each of us, plus a study for Geoff and for me. Land, peace, quiet, too good to be true. A good place to die, I thought, before I could stop it.

A good place to knit. Stand corrected. My father used to say that the Greeks believed, when a goddess came to the end of a skein, someone on earth had to die. Life is filled with so many skeins, of so many colors—and moving was like a little death. I didn't fear the challenge of change, but something in me was afraid. What if I got back there, way out in the cold, in the country, and Geoff was planning on going to Paris for a couple weeks, and I would be alone, and what if I got *really* sick, not knowing my doctor, in a new community.... No. I wasn't going to plow the road and merely pile snow up against the doorway. I would work towards confidence, and keep picturing the best.

III

Shining Seed

The Alternative Box
April

I felt like it was time to start seeking a cure. I had wavered from this side to that before, from allopathic to homeopathic medicine, not wholly sure about either, and yet wanting to take what each could offer. If only I had a pure faith in some method, perhaps I'd be better off. The over-eager skeptic's not so good for herself.

I wondered about new alternatives. Here in Berkeley, if you open the door, it's like opening Pandora's lid, the alternative box. But maybe that story would change in the New Age. Instead of nasty little evils escaping from the darkness, maybe tiny sun spirits would leap out from hiding and proclaim themselves Goodness and Mercy. In that light, I went looking.

I had a long phone conversation one evening with an older woman who'd had lupus for many years. She was articulate and chipper, extremely conversant with all the terminology and the new lupus research, but she was also hardcore when it came down to the subject of alternatives. When I asked her about diet, she insisted that a good, balanced diet was all one needed, and though she had met patients who had supposedly cured themselves with herbs or whatever, she was skeptical. She mentioned that a group of Western rheumatologists had recently been invited to China, and it appeared that even the Chinese seemed to prefer western medicine over acupuncture for lupus and rheumatoid arthritis, though it would not necessarily follow that acupuncture was never used or sought by lupus patients in China. I had my own doubts about alternatives, but cortisone drugs, which simply suppressed symptoms and offered no cure, seemed like no answer either.

Everyone had someone they wanted me to see. It was confusing, all the advice. Sometimes people were so eager in their suggestions, I felt forced to consider another route. But what a smorgasbord of therapies there were available in Berkeley. How was I to find someone who would share the same vocabulary and outlook. I suppose it's like looking for the right church to attend. I've never found one. Where is the minister I can talk to, who isn't stuck in some rhetoric or format that doesn't fit my intuitions or needs.

I was sure that there might be genuine healers out there, but basically, I thought I had to nourish something inside myself, and work on that first, alone. Perhaps this disease had come to challenge my life, bringing me to a place where I could be receptive to the spiritual world. I had been so caught up in my daily material life, and had avoided making a place for that quiet, deeper part of myself. Illness can almost be seen as an opportunity if viewed this way. I had been given a break from the daily trudge, and I think I had to experience inaction, so that I could reach into that other realm, where peacefulness sustains one.

Getting in touch with my own personal source, asking for further guidance and help from the spiritual world, seemed more important than the endless muddying of internal waters through psychoanalysis, looking for the subconscious gemstone. I wanted to reach up, above myself, opening, lifting my arms, as I did in eurythmy, moving with that verse—

"Light, and Warmth, of the Divine, World Presence—
Enfold, Me."

Sometimes, as I lay in my large, white bed, aching and turning, it came over me as a soul ache too. How unworthy I was, even to try and reach out. How prideful I had been, how short tempered with my children, how I hadn't even appreciated the man who was my husband. I felt this new tenderness for him, and a tenderness for life. The friends, and the fortunate circumstances, all that I'd been given, I had taken for granted, just as I had taken my healthy body for granted. I had taken, taken, taken. And what could I give back. How could I ever give back enough. What was required of me. How could I allow health to enter back into my body. How would I make way for that. Would prayer fulfill that demand, the desire to replenish. Returning to the world. That was the gift most needed, and yet my offerings were so puny. Why was it so hard? My aloofness made me self-conscious in my attempts to pray. I thought of a knife, bent on opening a walnut, (my old arthritic shell), trying to crack it just right, the naturally snug fit of those perfect halves, the self and the other, the inner the outer, the bitter bark wedged into the nut's sweet meat.

A Joyful Noise

April

Laughter and singing both seemed like the best remedies. I looked forward to joining the school's singing group, which met on Friday afternoons. In the past, at festivals, and at the Christmas Faire, whenever I had sung with this group of friends, it had been a true communion, especially when the entire school community sang "Jubilate Deo," in a three part round, voices braiding, over-lapping, until chills swept up and down my spine.

When I was sick in bed with a sore throat, I looked forward to those times of song again. But when I finally took the prednisone, the sore throat disappeared overnight, and so did my voice. My vocal cords had been affected by that month long exacerbation. The pain had been replaced by a broken voice that scraped like an old 78 rpm record, disappearing altogether at odd moments. Everyone told me how "sexy" I sounded, like Lauren Bacall, but I think it simply sounded like laryngitis. Dr. Ellman didn't know whether it was a temporary condition or permanent, and he didn't think a throat doctor would be able to do anything about it.

I decided to try complete silence, to see if that would give those hoarse vocal cords a break. When I awoke the next morning, the children were in bed, and I didn't say a thing. I felt full, funny, as if I held a hilarious secret. As I got out of bed, I motioned for them to both come, get dressed, eat breakfast, and they responded much better to my pantomime than they normally would have to my verbal instructions. Gesture can reach children readily, and what a delightful change. How often I've had to stop my own nagging voice, a mere repeat of that same old record I listened to years ago. Break it. Change the patterns. Make the bed. Keep the secret, smiling, though laughter's fine for this silence game.

I felt stronger as the day wore on. Holding myself in helped preserve what strength I had, as if talking depleted that energy, let it dribble away, a mere trickle, emptying the tub. I couldn't answer the phone. Wrote silly notes when I had to communicate. Soon others were giggling too for no reason.

Strange, going to *Berkeley Horticultural* that afternoon, and not being able to ask—What kind of plant is this? How much does it cost? Where should it be planted?—I picked up three of the beautiful, flowering plants, paid the uncontested sum, and waved goodbye like a moron as I left, still silent.

But now, a chorus of color, yellow, orange, cerise, sits in harmony outside my kitchen window.

Focus of Light
April

My friend, Linda, wanted me to meet a very special woman whom she'd worked with years before. It was hard for her to describe exactly what Carol Collopy did, because she didn't fit into any neat category or particular movement. When I met Carol, she did seem to be unique, not at all "Berkeley," and though one might call her a healer, she never used that word. She didn't look the part.

A beautifully young, middle-aged woman, who had raised four children of her own, she looked like she might have just come from the Burlingame Country Club, with her neat hair-do, attractive outfit, and gold jewelry. She was not trying to create an aura of externals, but right away I sensed a certain radiant strength.

At Linda's request, she had driven up the peninsula to visit with me. The three of us sat together in the living room. I was still in my bathrobe, convalescing. Because my voice was still bothering me, I had hoped that it wouldn't just be a verbal session. I was ready for the laying on of hands, but I didn't know what to expect. The house was quiet for a change, as a babysitter had taken Ayler, and Linda's daughter, Kirstin, to the park for an hour.

Carol asked me to tell her something about my lupus, and I proceeded to give her a quick run-down of my physical symptoms, how my disease had progressed on the physical level. But this was not where she was coming from, I realized. I felt incompetent to express all that I might have. A sudden sadness welled up in me, and strangely enough I felt like I wanted to get under this woman's arm, weep on her shoulder. I wanted to tell her the truth, how unworthy I was, how I needed to be mothered, but of course I checked that impulse, and was grateful to listen to her. She was warm and yet matter-of-fact. As she sat there and talked, I felt myself opening, receptive to her words, as if her words were warm milk coming from the source.

Her parents were both faith healers. While her mother's physical problems had been answered through prayer, her father had continued to work with a congenital heart problem, that should have taken his life when he was an infant. These family struggles seemed to have strengthened their faith. Even when faced with the most severe physical problems, they never used conventional medicine. She wasn't suggesting that I do the same, merely telling me her story.

Carol recounted two of her own personal healings. When she was a young woman, five of her vertebrae had disintegrated. During this time she was part of a committed group of people who prayed or meditated together at the same time every morning, each in his own home, but with a sense of common purpose, of unity. The group decided that they needed to do something for Carol as her condition worsened. They decided that they would all ask for "what was best for Carol." She too, sat on her bed, and prayed for this, receptive to what might come. Then one morning, during her meditation, she felt a light-charged blast. She believed that she had received the powers of miracle. When she went to the doctor and got x-rays, he was astounded. The radiologist pointed out five tiny seed like spots. They were indeed the beginning seeds of five new vertebrae, which would now proceed to grow. With excruciating but miraculous pain, the vertebrae returned.

Later, when she had had her children, she discovered that she was very sick. She went to a conventional doctor, who agreed to work with her, even though she didn't want to take medication. He was pleasantly gruff, a sincere pragmatist. He told her that she had leukemia, and that she had a very short time to live, a matter of months. Her response to this pronouncement was intuitive.

She found herself waking every night, when her husband and children were asleep. It was August and the evenings were balmy. She would go out into her midnight garden, find a place where she could simply gaze out into the sky, and after several nights she realized that she kept returning her gaze to this one star—she wasn't comfortable unless she could clearly see it. She felt herself actually falling in love with this star, and looked forward to that time she would have with it in the middle of the night, a very quiet time that seemed to be working on her—to open, to accept, and to love.

She had already struggled over the fact of her imminent death, wrestled with her fears and angers, maddened that she wouldn't be able to accomplish her life's work, whatever it was she was meant to do, but finally, with this focus of light, she let all of that go, and sustained this simple relationship with her star. It was then that she began to perceive divine connection, the interweaving of all things, and she knew with her entire being that everything mattered—"Each feather that drops is felt in the universe, every death is acknowledged and received, and every life has its meaning." A huge magnificent network was there and at work, pulsing and full of love. As she admitted this into her being, she felt a complete wave of peacefulness, and she knew that she could die, and it would be all right, that she was part of it.

After that experience, she sensed that she was beginning to heal. She returned to her doctor for more tests, and when he saw her sitting in the waiting room, he looked stunned, and whisked her down the hall to his room.

"What's with you!" he asked her.

She said that she felt very good, and though he was not a poetic type, he had to admit to her that he had seen a shining brightness around her, when he saw her in the waiting room. Most peculiar. He had even moved to make sure it wasn't just a reflection off the glass. She did look exceedingly well. So unusual. When they took new lab tests, there was no sign of leukemia. She had a complete, spontaneous remission.

She went on to describe to me how it was a continual process of learning and changing. What worked at one time, for one problem or for one person, wasn't a formula for everyone. It could be a painful process, finding one's own point of concentration, or focus, learning new ways in which to open, allowing health to enter.

She asked me if I prayed, and I said that I tried. I thought of my feeble attempts, like someone who wants to paint, who loves color, and yet who holds the ready brush above the paper, wondering— Now, what do I do. There was no one technique. Each person had to find her own style, her own expression—how to pray, how to ask, that was the hard part, humbling one's pride in order to ask.

"I ask that my body and soul be healed. I ask for health, for peace within me, no more civil war. I ask for light to enfold me, to protect me. I ask to be more capable of love, to be kind and gentle with those around me."

I found myself wanting to open my hands in the gesture of receiving, my head lifted rather than bowed. I still felt humble and small, yet glad in this upwardness, imagining light pouring into me, healing me, gathering me up and holding me, like an infant, given over. I could feel the need to bare the smallest part of myself, that tiny seed self, to expose what was essentially me, pitiful, painful, vulnerable, to hold that out, as if into shining rain.

I felt bathed by the long rainy season, lying in my bed under the eaves, with the white down comforter up around me. Everyone else complained about the endless rains, but I was rounded out by it, soothed. Then when the sunlight did break through, it was like the dramatic return of a travelling love. My arms would open, eyes close. *The unseen moves upward as the physical grows stone—Rise up from out your carved condition.*

> *Not who to blame, not even—Who do I forgive, just this need to be completely held. To give oneself over, to skin the shining seed—then to bury it. It was a long slow rain, and it was coming from me, pulled from me, aching, until even the smallest birds bathed in it, and new life came up on its own grief. I will have slept from the birth of light to the death of darkness, and then my time is come to term, this spring. Still, I have these hours, returning to the world, while the rainwater pours, streaming over the roof of this room, and I am deep in my comforter.*

I gazed at Raphael's *Madonna and Child*, there on the wall before me. It had come to replace the TV, which I'd dragged out onto my dresser. But each time I turned on the tube, I was repulsed by the noise and frantic action, by the low brow humor, the desperate attempts at overstatement in the effort to entertain. I felt dragged down by watching, and decided to just put it away, back in the closet, and then I hung this picture up in its place, where my gaze could go in the quiet hours, following the soft colors of folded material. The collecting curves fell into a harmony my eyes could follow in an ellipse of looking—there in its golden frame—rounded baby, flowing mother, softened colors, glowing frame.

I felt that all Carol had to say was true. Simply hearing her story affected me, stirred a positive force back up in me. From that day we shared together onward, I felt my strength renewed, though I didn't want to "work" with her or anyone at that point. I had needed medication, and I wanted to recuperate in my own way. I knew my energy would return, given time and sleep, and that I simply had to learn how to find that rhythm where the social and the private, outward involvement and inward creativity, movement and rest, breathed in and out, in balance.

After Carol left, Linda said to me—"You'll be part of her daily prayers, now that she's met you." I didn't doubt that it would help, that I had been touched by the life of someone with a gift.

Circles of Support
May

A friend, who's a therapist called me, "I've just started seeing this young woman who has lupus," he said, "and I don't think she's even talked to anyone else who's had the disease, so when I mentioned that I knew you, she seemed quite eager. I thought you might want to give her a call." I agreed and got her name and number, Debbie Howard. "Maybe you have some reading material you can pass on to her," he suggested. "I think she's been reluctant to find out about lupus. Afraid of knowing too much."

I assured him that I'd give Debbie a call that night, not that *I* knew very much, being a mere puppy of the lupus strain.

Debbie seemed almost relieved to talk on the phone. She told me that her rheumatologist was Chinese, and that he could barely communicate in English. When he first prescribed prednisone for her, all he had to say was—"Now you're going to be a very *chubby* girl." She had gained some weight, but she hadn't turned into Little Lotta. In short, she wasn't able to communicate with him, and she was worried about the quality of her treatment. She was single, and lived alone. No wonder she was seeing my friend, as she probably simply needed someone to talk to, and I had found out that you don't have to be a raving maniac to have such a need.

In the past year Debbie had had several extreme bouts with lupus. Hers had started as mine did, with progressive arthritic symptoms, which she tried to ignore. She was pushing herself at her job, and she was also exhausted. Without any other symptomatic warning, the lupus struck her kidneys. It was rather shocking to me, to think that such an attack could strike so suddenly.

Later in the year, she was back at work, and again, without warning, her central nervous system was dramatically affected. "Everything was so intense," she said, "the lights up above and then this exaggerated piercing sound. It was like a bad acid trip." Both times she was hospitalized, and Medi-Cal took care of the expense, but now, working again full time, she had no insurance to cover on-going lupus care, and the financial drain of going to see a new doctor for an initial checkup, usually about $100, was too much.

When I told Dr. Ellman about her case, he was generous enough to offer an initial meeting for a consultation fee of $35. Rare is the doctor, like him, who seems to be concerned with the cost of medical attention for those in an insurance bind. He had given me a financial break for my first consultation, because my Blue Shield didn't cover SLE. On the way out of the building, I kidded him that his secretary had just taken my last check, and he responded, "I hope not your last dollar too. You let me know if that gets to be a problem."

"I will," I said.

"It was good seeing you," he added with a grin.

I called Debbie back and let her know that she had this option. I encouraged her to see Dr. Ellman, as it seemed so important to find a rheumatologist who was relaxed enough to talk. I was sure she would like him as much as I did. She said that she would think about it. Since there is no ultimate cure for lupus, and it's a continuing process of flare-up and remission, one might as well try to find a doctor you genuinely like, for even if a doctor is giving you proper medication, if you feel fear and mistrust, some good is undone. One needs to establish trust, warmth and good communication, and then possibly the medication will be even more effective.

Debbie was eager to read the pamphlets I'd received from The American Lupus Society, and a book I'd bought, *Lupus: The Body Against Itself*, by Sheldon Blau & Dodi Schultz. It had been recommended to me as one of the clearer descriptions of what one can encounter, on the physical level, with SLE. It did seem important to inform oneself, as understanding can help to alleviate fear. I told her I would mail this small stack of literature to her, and suggested that we go to a meeting of the Lupus Society together. There were monthly meetings in Marin, and I could give her a ride as she had no car. She seemed as grateful as a younger sister.

It made me think of what it would be like to have this disease and to have no one turn to at all. Both of Debbie's parents were dead, and she had no siblings or family in the area. I'd heard of several young women who had gotten so sick, they went home and let their parents nurse them. One father worked morning, noon and night, making his daughter a special curative soup, called Beuler Broth, with fresh zucchini, green beans, onion, garlic, parsley and lemon. She ate nothing else for months and cured herself. I couldn't imagine such a regime.

I didn't know how a single mother would be able to handle a severe bout with lupus. I never would have been able to cope with two small children and a house all alone. I wondered if the Lupus Society had a support group for people who needed emergency at-home help. Here was this woman, all alone, who apparently had no one to lean on. It made me all the more aware of the circles of support surrounding me, and how fortunate I was.

I thought of how generous my sisters-in-law had been, coming in to help, and how endlessly uncomplaining my husband had been, extra money for housekeeping and babysitting help from my parents, letters and phone calls from siblings and cousins, aunts and uncles—it was like a lifeline of buoys keeping me afloat.

Then there was the circle of my closest friends, who also sustained me with the written word. Jill sent a carton of favorite books from her library. Others brought casseroles and soups, valentines and foot rubs, flowers and conversation, Gloria arrived with a load of grapefruits—sweet white light—which I devoured. I always told friends when I was too tired and that was understood.

The circle of school community friends was amazing to me. It was encouraging to know that this loving community, that cared about healing on all levels, was behind me. They also took turns bringing food, which was such a great help. One woman astonished me. We were only acquaintances, but she brought over a five course meal, each dish so beautifully prepared, everything delicious. An older woman in the community brought me two copper bracelets, copper being an old-time antidote for arthritis, and a lovely veil painting which she had made. Others helped drive Clovis home from school, taking him and Ayler when necessary.

Once I was able to hold a pen again, I wrote each person a thank you note, and was overwhelmed by how many good deeds had been done for me. I felt those good deeds to be part of a positive force that reverberated in the universe, multiplied there, expanding, and how in receiving those gestures of love, I had been truly helped, carried over some dark places.

Sometimes it's a surprise, when you realize you're getting help from some unexpected source. I had a long chat one day with a nextdoor neighbor, a young guy who spends every free moment at the drums, and on his way out, he turned and asked how I was doing, and I answered, "Much better."

He smiled and said, "Well I've been praying for you." A big smile went over my face as well, for here was this guy, this hip wit, and he was praying for me. I could tell that it hadn't been that easy for him to say.

"Thanks," I beamed. "I really appreciate that."

Finally I could acknowledge the circle of healers, those people and doctors who had given something of their knowledge and themselves.

There was also that Golden Circle, which I continued to ask for—to protect me, to help shield me.

It all made me feel responsible for someone who apparently had no one close by.

When the flyer from The American Lupus Society arrived, it announced another lecture by Dr. Juneau Pallen, which would be held at Marin General Hospital. Geoff and I had been fascinated by his talk last October, so I made arrangements to go again. This meeting was going to deal with local chapter business, but Dr. Pallen would also be speaking about the latest relevant research, and how it might affect our lives.

I called Debbie, told her I could drive if she'd like to go. I thought she'd find it interesting, as Dr. Pallen had been so direct and informative before. Debbie was up for it, and said that she'd take the bus to my house that evening, since I'd be getting the kids ready for bed, though I insisted on driving her back to her place in Oakland afterwards.

A small, intense-eyed, dark haired girl arrived at the door with punctual precision, introducing herself as, "Debra." She was dressed in black pants and pink tennis shoes, holding the stack of literature I'd lent her under her arm. I invited her in—the boys were romping about in their pajamas, and she seemed to enjoy their antics.

Later, in the car and on our way, she was quite frank, saying how much she liked children, but how impossible that looked for her now. "I guess I can never have a child," she said. "But if I were to get pregnant, I couldn't physically afford to have an abortion, and yet I can't have my tubes tied either, because an operation might set things off."

"That leaves room for about *no* mistakes."

"But my boyfriend and I broke up, so I don't have to worry about it."

What a relief, we tried to laugh, talking on about our short histories with lupus, all the way across the Richmond Bridge, enjoying each other's company, immediately established because of what we'd shared, though I could see how the severity of her disease made her emotional life more fragile. I could almost feel her shudder as she said, "Isn't it awful, having to stay out of the sun? Sometimes it makes me feel like I don't belong on this planet." I acknowledged the isolating factor which shadows our condition, but I wanted her to see beyond the gloom, the difficulties.

The mood of the meeting wasn't so serious. As we walked in, they were trying to elect new officers who would take some responsibility, but no one was dying to step forth. Finally, a few were cajoled with much good humor and congratulations, and then we went around the room introducing ourselves.

"I'm Bethany Mills. And I have SLE, and I'm sick and tired of it!" A few quick cheers of agreement.

"I'm Mary, and I also have lupus, and I don't like it either."

Everyone seemed to be in such good spirits, though Debra and I were a little reticent, newcomers from the East Bay.

"So you two were friends, before? Even before you got lupus?" one woman blurted out, amazed, her face and body, round, bloated and flushed, no doubt from medication.

"Actually, we just became friends tonight," I offered, and Debra smiled as the introductions went on.

"My lupus is in remission now," one very lovely, middle-aged woman said. "For those of you who don't know me, my name is Paula, and all I can say," her beautiful, bell-clear voice became even more sonorous as it quieted, "is that I'm looking forward to the day when the future's flowering womanhood, no longer has to succumb to this disease."

As we went around, I recognized the voice of the older woman I'd talked to on the phone, and who had been so informative. We exchanged hello smiles. During the last meeting I'd attended, she had been upstairs, in the hospital. Several women, hospitalized right now, were mentioned and thought of, while an attractive young woman, who'd had a kidney transplant, poured herself some wine. "I know I'm not supposed to have this," she laughed. "Oh well." And the meeting went on.

There had recently been a fund raising concert, which had brought in a profit of $1,500 towards the purchase of a tabletop ultracentrifuge, which Dr. Pallen needed for his on-going research. The machine cost $5,600, a long way to go, but there was still some hope that the national organization would help match funds.

Finally Dr. Pallen arrived, coming from the main part of the hospital where he'd been visiting his wife. They had just had a baby boy that morning. He was obviously taking it all in stride, as he got right into the talk, drawing diagrams and answering questions about the centrifuge. He graciously thanked the group for helping to raise this money and went on to explain how it would be used in his research involving monoclonal antibodies and SLE model mice.

"Each time that we use a monoclonal antibody," he explained, "whether to treat a mouse or to examine its cells, it is necessary to spin the antibody at very high speed to remove any clumps of antibody, which tend to stick to the cells. Because we use the antibodies several times a week, this is a frequent requirement." It had once been a very tedious process, requiring a terribly expensive, cumbersome and slow machine. For small volumes, the centrifuge did the same task much, much faster.

Then with a tantalizing twinkle, he announced that he had some interesting news. We all sensed his excitement. A woman researcher, Dr. Hahn, in St. Louis, and her associates, who had been treating model mice with monoclonal antibodies against DNA, recently found that the mice were getting better." This research was reported just a few days ago," he announced, and the information hadn't even hit the literature yet. We all felt like part of the vanguard. And yet right at this important time for research in immunology, funding was in such jeopardy, necessary funds were getting cut and more cutbacks were threatened. He encouraged us to write individual letters to representatives. It seemed criminal that government had such offensive priorities, and yet the mood in that meeting room was still incredibly hopeful—*Applause.*

By the time I dropped Debbie off at her apartment on the far side of Oakland, it was quite late. My tank was on empty, literally and figuratively. When I stopped to get gas, I could hardly keep my eyes open, slightly nauseous and dizzy from exhaustion. It made me realize that I shouldn't push it, that I needed ten good hours of sleep a night, and that I was still recovering.

Hands On

May

A writer friend who lives in San Francisco called and said that I had to go see her bio-dynamic therapist. "He's a real *mensch*," she said, "and his office is only two blocks away from your house." She told me how he had helped many other writers I knew. But for some reason I was nervous about it. She persuaded me to at least give him a call, and I agreed, but I called his office on a Saturday, so that I only had to talk to his answering service. A half-hearted attempt. I left my name and number, but curiously, he never called back, and I was almost grateful.

When I told my friend Judith about it, she said that she thought his approach would have been too forceful for me. "If I were you, I'd treat myself to something more calming once a week—Why don't you get a good massage. That would probably be better than getting yourself all stirred up." It was true, I didn't want to pound on any furniture or rattle my psyche at this point. I couldn't risk deep water in such a rickety boat. If I had unexpressed anger, perhaps it would have to stay unexpressed a while longer.

"If I were going to work with anyone," Judith continued, "I'd find a woman," and yes, that's how I felt too—that gentleness, less self-consciousness, less sexual tension. She suggested a woman named Zoee Esty, who had done wonders for two of our friends. Zoee worked with a system of bodywork called Ortho-Bionomy, which helps to bring about a profound release of stress, tension and pain. She had trained with an Osteopathic doctor, and now worked with a general practitioner several days a week, seeing her other patients at home.

When I spoke to Zoee on the phone, I imagined a buxom, dark haired, mood woman. She had such a slow, deep telephone voice, but when I finally came to her door, a week later, I saw a short-haired, blond woman in a cotton turquoise sweater, who happened to have the same voice. She was beaming, warm, and welcoming. I felt right at home. Her single bed was in the corner, and I sat on a chair and we talked for a while. I told her about my general physical pattern and progress, how I had attempted naturopathic methods of healing before resorting to allopathic drugs, which had worked for me, and how now, in this stage of recovery, I again wanted to explore alternatives in my search for a deeper cure.

She had a little stick of incense burning, which I didn't like, that sweet smoke. Later I smelled it on my clothes. Being an ex-smoker, I'm particularly conscious and wary of smoke, still craving and yet repulsed at the same time. Perhaps she used it to suggest relaxation. I did feel comfortable, though I was surprised that we were doing all this talking. I thought I had come for a massage.

She went on, asking me about my life, indicating that I should tell her what had been stressful in my life, but I proceeded to tell her about all the good things instead....

"So you've had no difficulties?" she asked.

"Well, I wouldn't say that. I've had an easy life, materially, and a truly lovely life in most ways, but I have had this on-going conflict with my mother. It still disturbs me." I could feel the tension of words catch in my throat as if I'd caught *the* fish on the hook. She didn't take it any further, but began to unfold her table, setting it up there in her living-bedroom. The table had a 6" covered foam surface. She placed a sheet over the table and I undressed. Wearing only my underpants, I lay down on my back under a soft white flannel blanket, and then she began to work very gently on me, pressing touch points in my neck, and then my skull. I closed my eyes and enjoyed it. Slowly, very slowly, she took her time going over all of my joints, from neck to shoulder to arm to hands to hips. She felt that my left hip was rotated and my left leg shorter, so she worked on improving that balance. She told me about a book called, *Rebirthing,* by Sondra Ray, which she thought I might read, and told me about a tape I could send for, a self-hypnosis tape I could play in my sleep. It was about parental approval, since some of my stress did seem to come from this conflict. She asked me what the problem was.

On my thirty-third birthday, several days before, I'd received a call from my mother, but there was no joy, no happiness for the memory of my birth. The call was cold, insulting. She was obsessed with the Steiner school, and how terrible it was for Clovis. Everything I brought up was negated. The used Peugeot I had bought to replace my old rusty van—"Those are awful cars." I told her of our decision to go to the country for a year, and she was flabbergasted—"Why would any-one go to that God forsaken place!" She seemed personally offended by our decision, and insisted that Geoff would lose his job, that it was ridiculous. Then she said how Uncle Chippy had called them, after he had dropped by to see me, and how he had said I looked perfectly well, insinuating that I had been exaggerating my lupus. Everyone could visit but her. I was obviously in perfectly fine shape.

"Your tone is very irritating to me," I said at last, in a low controlled voice, barely masking my hurt and anger. I couldn't believe this was still going on, after all these years, and on my birthday! But I was unable to acknowledge that she too was hurt and felt rejected. I hadn't called her for help. It was now five o'clock, and the children from playgroup were still at my house. I was exhausted. As I hung up, I felt like the call had been a slap in the face, perhaps to remind me of that slap on the butt thirty-three years before.

As I tried to explain this to Zoee, lying on my back as I was, the hurt welled right back up in me—I could taste my bitterness. I started to cry, shaking with the sudden forcing of emotion. I had needed that bit of talk more than I thought, needed to let go of those negations, instead of harbouring them.

Then the mood changed as quickly as a tropical storm passing by, and I settled back into gentle breathing as she continued to work on me, carefully, soothing. She suggested that I ask for the psychic ties to be cut between us, so that my mother could have her ideas and opinions, and I could have mine, but I wouldn't have to respond emotionally.

It was a nice thought, but I couldn't help responding. I also knew that my mother didn't need my opinion to argue against. It was as if she were arguing with life itself, or wrestling with her own dark forces. How often had I sat there absorbing her rant, in the name of honesty, truth, but is truthfulness without kindness, heart, a benefit to anyone? Am I doing her the same disservice here? And why did I always focus on this dark side of my mother, when she also had much to give. Was I simply miming her method, seeing "the bad" in order to feel better about myself?

Zoee said that I had to ask for love, so that I would be able to love her in a new way—pouring love back to her, for only with such love could she change. I cringed at the thought. I too was afraid of changing.

Fear. Was I afraid of this disease? Was I afraid of dying? Afraid of having internalized too many negations, and yes, afraid, that I was a bad mother myself. How to transform the patterns that had been cast, from her mother, to her, to me, and then mine. If I could not accept the voice of my mother, then I couldn't accept myself, the deepest resonance of my own femininity—self-repulsion on the cellular level. No doubt. If I rejected my mother, I rejected part of myself, exactly what my body was doing. Was life on this level but a metaphor? Translated like a bad dream?

Zoee had me turn over on my stomach and she worked on my lower back, my spine. She returned to the idea of these parenting tapes. She herself had bought the tape entitled, *My Parents, Myself,* because she had been having trouble with her own teenage daughter. "We couldn't do or say anything, without a big conflict!" she laughed. "So I wanted my daughter to hear this tape, and I put it on night after night for her to go to sleep with, and then finally she turned to me and said, 'Oh cut that out, will you, Mom?' And I realized then that *I* was the one who needed to deal with the message. Hey, I'm the one who has to listen to this, not her. And so once I dealt with my relationship with my own mother—our relationship just cleared up." She beamed down at me, opening her hands, in that gesture of—Simple. Whadyaknow!

I agreed that I would send for the tape. Zoee had worked on me for almost two hours. I sat up, and felt great, clear, realigned. She thought if I visited her three more times, then I might try seeing this woman in Atherton, Margret Simmons. She was a chiropractor and an M.D. and she worked with a psychic healer. They had had a great deal of success at getting to the bottom of an illness, cutting through to the root cause, illuminating it and eliminating it. I was willing to consider going.

So Called Normal
May

This week Dr. Ellman thought I looked quite healthy. And I agreed. I hadn't felt so good in a year. My color was good. I even felt attractive. I'd gained some needed weight. If I could only hold it there. He said that 3 mg of prednisone should no longer affect my weight gain. I felt especially vibrant, mildly ecstatic. Everything looked better. I wondered if it were because I was now a new and better person, or if it were simply the prednisone, a lovely delusion. Sometimes it seemed like the best part of a strong cup of coffee, when it hits with a warm rush—*ahhh, zip and zoom.* But this was even more radiant. Yet when I felt bad, depressed, I also felt worse, went lower, and I had to learn how to exhale, to blow those bad times out.

Dr. Ellman said that often when you've been sick for a long period of time, and then suddenly you're well, feeling "normal" feels Great. But

I could remember what "normal" was like, (it wasn't that long ago) and this was much better than normal. Prednisone does affect people in different ways, and sometimes it does make a person more speedy. I had a new lease on life, and I wanted to keep it, but I also wanted off the drug. Even if I had to readjust to so called "normal" me.

Dr. Ellman said that sometimes as little as one milligram of prednisone could suppress the illness. It didn't make sense, and it shouldn't work, but it apparently did in some cases. He had one patient who only took one pill of Plaquenil every third day, and that worked for her, but if she stopped, her hands became swollen within a week.

The less prednisone I took, the more anxious I became, as if I could hear the rumbling of a burning river getting closer and closer to the surface. I was surprised how long it took to gradually reduce the dosage. Decreasing the drug I felt high strung with energy, like a thoroughbred walking down a railroad track.

> Simmer, spit—No water in the pot. Easily rattled. Battalions inside. Not over. A stream tunneled under. Less now means more sooner. "Your old life's at the door!" Take on this bit, then also, or more so. Who knows to say No to. A strain to put wordless immensity in mouth. Freak leaping of long legged bug on black window. Running straight for the haystack when the whole pile swerved. Collapsible lawnchairs. The tackling of toddlers. Sugar fox sneaks over thin crust of snow.

Sometimes my cheeks flushed up red and my forehead burned but the fever never took hold. When I got tired, I became exhausted. I had to get nine regular hours, and that usually meant going to sleep by ten. I forced myself to lie down for nap-and-thought with Ayler in the afternoon. It was so nice to lie there under the comforter in the big bed with this little person snuggled up close, the hot smell of his hair as he slept. But when Ay was gone for all-day playgroup, twice a week, I didn't stop to rest. His rhythm helped patrol me.

Opthamology & the Gorgeous Orb
May

There was a remote chance that Plaquenil, the anti-malarial drug that I was taking, could cause eye damage, even blindness, so after two months of medication, I had to go see Dr. Sorenson, a recommended opthalmologist. I was on the look out for any color changes, but had seen none so far.

When I was led back into the corridor of offices, I was offered a chair by a big black machine. The cave-like darkness of the room, and the EM3W screen up above, brought my experience of sixteen years before, flashing back, making my stomach queasy as I waited, my eyes, brimfull, with nervous self-pity.

When I had been a high school senior, I found out that I needed a detached retina operation. My parents took me to Barnes Hospital in St. Louis, and it had been a traumatic time for me. The worst had been the long silver needles injected into my optic nerve, and then the weeks of inactivity, followed by months of restraint.

The operation had been a success, but I had always been afraid to have my eyes rechecked since that time. I had avoided this examining room for sixteen years.

> *The eye, that gorgeous orb, so soft, exposed, so telling. The eye in its dance does gesture. The eye does laugh and love and weep, the eye with its twin partner, wed forever, one making up for the other's failures.*

But now, asked to rest my chin on the black scoop support before the big machine, I was hesitant, and withdrew as the light rolled in at me and touched. I didn't realize that the machine was supposed to actually touch my eyeball, to test eye pressure. Once I understood, I relinquished instinct and sat there, taking contact. My eyes were dilated wide, and Dr. Sorenson let the light enter full strength, as I looked to the familiar far-right, far-left, both up and down. The light beam penetrating my eyeball, seemed to plunge with a sexual disturbance that made my innards squirm.

Moved to another room, I rested my eyes before the camera, where they shot a roll of flash pictures. The dazzling combustion of fireworks, flashing—More stunned than Greta Garbo ever was.

Later, when I saw the pictures, they looked like spherical moons, floating in black space. I had slight retinal puckering, most likely from my first operation. The Plaquenil wasn't affecting my eyesight, though I would have to have my eyes rechecked every four months to make sure.

Flower Drops
May

I went to see Zoee again, and she greeted me at the door with a warm hug, so cheerful—bright as the purple drape she had hanging in her sunny room. I got undressed and lay down on the table, pulling the soft flannel blanket over me. "My daughter gave me that blanket for Christmas," she announced proudly. It was almost like lambskin or cashmere. How nice to know your mother's tastes and inclinations so well, and to honor them.

Standing at the head of the bed, I could feel Zoee getting quiet, ready in herself, with her hands holding the ball of my head. She smelled of rose lotion, and that mild comforting essence made me sink deeper. I was tired from staying up late with my writer's group the night before, and I didn't feel the need to chat. I felt safe here. Soon I drifted off, as she continued to do her work. Then something popped me back to awareness—*Oh*, I hadn't taken my medication that morning.

"What do you think of that dent in my forehead?" I asked. It looked like someone was testing a cake and the thumbprint stayed on my forehead. I wondered if it were an aftereffect: of the prednisone, just as the shot of cortisone in my discoid lesion had collapsed that place in my cheek for several months.

"Right on your third eye, isn't it," she remarked. But then in her genuine way she added that maybe it was like an open window. Perhaps I was more receptive now, my third eye being closer to the surface. A nice thought, but I doubted it.

She told me how I did have the power to make myself well. I resisted that notion too, though I realized it was probably true on a certain level. "I've seen spiritual healing *work*," she persisted. I believed that she had, though I'd never seen it work. Was I spiritually complacent? Was I being urged to some end? I didn't want to feel totally responsible for my illness. Though no matter how hard we blame, cause usually boomerangs back to self. She mentioned this couple in Atherton for the second time, a chiropracter who worked with a psychic. "They cut right through, it's amazing," she smiled.

"That's a *long way* to go," I whined.

"A long way, sure, but for the kingdom?"

Maybe, we'll see, I thought. She considered these sessions with her a time for opening up, so that I would be ready for them. One place always seemed to lead to another. I always felt like I wanted to yawn when I was lying on Zoee's table. Trying to yawn, it reminded me of how shallow my breathing was. She suggested that I call the Seik's ashram, and inquire about the kundalini yoga classes. They weren't expensive, and they would help deepen my breath. "The Seiks are such a healing group of people," she said, going on to describe how strong and calm most of them seemed. She portrayed their ashram as a haven, and how wonderful they were with children. Sometimes, you wouldn't hear the children, you'd just see this row of tiny shoes all lined up by the door. Now we were to be quiet again. She was working to clean my aura. As long as I could keep from thinking about that, keep my cynicism in check, and open myself to the possibility, it might help. It couldn't hurt.

That's exactly what Zoee said about the Bach Flower Remedies. I was starting to get dressed when she pulled out a large notebook and started telling me something about them. "They're very mild," she said. "You can take them with any other medication. There's no conflict." Even though they were homeopathic, one wasn't limited to avoiding certain foods or substances. These remedies were made from the essence of wild flowers. I looked through the notebook which pictured each flower. Edward Bach was convinced that emotional, physical or mental stress was often at the root of an illness.

"If a person is subjected to a trauma or a problem and allows the emotional reaction to linger," she read to me, "then the problem could manifest as a physical disorder at a later date. The Bach Flower remedies are specifically formulated to assist in releasing that particular trauma from the cellular memory."

I glanced over the reference sheet that described thirty-eight different problems and the flower remedy for each: for inner torture, anxiety, weakness of will, dreaminess, self disgust, despair, for those who hate, for nostalgia, impatience, shyness, gloom, for exhaustion, inflexibility, for trauma, pride, and aloofness, for dissatisfaction, persistent unwanted thoughts, apathy, resentment, and then the Rescue Remedy, which was a combination of five different essences—Star of Bethlehem, Clematis, Cherry Plum, Rock Rose, and Impatiens.

I circled several of the flowers, and then eliminated some. Together Zoee and I decided that these three would be most beneficial to me:

Chestnut Bud: Refusal to learn by experience; continually repeating the same mistakes.

Vervain: Over-enthusiasm, over-effort; straining. Fanatical and highly strung. Incensed by injustices.

Walnut: Gives protection from outside influences and over-sensitivity. Link-breaking remedy for transition and change.

Zoee mixed a bottle of these three essences together for me. I was to take 4 drops 4 times a day, and to think about these affirmations which would help antidote my failings:

Chestnut Bud: I learn the lessons of my life experience. I am careful in my observation of life.

Vervain: I practice moderation in thought and action. I harmonize my will with the universal will. I allow others to follow their own beliefs. I feel relaxed, open, balanced.

Walnut: I am free of limiting influences. I follow inner guidance despite others' influences. I am protected from any negative influences. I break all links which hinder my growth.

When I read Edward Bach's book, *HEAL THYSELF, An Explanation of the Real Cause and Cure of Disease,* he explained that the conquest of disease rested on the following: "Firstly, the realization of the Divinity within our nature and our consequent power to overcome all that is wrong; secondly, the knowledge that the basic cause of disease is due to disharmony between the personality and the Soul; thirdly, our willingness and ability to discover the fault which is causing such a conflict; and fourthly, the removal of any such fault by developing the opposing virtue."

The point he made which I admired most was—"To struggle against a fault increases its power, keeps our attention riveted on its presence, and brings us a battle indeed, and the most success we can then expect is conquest by suppression, which is far from satisfactory, as the enemy is still with us and may in a weak moment show itself afresh. To forget the failing and consciously strive to develop the virtue, which would make the former impossible, this is true victory."

I liked it. It made sense. A gentle, honest therapy, little drops of wildflower dew, memory drops in spring water, a helpful nudge towards a positive route.

Whenever I left Zoee's house, I felt clear-headed, refreshed, and yet physically tired, ready for a nap. I could tell I was in better alignment, straighter shape, as I sat up tall on the quick ride home. I decided not to take my medication that morning at all. See what would happen if I dropped it.

Nothing much happened during the next few days without either the prednisone or Naprosyn, so I stopped them altogether. After two months, the Plaquenil had taken hold and was doing the job. I would continue with that one pill a day.

Why Mothers Cry
May, Bolinas

Do other mothers cry on Mother's Day, full of expectation and consequent disappointment? The commercial hype and material gestures, never give me what I want, what I could never even ask for, unabashed love. Somehow the husband gets hooked into this too, as if he's another variety of child, honoring Mother. *O Pie in the Sky.*

Ayler was too young to know what day it was, but Clovis, at eight, was the perfect age. He had even planned ahead, and made me a beautiful book, and bought a diamond brooch at a yard sale the day before. I adored it. But I especially adored his excitement, his involvement with giving. I hugged them both, my boys.

I had sent my mother a full sheet of bird stamps, wrapped in purple tissue, mailed in an envelope. Ten dollars worth of thoughtfulness, I couldn't help computing, but I knew it was the wrong gift, not sentimental enough, not romantic. Perhaps I was even chiding her for not writing me more letters.

My idea of a good Mother's Day was a family trip in the car, real middle class togetherness. It was Sunday, and that meant baseball practice, but Geoff agreed, after eleven, we would all drive to Muir Woods, which I'd never seen, and then on to Bolinas and the beach.

So I went to the grocery store, and *I* packed the lunch, got out the blankets and extra clothes. I did all the organizing, and then I was the one who began to feel beat, with my whimpery tot whining and dragging about my feet, tired too. What a treat. I had to push back resentment, as I collected everything we needed for the day's journey—I was the performing Mom, but a nagging notion kept tapping at my shoulder—Mothers aren't supposed to take care of everything on Mother's Day. Mothers are to be served for a change, taken care of, babied, loved.

We were off. I had my knitting, and my Red Zinger tea touched with honey, and the day looked great. Ayler fell asleep which made the riding even smoother. But Geoff was in a bad mood. Before we actually got to Muir Woods, he started criticizing me for some ridiculous grievance. I knew he wanted to make me feel bad because he did, and if he could only succeed, then he would feel better. I'd cry, and then he would be fine and it would be over. Where was my shield! He was nagging me about sending Clovis off to the evening baseball game equipped with a bowl of soup and a thermos of milk. Clovis always lost everything he took, so in the future, I was not to send along anything, even though the games were at dinnertime, and no one else ever thought to feed Clovis beforehand. I knew where all this was heading, the old control argument. Unfair!

Maybe he felt lousy because his mother was dead, and he had loved her immensely, and I wasn't his mother, but I couldn't imagine her approving of his tactics. "If anyone was ever organized, it was your mother," I said.

"Organized," he retorted, "but not over-organized."

Oh go eat Cheesits!

No wonder I had a cup of coffee and a cigarette from the pack left on the little round table outside the cafe in Bolinas, as we sat in the sun after a windy walk on the beach, watching the children ride their ponies on the dirt sidewalks, surrounded by flowers and Victorian cuteness in the midst of California's immense majestic landscape— that huge sweep of sea cupped in the curve of beach, rolling back into the coastal mountains. Those white birds nesting in the Audubon trees, herons walking in the shallow bay, light multiplied by light, on the water, the sand, on the street, and the mesa. The smoke and coffee tasted so good. This is how I used to feel, when I was well. Satisfied, relaxed, in love with life. Maybe I was getting well now, too.

My singing voice had returned, and as I drove I sang, until all three of them were asleep. I then gratefully drove in silence, knowing the way.

That's what a mother wants, to be included in the middle of movement, but to have this quiet, the pleasant aftertaste of such a day, the wind-blown rouge of gladness.

Breath of Fire

June

When I went to the Seik's ashram near campus, I knew very little about kundalini yoga. I had taken a prenatal yoga class three years before, but I knew that this would be more vigorous. I had heard about the cleansing breath of fire, and thought it wouldn't hurt to try.

The ashram was quiet when I arrived, a young girl playing on the steps with her dog, a few women in the kitchen, one yoga student in a purple leotard doing warm-up exercises on the baby blue carpet of the wide-windowed white room where we would be. It was still light outside, but heading towards dusk. I took off my sweat shirt and realized that my cowboy shirt was a bit tight for strenuous exercise. I sat down on the bare rug and waited. Even then my knees felt sore and stiff.

Two men and another Seik woman arrived, followed by the teacher, who was dressed in the traditional tight white cotton pants, long white coat and turban. I stood up and introduced myself, saying that this was my first time here. I didn't have a chance to explain that I was also recovering from... that I hadn't exercised much since... We began.

I already felt awkward, out of place, but was thankfully at the back of the room, where I could mimic the moves without being on display. The two men were up front, closest to the raised box where the teacher sat. Both of the men in the class had a much stronger presence, doing the exercises with so much force, louder and more urgent in expression. I felt like the fifth echo down the canyon. We imitated the tones the teacher started, exhaling to the deepest most empty part of the lungs, a great gasping inhalation and again pushing all the wind out. I realized, dramatically, how shallow my breath was, and how shallow my understanding of this process was also. My search had taken the route of a skipping stone, and I felt like the typical Berkeley dilettante, dabbling in alternative health, but endless medication didn't seem the answer either.

"Now the breath of fire," the teacher said, coming over to explain it to me. "You breathe with your diaphram," he demonstrated, "pushing your stomach out on inhaling, drawing it in, when exhaling, exactly opposite to our usual method of breathing from the chest." The others were all pumping with the rhythm of a steam engine, while I proceeded slowly, confused, disoriented. When I tried to *think* about the *in* or the *out*, I got all messed up, and the exercises were beginning to wear on me. I was shaky. This was too much for me.

Now the other students were performing "the plow" (where you lie flat on your back, lifting your legs up and back over, so that your toes touch the floor behind your head) at an unthinkable pace, over and touch back down to carpet, over and touch back, eight to ten times. Then breath of fire, blasting air in and out like a fire bellows. I pushed myself as far as I could go, determined not to give up, but all of this would have been hard on my pre-flare-up body. I felt that little dwarf, Grumpy, growing in size. Did illness make me more of a complainer?

He had us rest our heads down. It smelled vaguely of puke on the carpet. I thought fondly of my more feminine, fluidly slow, eurythmy classes, how that was more my speed. Now there were positions I couldn't perform at all, as I couldn't sit up on my knees, which were slightly swollen and sore. "Why am I here?" I kept asking myself. "I will appreciate the fact that this class must end."

I gave the teacher four dollars and thanked him, walking out on some pretty shaky legs, and yet I was warmly invigorated by my elementary efforts. It made me envy those men and women who were in the position of challenging their bodies—how good that makes the healthy body feel—and it made me realize how little physical activity of any sort I was getting. Hard, trying to stay out of the sun during the day, and going to bed early at night, difficult to find the appropriate, soft, physical activity that wasn't too strenuous for the recuperating body. Indoor swimming would probably be ideal, or twilight bike rides with the perfect partner.

My Highest Aim
June

It only took me one rather relaxed hour to drive to Atherton, instead of the hour and a half I'd figured on. By 10 a.m. I was filling out my medical history when Margret Jane Simmons walked into the Health Center, her crisp energetic, "Good morning," sweeping by me. She was followed by a smooth, soft faced man in a creamy Indian shirt. He was auburn, and looked like he never went outside during daylight hours, while she was well sun tanned, perhaps naturally dark, but also cool and quick and trim. The man behind the reception desk put on some celestial space music, which was amusing and pleasant, if not a bit too appropriate. Nervous, I went to empty my bladder, before I was invited into the examining room by the receptionist. The fancy chiropracter's table in the middle of the room looked terribly official.

"Please take off any jewelry," he said.

"But I can't get my wedding ring off."

"That's o.k. Just your necklace, that might interfere."

I felt alert, slightly anxious about this encounter, as if I were anticipating a double blind date. Be calm, I said to myself, as I sat down in the chair closest to the door.

They entered together, and I was asked to move to the other side of the room, before the window, while they sat in the two chairs opposing, the set up now obvious.

"I'm Jane," she introduced herself, "and this is Bernard."

I was slightly taken aback. "So you're not Margret Simmons?" Was I getting an assistant?

"Margret Jane Simmons," she elaborated. "I dropped Margret. I have made some progress in this life." Her head dipped to scan my freshly marked papers. "You've had a lot of troubles here," she paged through, but I hastened to tell her that I had marked down all the symptoms I'd experienced *during* my lupus flare, before I started taking prednisone and plaquenil. The medication had suppressed most of those symptoms, but if I were to stop medication right now, I believed that many of the same symptoms would return, possibly even in an aggravated form, as my sedimentation rate had continued to climb up into the 50's even after I began taking prednisone. I was directing all of my attention to her. She spoke and I responded to her, while Bernard seemed to be the passive partner, the seer.

She asked me about my diet, how much bread I ate a day (good bread, about four slices); how many cups of milk products (around two or three); Rice? (twice a week); Other grains? (not much); I spoke up for my well-balanced diet; What about other wheat products, pasta, pizza? (maybe once a week) Vegetables? (lots); "I still eat chicken and fish, but I cut out red meats a while back."

"You're going in the right direction then," she nodded. "But are you willing to make some big changes in your diet while we're working with you?" She looked at me directly. It would be hard to contradict this woman, I thought.

"As long as it's not too radical," I laughed.

"Well you're going to have to make some changes." She lifted her eyebrows slightly, though she didn't indicate what those changes might be.

I had hardly even made eye contact with Bernard. I stole a glance. He was sitting to the side in his chair, hand on chin, bored? He didn't look like he was perceiving much. But maybe it wasn't time for him yet. The music coming from the reception room was now a chanting chorus of women, a bit like Hari Krishna chanting. It sounded like they were singing, "No one, here can love me. Oh no one, here can love me," over and over in patterns, slippery as cream cheese is lulling to the tongue.

She engaged my attention. "We work on the physical, emotional, psychic and spiritual levels. Whatever is necessary for each patient. What I'd like you to tell us right now is how *you* would like to change on each of these different levels." I must have looked startled by that major blue book question, readjusting my seat.

I grabbed at the easiest—"On the physical plane," I began, "I would like to be truly well, not dependent on drugs. I guess I want to feel clean." She nodded, understanding, agreeing, but I was beginning to show signs of fright, a dry mouth, tacky, a slightly quavering voice, short of breath, as I anticipated all the rest of the heavier changes I needed to make on all the other levels of being. Not so easy for me to articulate. I wanted to speak, but I was holding back, maybe because I felt no warmth here, no compassion. "Personally, I think I have a rather obsessive personality too. I set patterns easily, and then stick to them, even when they're bad for me. I'm a bit hard-nosed about my opinions. . . ." But all this seemed beside the point.

"How long have you been off nicotine and caffeine?"

"Since last fall, though I've started drinking a little black tea again. It's funny, when I was sick, I felt so pure, but now that I'm taking medication and feeling better, those old temptations are creeping back into my life." I made a creepy-crawly motion with my fingers. I was avoiding the real topic of conversation. What *was* bothering me. What was at the bottom of all this. What emotional and spiritual disturbances were encouraging my illness.

Perhaps she sensed I'd divulged enough for now, or maybe she just wanted to get on with the exam, for she suddenly announced, "Ok, stand up with your back to me."

"Like this?" I asked, startled by the shift.

"That's right. Your left shoulder and hip are higher than the right. You can lie down now." I was completely clothed in a red print dress with blue cotton tights, though I'd dropped my hat and moccasins beside the chair. As I lay flat on my back now, she stood behind my head, gathering my hands in hers, so that my arms lay back. She told me to relax, as she began to shake them, pulling gently back and forth. She would say something to Bernard, then she'd stop and jot something down. Medical terminology, spliced with more surprising tidbits such as, "Any physical, emotional, psychic or spiritual parasites?" I immediatly pictured a lethargic grey form clinging to my soul. But he shook his head, un-un. I realized that she was asking him what he saw, jotting down his answers which were delivered with silent nods, yes or no.

I heard the door open, the receptionist asking for Bernard, an important phone call. "Oh that must be Dean Jokelson," she sounded excited, leaving with him. "We'll be right back." I lay there with my hands together on my stomach, feeling better alone. Why did it make me nervous to talk about myself. What was I afraid to reveal?

When they came bustling back in, he said, "You really are lucky to have come here."

"Yes, you came to the right place," she added. "Don't you feel better?"

If I did, it certainly wasn't remarkable, but I could afford a smile.

She moved with deliberate quickness, as if she wanted to move *through* all this. As I looked up at her from my prone position, I saw the sharp angles of her face, her short styled hair, dark piercing eyes. Zoee had told me how this couple cut through to the underlying cause of a disease, right to the root. She even used that slicing gesture to describe their process, and that cutting movement seemed to reflect her style, cold cuts. Near as she was to me, no closeness. But was it a physical, emotional, psychic or spiritual chill.

She stood by my side and began to test my strength. I had been to a chiropracter once before and this was somewhat familiar. I raised my right arm and she said, "Be strong," and then she pushed with a flick of her hand.

But no, "Take the thumb out of your fist," he interjected. "That represses the will. Always keep your thumb outside."

I raised my left arm. "Be strong," she pushed. Not so strong, it gave.

"Retest," he said. She pushed down on both sides, once again, and then once more. She looked up to him, murmuring something about schizophrenic thought patterns, and I wondered, Who Me? Was this for real? Or a bogus picnic on naugahyde.

But then she said, "Now repeat what I say," and each time she said a line, she pushed down on my arm right after my repetition.

"I know myself."
"I know myself." (strong)

"I know God."
"I know God." (fairly strong)

"God knows me."
"God knows me." (strong)

"My highest aim is to know God."
"My highest aim is to know God." (weak, arm falls right down)

She looked up at him, "*This* has never happened before." She sounded amazed, but slightly disgusted. "She knows God, but not her highest aim." Perplexing.

"This is unique," he added. "We'll have to leave the room for a moment."

"We'll be back." They hurried out. What have I done now. Have I offended God somehow? *I* felt offended.

Words falling like cardboard birds through the air. Flat. I lay flat on my back, waiting.

When they came back in they didn't sit down. "Lupus is really quite easy to solve," she announced with a shrug. "No problem. You can sit up."

"Really?"

Yes, they could take care of the lupus, they could clean that up, that was just like housework, dusting. "But you can't go into a building to clean unless you have a strong foundation, because the building might topple down on you," she explained. So they had to work on building a strong foundation, and then they could clean me up. "All of us know that you know yourself quite well."

I nodded, smiling.

"But we can't do any more work on you today. You have a homework assignment now. During this coming week, you have to think about knowing God and your highest aim," she said, and I assented. "So you think about that," and then both of them headed out the door. "We'll see you on Monday."

Surprised by her selection of my appointment day, I walked back to the receptionist who also seemed a bit surprised. So soon? They usually spent two hours for the first check-up, he'd told me on the phone, and I'd only been in for half an hour, including all the entrances and exits. "That's $85 dollars," he said, almost apologetically.

"How much do follow-up appointments cost," I asked, slowly subtracting the amount.

"Forty-five," he said.

"Monday?"

"Morning or afternoon."

Something else was scheduled for Monday, but I couldn't remember what.

"Afternoon I guess."

"You can come in anytime between 4 and 7," he explained.

"We don't give definite times, first come first serve."

No music was playing now and I was ready for Berkeley. I drove fast on the highway, faster than I'd driven in a long time. Thoughts peeled by to the side, though my assignment lay flat on the windshield. Highest aim. It still took me exactly one hour to get home.

The rage I felt was slow to dawn. At first it was self-pity. I was unworthy, spiritually at fault. Default. Disappointed by the abrupt end to the session. Reprimanded, fooled. A hollow ring was the after sound inhabiting me. I could only trust my intuitions and they said to Stay Away. There was something unholy here. Part of me wanted to believe that I was being challenged, that I should go back, and this duo would dig out some mouldy root that was infecting the whole, but strange as their tactics seemed, it was their feeling-tone which told me to forget it.

I also felt financially ripped off. I didn't have time for endless ongoing sessions. We were leaving for the East in a month. What exactly had I hoped for, anyway—an intensive, extensive one-time archeological dig, finding the shards of my past and present, pointing like arrows to some answer? Stupid of me to expect any easy answer. If anything, they did, put it back on me. I couldn't look to blame anyone outside. I had to engage my higher self, so fleeting these days. What did that self demand of me. What was asking to be acknowledged. I could sense that I was succumbing to my lower self as usual, to my instinctive desires, impulses, angers, wishes and hungers. Was a cut and perm on Monday the only change I needed? I knew better. I could be harder on myself than they could. But why did I feel even more lost now, sad, not knowing how to proceed.

Perhaps they had planted a seed, and I resented that. I resented the wait and work involved in the gardening of the soul. I hated dirt under my fingernails, dry earth on my hands, the dirty work of digging. It was as if I knew there was this tremendous garden to plant. It would be dazzling, a radiance of color, from the highest to the deep, but I would be responsible, for the upkeep as well as the enjoyment, and I hadn't even located an appropriate plot. Even the wildest bit of weed looked acceptable to me. It was a discipline of the will I needed. To begin immediately, on myself, for ground, find the flowers and nurture them first. Water what's worthy and yank the rest.

To know God is your highest aim. It was as if the same headlines kept reappearing each morning until I took note. To *know?* Was that enough? As if that were easy. To *express,* I recommended. To express, in art, that might be my highest aim. Or was that simply self-love. How can one lose oneself in the gesture of returning, returning to the world, when like the infant, one is contented in the center of the universe. My flawless egg. May God have pity and crack the shell. Even if it hurts, let that light slam through a little.

In wordless simplicity, in spiritual ignorance, a true illiterate of the soil, I got down and started to dig.

Home Alone
July

The first dog had fur of roses, white roses tipped in red. Suddenly, I was wearing his coat next to my skin, blooms over-opening against my chest. But the dog that amazed me most, looked like a tiny deer, with a green back, and soft fawn spots. His name was "Ugly." The old man who owned him was my favorite person. He lifted the deer dog and it kissed me incredibly. We were all on this steep dirt road, going above Baldwin Hill House, which already rests on the top of a plateau. "Ugly" had the face of an ancient, or if you looked again, it resembled an oval, one third of an egg, smoothly painted with the face of a Madonna. Climbing the hill above the mountain, white clothes flapping in the blue, up the just-turned golden road, while Ugly sprang amongst us, on his spindly legs, charming as Bambi, prancing through that grin of animation—Suddenly as scent they—mother and deer child—fleeing from the meadow, faster and faster. The little one makes it. It's snowing. He's calling, "Mother? Mother!" In the falling snow. Out of the lost grey blue a stag appears, "Your Mother can't be with you anymore. Follow me."

○

The morning after Independence Day, I received my own temporary but tasty bit of liberty and freedom, as Geoff pulled out of the driveway in the packed Peugeot, taking both boys to La Jolla for a week. I threw kisses to three departing faces, before I closed the front door, turning toward my own quiet space.

My idea of a vacation was when everyone else left town, and I got to stay home alone. Time to type and retype, talk and lollygag a bit, gliding from errand to appointment, without the pressure to get home, make dinner. I went out each night with different friends, with a happy heart and a bright, light head. How easy life was, how delightful.

It made me realize the amount of stress involved in living with another person, with two boys and their constant noise, clutter and demands. Tiredness, frustration and low grade anger can become such constant conditions, one hardly notices them for what they are, just as when you smoke all the time, you don't notice that your chest and throat actually ache a bit. You think that's just the way you are. That's life.

I was infatuated with my own sudden singleness, not that I wanted it for all the time. It was enough having this good short break. I was happy, yet I felt an undertow of sadness—I'm leaving all this? For what, for some dream? I'm leaving my good friends, god daughter, my doctor. I'm leaving this house with my books and this study window, leaving the school community, the network of people in this neighborhood. I will walk away from here without a safety net. Leaving made each contact tender. I suddenly felt urban. I didn't want to go. I didn't want to let it all go.

Stay in the moment now. Don't get sad. No time to lose so turn your head. Catherine and I went up to the top of Tilden Park and rented horses for a long afternoon ride. It was clear and bright, but I was well shielded with *Eclipse 15,* a scarf laid out under my net and straw visor, as if ready for the far Sahara. But this was the land of vision, of ripeness—Sweet California, and this was our farewell gallop. I loved it here. What was I running away from. We were on the crest of the world, that ridge, where the waters on both sides gleamed, and the bonelike descent to the Carquinas Straights rode steadily under the grass brown heat.

I urged my horse at the right moment to respond, Catherine behind me, making mine speed, making our free wheeled, unwound way— snatching an image to remember, to return, and the horses did the rest, neck an' neck.

Walking the horses back to cool them down, I sat up straighter in the saddle, just to think: No bones to ache, no fever to bake, no fingers to shake, no fear.

Though there would always be another layer of fear. Late that night alone, I went through my self-protecting light switch ritual, making it look like a happy houseful was at home. I never have loved solitude at midnight, but tonight the full moon was going to demand all of my attention, scheduled for a full eclipse. I sat at my desk, reading this manuscript, making changes, watching the shadow of earth as it ate into the light of the moon, nibbling her wafer, edging her out.

I had never been a woman of the moon, resisting her charms, but now, in search of the nurturing mother inside me, I wondered, can the milk of kindness come from me too? Will I look forever to my women friends, for mothering, comfort, help? Or can I find that curve inside myself.

I looked back to my childhood album, with its green leather cover and torn off spine. Little eyes gazing at the first one I loved. We were one, indivisible, then separate forever. I didn't have to get even any- more. I could stop my resentments and simply not answer. I didn't have to hold onto my illness or anger. The sun and moon could con- tinue their relationship, while I continued mine, on earth.

The wolf still followed at my heel, the shadow of disease. Someday it might go berserk. Someday it might retreat for good, go back into the deep dark forest from whence....

I looked out the window and faced the moon, watched her go, bit by bit, sentence by sentence, and as she darkened, I felt friendly towards her. O sphere who attends to earth, sisterly sphere, I see you in space as something fragile, a celestial twinkling wraps your nest. Light *is* what makes the moon for man, and now in perfect alignment, she was nothing, but a rosy glimmer. The veil had dropped over her entire face.

The clouds flew in to defend her, to smother my wonder. They allowed me to sleep, to howl no more, in the dark, in the deep, eclipse.

It wasn't just luxurious life alone that week. It was time to put our house in order, and a mild form of packing panic energized those days. It felt like molting—the cast off parts being replaced by new growth, but *these* wings wanted to go wild, as if a body could turn itself inside out, and soar recklessly inward forever.

All of the clothes, toys, kitchen utensils, objects that could break, paintings to be stored, everything had to be considered. I made a stack of cartons TO GO in the hallway, and the boxes (to stay) began to fill up a closet. Even though I'd given three carloads to the school yard sale, we still were burdened with material goods—what to sell, to give, hand down or save.

I believe it's an irksome but undeniably feminine instinct—that urge to clean up, make order, before making a move. But what I really liked was, once it was clean, it *stayed* clean. No big and little dirty feet here. There was lots of time for the long list, all those errands and appointments, back to the eye doctor, everything was fine, over to the vet, who insisted that Tango was the friendliest chow on earth. "Why do the best people always leave," he complained.

He offered to let me xerox this manuscript on their new trial machine for free, and I answered, "Where else could this happen but in Berkeley."

I took the fresh copy over to Dr. Ellman's that afternoon. I had no complaints for him that day, no aches or pains, and he considered me clinically in remission on Plaquenil. Together we decided that it would be best to stay on the Plaquenil through the summer's most intense ray days, and then I could try to decrease that coming fall, but he also warned me about the sun glare off snow, if I were to do a lot of skiing.

My blood pressure was normal, as usual, and my hands looked perfectly normal. I almost felt like I looked better, riper than ever before. In such good health now, it was hard to imagine that the disease would ever seriously return. I didn't want to have to learn what "chronic disease" meant, but Dr. Ellman warned me that if I were to get sick, with the flu or an infection, my lupus would probably flare back up again. It was the first warning he had ever given me.

Because I was the last patient that day, we had a long, lingering chat. We talked about writing, small presses, the new lupus research. I had known that Dr. Ellman was the rheumatologist at UCB, but then he mentioned that he was also one of the many doctors at USSF who kept track of 400-500 SLE cases in Northern California. What a job. I was surprised that there were so many of us. Lupus had once been called a rare and usually fatal disease, but it was no longer rare, and it was uncommonly fatal. "You walk into a room filled with lupus patients," he said, "and they practically all look normal. Very few people die now. Lupus can almost always be well managed." He was frank and open with me.

"I'm not exactly morbid," I got up to pour myself two quick cups of water, (they still used those paper pleated cups) "but I do worry about my kidneys. Is it true that all lupus patients have some renal involvement? And that the blood and urine tests don't always show everything?"

It was probably true that all lupus patients would probably show some abnormality on their kidney biopsies. "But we can't give everyone a biopsy," he answered with warm concern. "I can see no danger for you." There were different intensities of lupus, but they still shared that common name. I had a milder form, not because I hadn't suffered, but because there had been no major organ involvement.

But now I had to face the future. It was time to say good-bye. And hard, trying to hide my feelings. I was unsettled by this good-bye. I put out my hand to shake his, eyes downcast, but then he gave me a big, generous hug.

Walking down the hall, I suddenly felt like a dinghy cast out onto open sea, on my way, all alone, my own course through the universe, no one to hold onto forever.

Back to the Beach
La Jolla, July

When I talked to Geoff on the phone, he sounded tired. It had been a drain travelling with the boys. He didn't want to have to drive them both back home. He wondered about returning Ayler on the plane.

"You can't put a two year old on a plane without an adult," I said. He was succeeding in getting a maternal response, but I resented having to react to his misjudgment. I could tell that my few days of independence were dropping their curtain and the carefree show was over. I resented having to rush in to take care of things, when Geoff would have two free weeks this summer, and another two weeks this fall when he planned on going to Paris alone. I could have said kindly, "Oh, you'll mangage." I could have sent Summer to La Jolla on my ticket, dressed up in my overalls, but I was riding on a got-to-keep-movin' mood, and agreed to go.

Greeting them all at the airport was sweet. Clovis gave me a big kiss and hug, Geoff had flowers, and Ayler jumped into my arms and wouldn't let go. A bushel and a peck and a hug around the neck, but what was this—five nickel sized open sores under his arm. Looked like impetigo. Poor babe. "Hi Bo!" Geoff's brother had driven them all to the airport, because Geoff let the Peugeot run out of diesel fuel halfway there. I could tell Geoff wasn't 100% but I had little sympathy for him. I wanted to be in a good mood, as we returned to the La Jolla house, Bo rapping away in his always shining manner, a riff and squeeze a minute, but I was sad that my sister-in-law, Michele, wasn't there. She'd flown back east for her brother's wedding.

Bo had been helping Clovis with the piano, and they both played me a few new tunes, while Geoff cooked up a savory shrimp and veggie evening meal. We all joined hands and sang the sailor's grace—*For health and strength and daily bread we give our thanks Amen.*

It was clear that Geoff had been spending a lot of his vacation time with a woman artist we both knew. She was single, and I knew they both liked each other. I admired her too, but now I was jealous, angry that he was inviting her to accompany us to the beach, our one full day together. I guess I needed some focus of anger, and unfortunately it was her. He made plans for us all to meet at noon by the checkered flag at The Shores.

Even though I spread *Eclipse 15* from head to toe, and wore long mint colored cotton pants, a long sleeved shirt, big sunglasses and a wide brimmed hat, even though we rented a huge beach umbrella, I still got burned during a twenty minute swim in those salty, exciting waves. It can take a while to get used to the fact that one's body has changed. Two years ago, on this same beach, I basked in the sun, was brown as a berry, was smoking and drinking my regular coffee, and all I had were a couple of spots on my face. Big Deal. But now the sun could light my fuse, sizzlin' & sparkin' by the time we were ready to leave at three.

As we all stood up to say goodbye, Geoff, the Aquarian includer, invited this same woman out for that evening. We could all go to the movies. Our one night before I returned. Then she casually mentioned that she'd be coming up to Berkeley soon, and how grateful she was for his hospitality.

This news stopped me. "Oh? When?"

"At the end of the month," she said.

Interesting! I'd be in Wisconsin, Geoff in Berkeley, cleaning up his supposed room. Sure. Spreading dust on his morning toast. I felt like this whole beach scene was a set-up, and I'd just walked on as a figure of convenience.

Back at the car my hostility and sun reaction were shimmying together in a confused criss-cross. I told him what I thought of this sojourn south, "Did you just want me to come down here to witness this? I don't know why the fuck I'm here. I was so much happier alone."

"We can always get a divorce," he said, as if he'd been saving that one up.

"Oh Cute!" I sat in the backseat sobbing, sun burned, frazzled, shaken from the inside out.

"You're being absurd. I can have a woman friend without bothering her body."

"Don't lie to me!" I yelled, blurting out—"I'm having a sun reaction."

It was a warning, a good strong warning—Don't play with fire— emotions, or the sun.

Heart's Field

August, Oconomowoc, Wisconsin

Anything less than pristine seems to speak of an impure parting. We had just one week to pull all the strands of our lives together before departure, but I felt like a bird in anxious confusion, pulling all the strands apart, slowly deconstructing, yarn by yarn, thread by thread, the nest that had been so carefully molded, all that a family of four accumulates in eight years, all the good friendships, and long good-byes, piled like gifts together, those last few days of fresh grilled salmon, champagne, park picnics, frantic phone calls, last minute changes, extra bags, farewell tears, talking to the locals, buying something just one more thing, telling the tale that had been told a few times now—"We'll be gone for a year, to Great Barrington. Yes, an old Victorian farmhouse, on the top of a hill, acres and acres of peace and quiet and apples and arbors and lawns and luscious bucolic splendour..." But the closer the date came, the less real it felt, the more afraid, the less I wanted, the more anxious, wired, the more I roamed, trying to escape, dropping in, driving on, in search of a borrowed smoke.

Moving was like leaving the heart's wide field, freshly trailed with clean swipes from the fork blade, overturned and ready to be sown by someone else. My past had been gashed, exposed in goodbye. But I had it together now, *all* together.

Once on our way, it was an easy flight, just me and the two boys, my chow in her kennel, six suitcases and four carry-on bags. Clovis and Ayler were both perfect that five hour cruise, and then, just as anticipated, Wisconsin wrapped its big muggy arm around us all, and lay us back into a dark and primal sleep.

But everything was so familiar. I hardly had to open my eyes. The green was the identical green of every other year, and I felt empty. I started bumming Uncle Chippy's smokes. I knew I was getting sucked back into my habit, but I needed company, so, why not. Finally, reluctantly, I decided, No—better to get off the regular ration and enjoy the occasional toke.

I started to swim long laps around the raft, and after a week, I mellowed out into the country rhythm, and was glad to be here. Now Berkeley seemed crazed in comparison. I succumbed to the water lap, horse lip, leaf sway, long walk, lazy way of the eternal dip, into amniotic mildness.

A year ago, this SLE had reared its ugly head. But the future didn't look so bad. I was writing again, knitting and writing both, hands and heart and head. Working on a royal blue sweater with cerise red hearts for Joanna, my goddaughter. We carry the ones we love with us, we do. We knit them in our thoughts. And perhaps the knits and purls of that will make a fortuitous pattern.

Love, what we long for and fear the most. Why can't we be more happy in our lives. More glad. Sow, sow, reap what's sown. I would spread the just turned memory field with brilliant hearts, from coast to coast, a shining track to trail us both ways, back & forward. At night, in dreams, those flowers bloom. And I have begun my garden.

We hearts grow across the country. The abundance of it comes in seed and stag, as summer heat—rising to the rain, out of sand and soil, under simple sheets, over land, we come, to water. We fly our notes that write like net, that sparkle and connect with spray and Boom. Our garden of tunes, our resting field. We brain— We heart— We will.

Chronic Admissions
August

Feeling so healthy and strong, I almost thought that I had it licked— Lupus wouldn't get *me* down again. I guess it's true, as one doctor told me—"Most people with a serious chronic disease exhibit what psychologists call 'denial' to some degree." I had believed that saying NO, was part of my positive outlook, part of my strength of will, but perhaps it was a mere function of pride or fear—*No*, that won't happen to me again. Lupus won't consume *me*.

You can take almost anything once, it's the repetition that's hard to digest, the mere thought of that menu, disgust. The mere idea, that no matter how hard you try, no matter what you do, or how good you are, you have a potentially life-long disease that will shadow punch you flat every chance it gets.

At first, months ago, it seemed everyone else wanted to deny the existence of this disease that was working on me, my husband, my parents, my doctors, while I just wanted to get it named, but now I was the one who had to struggle with denial, and what "chronic" actually meant: Of long duration, continuing, constant, prolonged, lingering. Compare acute.

True, it might drift off someday, go away completely, but it hadn't yet.

When I walk, it heels. When I stop, it sits. When I go, it comes. Obedient to my blood.

Lupus, at least, was faithful. Here in Wisconsin, Tango was total dog, no urban pet. Loose all day, she hunted prey and one afternoon even cornered a badger under a lawnchair. She swam through fields of heavy growth and came out solid green with burrs. As she became more active, I became more relaxed, and only now could I see the state of emergency I'd gotten into, trying to leave Berkeley, getting sun burned and upset. I had set the disease in motion, so when I hit the Midwest, with its daily weather changes: windy on Monday, muggy on Tuesday, raining on Wednesday, hot on Thursday, humid on Friday, cool on Saturday, I was sick on Sunday with a bad head cold, and soon that reminiscent sore throat reappeared. My knuckles, which had felt so free of symptoms, began to ache, and again I noticed that it bothered me to sit down on the toilet seat, not painful, just painfully aware.

I was tired, deep inside myself, not the kind of tiredness I could sleep off in an afternoon, but dragging, off balance. I began to perceive the old signal—that cellular shimmy, and all of a sudden, fear felt physical and my body panicked—Oh NO, not me, not this, again. I was over-reacting emotionally. My fuse had been burnt to a stub, and now it took but a second, one phrase to ignite it. When my mother aggravated me, I flew off the handle. That made the seesaw slam. Later, I apologized, still frantic with emotion, "I'm sorry I said that, I'm just so scared. I think I'm getting sick again." I couldn't help crying in front of the children. I dragged the groceries up the stairs, put myself to bed, and stayed there, taking massive Vitamin C, letting my mother and the babysitter take care of the rest.

Lying there, listening to the cardinal, that had come with sudden redness to my window to woo me, I whistled back, and he whistled right back, until we had a true duet. *Ooooop, Oooooop, through through through*, he sang. My heart wanted to rise up and call that way. But something seemed missing from my life.

My appearance had dropped from attractive to poor, as if I'd fallen suddenly out of love. I noticed a dark and unsightly area of skin on my upper lip, that seemed to shadow my mouth. The downy hair was still blond there, but the skin looked dirty underneath, most likely a side effect of the Plaquenil.

I had been knocked down a peg. Aware that no battle was won, just fought, fought back, and how long could I hold out, with military metaphors bivouacked on my doorstep. I thought I had made peace. Would I always be divided into sides. I grew up on the Civil War, with a father from the North and a mother from Augusta, and knew that even that sacred union could be a battleground. That wasn't what I wanted for my life, my family, marriage, body, a never ending struggle against unity, harmony and self.

But if a little cold could set me off and make me feel like this, what would a big bad virus do, or a serious accident, infection, operation. Could I walk behind a golden shield? Could I make my brain slow so far down that it would only send calming messages out—elliptical waves, lemniscates lulling the little panicked antibodies that were over-achieving again. O lullaby, my body and soul, with a soothing, smoothing song.

I would have to learn from my life experience. Not—I can do every-thing, but—I can maintain. I should also be ready to go down, ready to face it, not ferocious, outraged in the face of it, but prepared. And ready to rise above, to regain and continue *through through through*.

Admittedly, I've never cried so much in my life as this past year. It used to be just once a month, predictable, but now hot tears came cheap. I didn't always like what I saw, and sometimes my whole body seemed to squirm, as if life were a dress that didn't fit.

Geoff was soon to arrive, and he never let me stay down in the pit of self-pity for long. The packed Peugeot was on its way, rolling through Utah, Nebraska, and Iowa, until finally, eleven miles west of Oconomowoc, the headlights gave out in the pitch black night. Geoff locked her up, flagged down a ride, and crept up our steep carriage house steps, way past midnight.

Here in the Kettle Moraine, where the cardinal calls, lavender lilies with golden throats bugle out their song.

We were ready to recover and go on.

IV

And Beyond

On Top

We whizzed down the highway to the little Waukesha Airport, big cumulus clouds in the distance, a ripe, cool, clear end of summer day, and Uncle Billy, our pilot, was right on time, sliding the big doors of the hanger open to pull out ECHO ROMEO, a yellow, two-prop plane. Tango was stationed in the tiny backseat, while Ayler and I took the middle. Clovis was given a set of headphones, informed that he would be co-pilot, up front, which was both a *gulp* and a thrill.

Up in the air, all the worries of planning and moving, time and place, dropped away in the unoccupied blue. I could understand a flyer's desire to get away into this perfect space. Surrounded by a peaceful hum, we cruised. Then that leaping delight, as the plane went right into a big billowing cloud, as we made our way over a storm front, the dips and bumps that make a plane more intimate than a station wagon. We all ate voluminously of cold fried chicken, garden tomatoes, hard boiled eggs, plus apple juice and cookies. Ayler, lulled by the steady vibration, put his head down and went to sleep.

When he awoke, an hour and a half later, we were well above New York State, and descending. Rounded green mountains were humping up, the whole landscape intimate and sculpted, cozy and gorgeous. We had arrived early. It had only taken three and a half hours instead of four. Good tail winds. We sailed down safely onto the small runway, climbed out on the yellow wing and hopped down. Great Barrington, Massachusetts.

Then Jill and Willa appeared in the little terminal house, Jill, big and round, at the end of her pregnancy, and Willa, in her shyness, just stared at her celestial twin. Ayler and Willa had both been born on the exact same day, which was always cause for continued, mutual awe. There was something similar about them, with their white blond fly-away hair, both of them, tall, thin, bright, but akin to like magnets, repelling. Willa made up for her shyness with a gigantic voice, "Why did he SAY that!" and then Ayler withdrew, hunching his shoulders in glee, glad at having affected her. Geoff pulled up in the trusty Peugeot, and convinced Uncle Billy to come take a peek at our place, before flying on to New Hampshire. We filled both cars and headed up the road to Baldwin Hill, just two miles away.

The tar road turned gravel as we went up the incline, and then I saw her from across the field, inviting us on, that lovely white Victorian with embracing porch, and big red barn like a boyfriend on the side. I walked through the house in a kind of daze. This was really some house, terribly grand, yet comfortable too. We fell out into the yard, and Jill and I wandered around with the two little ones in a stunned frame of mind, both of us incredulous, as if our eyes couldn't dilate wide enough for the surrounding views, ripening apples, field of cows, the mountain rising, but above all, the quiet.

Then with an unexpected thrill, Uncle Billy's plane buzzed over the house, making an arc up into the blue. Seeing him soar away, meant we were really here. We had landed, but we were still flying, halfway between heaven and earth, on this high meadow in the Berkshires. The air almost seemed mentholated with freshness. Dill and mint were abundant in the garden. A tractor rolled by on the gravel road out front. We discovered a pony in the barn. A grape arbor, laden with heavy bunches, stood at the end of the lawn. We could see a path through the bushes, made by children and heard the neighbor girls chasing chickens in their yard. Grace must have landed us here, for we were clearly in that state, hovering on top, filled with the fullness of the land and the generosity of friends.

The night was large and silent. Then sunrise appeared in a blaze at my elbow. I dozed back to sleep, and woke again later, the valley in the distance, creamy with morning mist. The bay windows opened in a curve onto this spread of uncluttered landscape, God's own breakfast bowl.

Dr. Incao
October

What a liberating feeling to be zipping down a glorious autumnal valley road with the maples glowing like huge unearthly lanterns. Somehow this land felt like home to me already, and Jill was like family. Alone together now, it seemed to be an adventure, even if we were only going to the doctor. I was driving, but glanced over as she spoke. "Now you really have to *talk* to him, Laura. Draw him out. And remember what he says! I want a full report." That tickled smile she kept half-tucked in like a hanky, her humorous wholesomeness, made me smile back. Jill's rich brown hair had a lovely thick lustre, maybe due to her pregnancy, which also gave her a solid sureness.

As we pulled into the little valley that held Harlemville, she pointed out Dr. Incao's house and office, sitting off alone up the road to the right, while the Steiner, Hawthorne Valley School and Country Store were down to the left in town. They were the town. We went to the store and stocked up on good organic grains and vegetables, beeswax crayons, and I couldn't resist some Weleda soaps and a wooden merry-go-round toy for Ayler's birthday. They sold fine materials and special handmade items, soakers, slippers, placemats, candles, baskets of wool, and I fondled a delightful fleece pillow made in the shape of a lamb.

We made it back just in time for our appointments. I had heard so much about Dr. Incao, and felt right at home in his warm yellow waiting room, though I also felt an old anxiety rising. I had always felt this way in the past when I met someone whom I thought was "in touch," as if he would discover something about me I had carefully hidden, or perhaps I was simply afraid to unearth old worries and fears, afraid to cry.

He was a small, wiry man with a dark complexion. He didn't seem to look "at" me so much as his look seemed to support a feeling "for" me. I had the strange impression that he was saddened and concerned for the weight of something I couldn't even name. Being an anthroposophical doctor, working from the insights of Rudolf Steiner, he took a special approach to medicine, that extends the art of healing, taking into account the biological, psychological and spiritual entities, encompassing man's body, soul and spirit. Professor Lievegoed's article, "Rudolf Steiner's Medical Impulse," briefly describes this art of healing:

> A delicate ecological balance also exists for the biological processes in man. Though man has considerable elasticity in his biological equilibrium, once this collapses, ill-health will result.

> The psyche (soul) can have a regulating effect on the biological ecology, or it can have a disruptive effect, due to excessive stimulation, excitement or greediness. A person can work towards making his life rhythmical, with moderation and self-knowledge. Artistic endeavor can also provide a valuable therapeutic tool.

Illness and restoration of health are always a matter of totality. A genuine therapy will always start from the ego and
encompass the whole organism. The ego may be recognized by the particular response of the person to the events
of his life, the thread of his biography. Life is given its form
and direction by the ego, and a way of life guided by
spiritual principles subdues avidity and dissatisfactions. A
positive approach even to illness gives rise to healing
forces.

Treatment of the soul is needed particularly in conditions
where the influence of the soul on the life-sphere leads to
overreaction, when external factors influencing our lives
have not been properly coped with. Early degenerative conditions have their root in the psychic sphere. The biological
controls are undermined, so that environmental toxins can
not be eliminated by the "natural purification system."

Modern medicine has very effective means of suppressing
overabundant vital processes, but it can do very little to
counteract degenerative processes. Anyone with a knowledge of anthroposophical medicine will know of its infinite
superiority in this particular area. Once the limits of elasticity have been exceeded, generative processes have to be set
in motion again.

In anthroposophical medicine, the endeavor is always to
make treatment total, for body, soul and spirit. This also
calls for a highly discerning diagnosis of the vital processes
involved in generation and destruction. It is then possible
to give differentiated treatment to individual patients,
using potentized remedies for biological processes, artistic
therapy for processes in the sphere of the soul, and the
biographical encounter for processes in the sphere of the
spirit.

As I talked about my past history with lupus, I kept gazing about his
office, which was painted in the Lazure method in varied shades of
blue. The eye didn't stop flat against the wall, but travelled with the
impression of blue ever changing. I asked him if homeopathically
prepared remedies didn't actually stimulate the immune system, and
if that might not be hazardous, considering that my problem might be

centered in an over-active immune system. He heard me, and considered what I said.

When I went on to describe my strong reaction to *Viscum alb.*, he thought that perhaps some less powerful medication would be best, to stimulate the warmth and healing processes, so that the symptoms weren't totally repressed, but so that a crisis flare wouldn't be brought on either. It would have to be a very delicate balance, and I would have to be watched closely. But he in no way wanted to make me feel pressured into taking this route with him. He realized it would be demanding for me, and at that point I had wavering enthusiasm.

"When symptoms appear on the skin," he explained, as in discoid lupus, "and the symptoms are repressed," (as mine had been with cortisone shots and cream,) "then the problem looks for a deeper outlet. A skin problem can become transformed into an arthritic problem, involving a deeper level, the connective tissue. And if that expression is also repressed " (as mine had been with prednisone and Plaquenil) "then it might eventually come to manifest itself in even deeper metabolic ways, in the organs themselves." Rather than pushing the disease down, into a more vital region, he wanted to see it work itself out, even if that meant some transitional difficulties. I would have to be willing to experience some constriction and pain again.

I had almost believed, or hoped that after a period of medication, my lupus would just drift away, like the weather—here today, gone tomorrow. The flare-up would have dissolved, and I'd have a new grip on my life——But— I realized now, that that was just naive, wishful thinking. I was afraid to face the payments due, over due, as if the prednisone had put me in deep debt, and the prospects out were too painful to consider.

He asked me about my past, and questioned me at one point—"Did you have much to do with horses, growing up?"

I laughed, and answered, "That's a funny question. Why do you ask?"

"Well," he said with that candid carefulness, "dealing with horses in the early years, can have a hardening affect on the physical body." It seemed preposterous, but then, when I thought about it, all that exertion and controlled strength, it did make some sense. The stress of early academics could also eventually manifest itself in the premature hardening of the body. I told him how I'd gone to a strict, academic school throughout my childhood, and how I'd ridden horses since I was four years old. I had been a tomboy. He wrote all of this down.

Just mentioning that word, "tomboy," made me consider the difficulty I'd had in accepting my femininity all through my life. I had gone to an all girls school, and had always played the boy's role, until my more romantic years, but even then I was often the leader. All of my female role models had been very strong and willful, uninterested in domestic things, and I had been proud of my worldliness. The women I did emulate, had a strength of character, and a drive that was outwardly oriented, physically competent, unafraid. These were all qualities I still admired, but I could see how they needed a certain balancing with the inward, calm, traditional realm of the feminine, how those qualities have actually been demeaned by our hard-edged, product-driven, masculine culture. As a young girl, I had never stirred a cake batter in the warmth of a kitchen, or played with dolls on a sunny windowseat, or learned how to sew. I had been pushed to excel in sports, where I was always number one, and pushed to strive in academics, until I became an "over achiever." I always had the feeling that I shouldn't be satisfied with who I was. I had to be better than myself. The best.

I could see how the lives of my women friends, here in the country, were different, expectations were different, the air we breathed called forth different forms of delight. Jill and many other women I was meeting, were home oriented, and their lives remained close to that protective circle, taking care of small children instead of sending them off to daycare or nursery, taking joy in the presence of their children, and even the children seemed different, as if they knew they could flourish in that garden of feeling. And the vegetable gardens were monumental, almost intimidating to me with my garden of metaphors, my salad of words. But here was such colorful, physical abundance, so much to gather and cook, can, bottle, and bake. This was not an easy life, and these women were not dull in any way, but everything was done beautifully, with care, as if for art. I pictured country life gesturing in a curve, extending the hand from the inner—outward, giving and welcoming, nurturing in turn. There was an appeal in this cycle, and I felt that perhaps they understood something of the feminine curve I'd always tried to sidestep in trying to make those straight away hurdles. I was always in a rush. But children shouldn't be rushed, and art, and life itself, can not be rushed.

"You know, when I get sick with something like a head cold," I described to Dr. Incao, "I feel so deeply exhausted." He nodded, saying how it was difficult now for my body to work through a problem.

There was a heaviness there, an opaqueness, while a small child was still so transparent. Even if he had a temperature of 102 degrees, he might sit on the floor and play with his toys. The sickness would burn right through him, and readily work itself out.

He wanted me to try a diet which he'd had great success with, and this diet wasn't terribly extreme, but it eliminated all sweets (except natural fruit) until after dinner. He described how the liver is confused by the intake of sugar in the morning, and how only in the late afternoon does it begin to gather in sugars, which it then sends out again the next morning. He also thought that I should try and limit protein intake, eating like a queen in the morning, a princess at lunch, and a pauper at dinner. Eating a savory breakfast, where the protein would have a greater chance of being digested and used. The protein heavy diet of the American dinner was often not processed and could be damaging, polluting. I was to avoid: canned, frozen, artificial fruits, alcohol, cocoa, pekoe tea and coffee, white bread and white flour products such as pasta and crackers and snack food, processed cereals, no white rice or cheese or commercial milk, no sprayed, frozen or canned fruit, or sulphured dried fruit; no shell-fish or red meat, no shortening or margarine, roasted and salted nuts, especially peanuts, roasted and salted seeds, white sugar, chocolate, salt, sprayed, frozen or canned vegetables.

But I could eat large amounts of fresh vegetables and fruits, whole grains, brown rice, cornmeal, cracked wheat, yoghurt, kefir, cottage cheese, and raw milk, fertile eggs, tofu, fish, chicken and turkey, if naturally raised, most fresh raw nuts and seeds, honey, maple syrup, sorgum and date sugar, lots of cayenne, ginger, horseradish, for their warming effects.

I felt like such a diet would be good for me, but I also felt unenthusiastic about a serious regime. I was grateful for these guidelines, despite my underlying hopelessness. I was beginning to feel like there was nothing much I could really do to turn this disease around.

We had talked for almost an hour. Jill was sitting there patiently knitting. She took her turn, and he said that the baby was big enough to be born, but that the head wasn't engaged, and he didn't think it would be born this week. Jill seemed to carry the weight so well, and hadn't gained a lot in other places, her face or arms or ankles. She looked great, and I felt confident about this, her second child. I kept telling her how much easier it would be, and hoped to be there for the delivery.

On the way home, Jill told me to slow by the graveyard. We were going to take a left. I pulled out and only then saw a huge truck barrelling down the hill right at us. I gunned it to make it across, while the truck swerved, *right, left,* and whirred on by, hearts pounding as we headed up the hill. I hadn't pulled out far enough to look before making my move, and the truck had been going too fast. I apologized for the awful panic. Little instants like that, make death seem clumsy as a fast truck, sudden as a bad decision.

Returning home, I received a letter from Summer. She said how she'd just seen Saskia, and Saskia related a newspaper article which described a new breakthrough in lupus research, regarding blood cleansing, because the disease's mechanism had been connected to protein build-up in the kidneys and liver.

Summer had just been to New Year's services, and she wrote, "One part of the service is a group prayer for the sick, where you name out loud. And when the womens' names were named, I said yours, and it felt so regenerative to have it reverberate in the room. After each name said, a *Baruch* is uttered as a blessing. So be it with you, my dearest."

For some reason these words made me cry, her acknowledgment, her wish for me, while Geoff on returning had asked, "How did it go?" And when I began to tell him how Dr. Incao thought I might need some new medication, which would be less powerful than *Viscum alb.*, he almost lashed out—"Why do you need to take anything more? You're healthy!" I turned my back on his caustic comment. I couldn't believe that he wanted to rub me wrong right now. Hot tears built up, but didn't let go. He seemed angry with me, or was he just angry at my disease, angry at his own dependence on me. He didn't want to rock the boat, when things appeared stable. He didn't recognize the leak, or see that my feet were already wet, the bottom of the lake, unfathomable.

Baldwin Hill
October

From the height of this hill we could see the weather travelling, and the undulating thousands flying before it, swept towards some warmer clime, but first, before us—bursting into shapes—chrysanthemum—a midday explosion of birds, which then swooped low, only to rise again and light in the giant maple, becoming a choir in jubilation for that glorious, inevitable end. Sweet cacophony coupled with color, woke up every fiber—A liveness packed the air.

The corn field beyond seemed to be condensing daily as Farmer Proctor cut in on its square, closer and closer on each edge, making the earth appear shorn. Each day was an awakening—Opening my eyes at dawn, to that lavender hill with gold let loose before it.

After hanging up the morning clothes on the line, I walked further back into the fields, and approached the huge wasps' nest in the little pear tree. I noticed, up close, the marvellous texture of colors, palest green and grey and pink in a streaming pattern that would put the best handmade papers to shame. Tapping the papery nest, a few fell out to alert me. Winter had not come yet. The bright string of clothes on the line seemed alive, billowing to dry, October.

"But that isn't the real world. You're just trying to escape the real world," I could hear certain friends accusing, and stepping back I wondered, which came first—the land, or the lack of it. This must be as real as manmade confusion, violence, noise and pain. This hill seemed more real than a street steady with traffic, or fights on a playground, or Pac Man handy at the corner store, or 'A WOMAN WAS RAPED HERE,' stencilled in red on the sidewalk. All of that seemed a violation of the real, natural world. Reality finally came down to a decision, and the question of staying had already occured.

I was slightly afraid of winter's white-out coming. There was talk that the bees were building their hives up higher, and ponies were growing even thicker coats—signs that this winter would be colder, "Harder than this generation's ever seen," said some old timers. Or perhaps this winter worry talk was how they excited and prepared themselves, a game to unnerve us wanderers. I worried that winter would make Geoff withdraw from the idea of staying, but it had been a long, generous Indian Summer, and Geoff had noticed how Clovis had begun to bloom, at peace with himself and his school. The children here were free to roam, inventing and playing simply, as the wind took golden leaves from the maple, took them, tore them, set them free, as the children held open their arms, as they danced to catch leaves in the afternoon air. "I don't ever want to leave this hill," I said. The glory of these trees broke a fire open in my heart—season of warmth and preparation, stocking up fuel—but I felt this beauty igniting inside me. This was something I'd always longed for, a place I could work for, to make my own, beyond inheritance, heredity, the past.

The field out front stood up in frost one morning. The first sign of winter had breathed on the fields, which had risen to reckon with arrest. The travelling thrill-cry of geese, made me rush outside, alert as a happy animal, as they flew into perfect formation, their call making me yearn, following their chevron, as if it were an arrow—*Hearken.*

We hurried to shake the trees for apple thunder. The thudding of thousands landed ripe on the ground. One tree had waxy yellow apples that blushed, one had dark, dark apples with rosy veins, one had archetypal fruit, white as snow, red as blood, with a flavor that was pink and which popped.

At sunset the colors fused, rubbed and blown and collected. Shapes stood out at dusk. Trees exposed their framework, their brooms against the sky. Walking with the children, on the cut field out front, my neighbor, Anne, and I suddenly stopped. The full moon had begun to rise, huge and singular over the rounded earth. Keenly, we sensed ourselves, right there. Earth as planet. Moon as moon. But how quickly she came, how pregnant.

Taking Hold
October

Confused, I didn't know what I should do. I didn't want to get sick again. I wanted to get well. I wanted Geoff's support, but I wanted to experience my own strength. I was afraid of being reduced to invalid status, reluctant to re-experience pain, but hungry for something to believe in, some course to follow. I had dabbled in too many possibilities without taking hold. I lay in bed, alone at nights, crying, almost rigid with exasperation, as if some realization were being forced through me, against some part of my will, as if I needed to be broken, in order to be whole—Sick, in order to be well.

When I returned to see Dr. Incao, I had decided that I wanted to accept what he had to offer, and I wanted to stick with it. As I greeted him this time, I felt less threatened, though still on edge. He was extremely careful in how he said things, words which would have made me back away if they'd been spoken in a cooler, less sympathetic tone. The beam he held was soft light, gentle indications. He seemed to understand how fragile we actually are behind the carapace of appearance.

He saw lupus as a soul struggle as well as a physical problem. I felt myself close to tears, as he said, "I think that you have to decide that you deserve to be healthy." It almost hurt him to be so forthright, but he saw the disease, on one level, as a form of self-punishment. I recognized that masochism in myself. I had learned to "take it" from my mother, and then from my husband, as if that showed some strength, but maybe it was just a habit of weakness. I had to stand up for what was best for me, for once.

Nevertheless, I felt defensive about this soul struggle business. My rational mind wanted only to consider the physical side. I asked him if he saw diabetes in a similar light, as a soul problem, but he grew grave and said that no, he thought that diabetes was very different, buried so deep that consciously there was nothing to do, whereas he thought I could turn my problem around.

It wasn't so much that I had an over-achieving immune system, as a misdirected one, he said. And he thought that the remedies would help redirect that action. He moved his hands in an outward motion, making a pathway, flowing outward. The Plaquenil and prednisone had simply frozen the process temporarily, so that I was numb to it for the moment, but I had just recently seen, after stopping the Plaquenil for five days, that the arthritis was still just below the surface. The stiffness in my hands, coupled with a cranky, short temper, came back so readily, I was shocked. "Ignore it, and it'll go away," wasn't realistic.

I was frank with him, and told him how I was really afraid of that place where I had been, and I didn't know if I was ready to be that sick again, though I did believe in this homeopathic route. He seemed to understand that perfectly, and indicated that he didn't want to see me in a crisis state either. I could tell that he had thought a great deal about my case, and yet I was surprised when he showed me the long list of prescriptions he would send off to Weleda, the anthroposophical pharmacy, if I wanted to go ahead. "It will take a great deal of conscious effort on your part to go through with all this," he said. Rosemary baths twice a week, birch leaf and horsetail tea, an ointment to rub on my kidneys before bed, plus drops before each meal, and six shots a week. I would have to give myself shots in my stomach: my solar plexus, four fingers below my belly button, and over my liver. Just mustering the will to give oneself a shot was part of it.

Geoff was leaving the following week for France, and somehow it seemed appropriate that I begin this alone, that I take hold of my own life, in my own hands, not look to him or anyone else to take care of it. I felt the sword of Michael strengthening within me. The day I began my shots, I also decided to stop sneaking the two-cigarettes-a-day I'd been indulging in. The paranoia, guilt and awful, clinging smell, weren't worth the moment's illicit dizzying pleasure. It had become nothing but a panic treat, and I was enslaved to this small dragon. But that sword of light, I'd felt a year ago, seemed to be cutting through my life once more, showing me what was good, and true, and healthy.

As the two weeks sailed by, I felt stronger and better, with a renewed strength of will and vigor. I felt like I was riding along in an unbelievably good dream, up on this heavenly hill. I had found a seventy-eight year old riding partner, Bunny Kirchner, who rode like a cowboy, and talked like an old-timer, telling me the tales of every acre and owner, as we went on through field after field, galloping down dirt roads, climbing the pike that overlooked it all, the horses hot and eager, the expansiveness of space and view, the geology laid out like a topographical map, one could reach out and read like braille.

I thought about what Dr. Incao had said to me, on leaving, at our last meeting, "You will have to let go of some things you dearly love. You have to believe that you deserve to be healthy." He said it so sensitively, that it was only now drifting down around me like some mere misty mention that had finally draped my conscious mind, but now the mist seemed to open like a robe, and a glow rose through me. Here. Health. Baldwin Hill.

But then Geoff returned from his two weeks in France, and the mood of the household changed, as if someone had just jumped off the see-saw. Imbalance is a shock. And ours had to be regained. I had been looking forward to his homecoming, I thought, but was also apprehensive, with a load of resentments in store. Even though I thought the trip was a fine idea, I also felt abandoned. Why didn't we ever travel together anymore. At the same time, I had enjoyed the relative calm of the household, no loud music, no quarrels, and when he burst back into our lives with his energy and critical comments, "Why have the children been in my room," I cringed. The boys reflecting their father's intensity, began to act up at the table. "I'm used to being around well behaved children," he said. Oh really, whose?

Before leaving, he'd promised me that he wouldn't look up an old love, who now lived in Rotterdam. She was divorced, and her letters to him seemed encouraging, and I was not comfortable with a rendezvous situation. But now it became clear that he had broken that bond of trust and had seen her anyway. There was no apology. My feelings meant nothing. I felt something inside of me lock. My hostility froze at a deeper level. The unhappy heart constricts, tightens around words that aren't really meant, "Why did you even come home."

I had come to understand lupus as stress related, and these upsets couldn't be any good. Why were we locked into this destructive pattern. Why couldn't we find what we needed from each other. What was he looking for out there. Feeling rejected I did my best to reject, and told him that night, tight with tears, that I realized he had this need to punish me. It all seemed clear to me now, what we were acting out. I told him that I thought he had a great anger towards his alcoholic father, and identifying with his good mother, he felt justified in hurting me, while I too identified with the opposite parent, and in my case, like my father, I had learned to take it, but now I wanted out, out of this sickness. I would not sleep with it anymore. I demanded to feel my own health, in body and mind and peace of soul. This venomous cycle had to stop. Silence. But he heard me.

On leaving Dr. Incao's office, he had passed on to me a few sheets he'd received from Veronica Reif, his friend and my curative eurythmist. Veronica had mailed him these suggestions from Carol Collopy, the healer I'd spoken to in Berkeley last spring. Perhaps the hurtful circle, of which I'd played a part, could be replaced by a helpful hand-holding, a circle of health that had roots in a firmer love. Receiving Carol's words, confronting her simple honesty, made me want to loosen the anger I felt.

Simple Suggestions from Carol Collopy:

1. Take your time.
This does not mean that everything must come to a total standstill while you wait for self-renewal. But it does mean that your commitments, either to the old situation that you haven't yet left, or the new situation that you haven't yet invested yourself in, are going to be somewhat provisional. And it means that you cannot rush the inner process whereby this state of affairs will change.

2. Arrange temporary structures.

Years ago when we were doing over our home, we tolerated for some time a living space in a small area that scaled-down our functions to a minimum. The walls were in stages of disrepair and were quite ugly, but it provided us with the protection we needed to go on living in a space that was being transformed. So it is with transitional situations in love and work: you will need to work out ways of going on while the inner work is being done. This may involve very limited engagements socially, agreements to do some work on a provisional basis, or it may simply involve an inner resolve to accept a given situation as temporary and to transfer your energy to what will be replacing your former connections.

3. Don't act for the sake of action.

The temporary situation is frustrating, often frightening, and there is the temptation to "do something—anything." This reaction is understandable, but it usually leads to more difficulty. The transition process requires not only that we bring a chapter of our lives to a conclusion, but that we discover whatever we need to learn for the next step we are going to take. We need to stay in transition long enough to complete this important process, not to abort it through premature action.

4. Recognize why you are uncomfortable.

Distress is not a sign that something has gone wrong but that something is changing. Understanding the transition process, expecting times of anxiety, expecting others to be threatened, expecting old fears to be awakened—all of these things are important.

5. Surrender to the emptiness.

Stop struggling to escape it. This is not easy. An understanding of its purposes may help.

a) The process of transformation is essentially a death and rebirth process rather than one of mechanical modification. While our own culture knows a great deal about mechanics, it has a great deal to learn about death and rebirth. In keeping with our mechanistic bias, we have tried to make do with recharging and repair, imagining that renewal comes through fixing something defective or supplying something that is missing. In fact it is only by returning for a time to the formlessness of the primal energy that renewal can take place. This empty place is the only source of the self-renewal that we all seek.

b) The process of disintegration and reintegration is indispensable to any new creation. This chaos is not a mess, but rather it is the primal state of pure energy to which one returns for every true new beginning.

c) The emptiness provides a perspective on the stages themselves. Viewed from that emptiness, the realities of the everyday world look transparent and insubstantial, and we can see what is meant by the statement that everything is "illusion." Few of us can live in the harsh light of this knowledge for long, but even when we return to ordinary "reality," we carry with us an appreciation of the unknowable ground beyond every image. This experience provides access to an angle of vision on life that one can get nowhere else.

6. Take care of yourself in little ways.
This is not a time to be living up to your highest self-image. But it is a time to keep an agreement with yourself; namely, to be sensitive to your real and immediate needs. Find little continuities that are important when everything else seems to be going out of your life. Doing unexpected and unplanned things. Avoid expeditions and enterprises! Do not do things to fit into a value system. (And do not take this "do" and "do not" literally! Find the spirit and heart of it for your purpose.)

7. Do not share your anxiety, confusion, or whatever personal experience you feel might explain your "delicate condition" to inquirers and most friends.

Many will simply respond to you with concern and alarm and will become involved in trying to get help for you. Others will be put off and threatened by your situation that threatens their own equilibrium and feel they are being drawn into a demanding situation. Quite simply, they do not want to become involved.

Finally, the way out is the way in. When wheels spin in loose gravel, you need more weight. Tempting though it may be to do something else and wait for the experience to pass, it turns out that it is one of those things that is going to wait around until it gets your attention, and cooperation.

Carol then included this except from Thomas Merton's *Dark Path:*

> It is my joy to tell you to hope though you think that for you of all men hope is impossible. Hope not because you think you can be good but because God loves us irrespective of our merits and whatever is good in us comes from His love, not from our doing.
>
> The message of hope this contemplative offers you, then, brother, is not that you need to find your way through the jungle of language and problems that today surrounds you; but that, whether you understand or not, God loves you, is present to you, lives in you, dwells in you, calls you, saves you, and offers you an understanding and light which are nothing like you ever found in books or heard in sermons. This contemplative has nothing to tell you except to reassure you and say that if you dare to penetrate your own silence and dare to advance without fear into the solitude of your own heart, and risk the sharing of that solitude with one lonely other who seeks God through you and with you, then you will truly recover the light and the capacity to understand what is beyond words and beyond explanations because it is too close to be explained: it is the intimate union in the depths of your own heart, of God's spirit and your own secret inmost self, so that you and God are in truth One Spirit.

Terrible Privilege
November

As we walked out to the car, Jill commented on the bouyancy of the atmosphere, full of moisture and breeze. "It's like being by the sea, isn't it?" Even though she was almost three weeks late, she carried herself so well, so nobly, that her largeness never seemed extreme.

I encouraged her to go in and see Dr. Incao first this time. Perhaps they would talk longer then. As I sat in the waiting room, knitting, I could hear bits of their conversation. He wanted her to go back up to Pittsfield for a second stress test. He said that he would not be confident about doing a home delivery unless she had the test again. He was having some trouble hearing the baby's heartbeat through the preliminary contractions she was having.

When Jill came out she looked concerned, in a hurry. "We'll have to postpone the pizza," she said, but I only encouraged her saying that it was best to be safe, and if having another stress test put Dr. Incao at ease, so that he could go ahead and deliver at home that evening, Great.

It was my turn to go in. I had been taking my shots for a month now, and I told him how I was actually beginning to feel better, stronger, but now I was also curious as to what these medicines *were* exactly. He described in a brief, generalized way, what the medicines were doing for me.

Monday and Thursday evenings, I gave myself a shot in the liver area, taking one ampule of *Formica*, derived from red ants. Steiner saw that red ants were incredibly quick at bringing dead matter back into the life cycle. I was also taking one ampule of *Magnesium phosphoricum*, which helped bring more light, for lupus was partly an inability to handle light.

Tuesday and Friday evenings, I shot (always subcutaneously) four fingers below the navel, using *Carbo Betula*, which was a coal made from birch bark, the birch tree having youthful, supple, yielding qualities, and *Melissa Cupro*, a form of copper, which related to Venus and the kidneys. The kidneys could get too contracted, tense, cramped, and this remedy helped counteract that in an expansive way, helping the kidneys to breathe.

Wednesday and Saturday morning, I gave myself a shot in the solar plexus, with *Ferrum Sidereum*, meteoric iron, which worked in a centrifugal way, as sparks shoot out from struck iron—throwing illness off from the periphery, helping the pancreas, which is the master gland relating to the ego. I was also taking one ampule of *Equisetum Formica*, red ants and horsetail, which also helped the kidneys in the process of elimination.

Sunday I rested, no shot. It was good to have a bit of a break, though I had found it amazingly easy to give myself these shots in my stomach, such a vulnerable area, but it was actually less painful than when I'd taken Iscador in the thigh. Sometimes I would hit a sensitive area right on the surface of the skin, and then I'd try a slightly different location. I found that I preferred giving myself a shot while in the tub, or while standing up, and once the needle was inserted, I didn't look, just pushed the liquid slowly in. One feels somewhat removed from one's own physical body in the act of jabbing a needle into one's own

skin. Will above matter. I was glad I could overcome my squeamish-
ness.

But the regime went on, and Dr. Incao had more to tell me. Every
morning, before breakfast, I had to boil a cup of strong, bitter, birch
leaf tea. This was a general blood cleansing remedy which was also a
Scandinavian folk remedy for arthritis. After dinner I took two cups of
a very mild, soothing Equisetum tea, made from the horsetail plant,
and like the shot, it helped my kidneys in the elimination process,
when salts and other harmful toxins had trouble being eliminated. The
silica in this tea was also beneficial, aiding the process of elimination.
He felt that I had a tightness in my kidneys, which he considered to be
the seat of feelings, and this tightness made me retain too much salt
and toxins. At night I had to rub a copper *Cuprum ointment* on my
kidneys for warmth, and I also had to take Rosemary baths twice a
week, resting afterwards. The Rosemary was good for connective tissue diseases, good for diabetes as well, he said, and it helped fire up
internal warmth.

Then, three times a day, before each meal, I took seven drops of
Absinth/For/Resina Laricis, an extremely bitter digestive, which helped
bring the head forces down into the metabolic. During the waxing
moon, I took seven drops of *Antimony Dil D8/Bryophyllum,* antimony
being a mineral, which like mercury, helped things to flow when they
got stuck, keeping me from stagnation, helping to bring things into
motion. Goethe saw Bryophyllum as the archetypal plant, all leaf,
leaves that sprouted more little leaves all around their edges, leaves
being the expression of the rhythmic area. During the waning moon I
took *Echinacea D3/Ferrum siderium,* and he explained that certain
medicines seemed to work in an expanding way and were best taken
during the waxing phase, and others worked in a contracting way,
waning. The archetypal polarity was taken into account here, the breathing of the universe.

When my father found out that I was taking some medication
according to the phases of the moon, he mailed me two cans of beans,
one of kidney beans, labelled—*Eat Only During the Waning Moon,* and a
can of wax beans—*Eat Only During the Waxing Moon!* He always did
help me keep my sense of humor.

Incao agreed that it was a lot to remember, but he thought that if all
went well, I'd be able to reduce these shots gradually, reducing the
Plaquenil gradually too. I was now taking Plaquenil every third or
fourth day, and felt no arthritic symptoms. I told him I was planning

on seeing a new rheumatologist, Dr. Volastro. I wanted my blood and urine to be checked regularly, and to have an allopathic opinion about my condition too.

As I came out of Incao's office, it was past five, and I could see that he had also been thinking about Jill. She sat waiting for me now, and he said, "I haven't been able to get in touch with Dr. Haling yet, but I think you should go home, get Alex and go right on up to Pittsfield. Don't wait to get in touch with Dr. Haling." He was very calm and soft spoken, but clear and firm. "I want the test done tonight." Jill borrowed the phone and called home, but couldn't reach Alex, so she called a neighbor friend, and asked her to come up and babysit for Willa. Everything was fine, mere routine, Jill assured her on the phone, but I could hear the controlled anxiety in her voice.

Of course she was unsettled, but I tried to make her feel more lighthearted. Everything would be fine. Of course she was tense, being so late, but I thought it best that Dr. Incao was being careful. She said how the whole process of pregnancy, the birth, had all begun to seem unreal to her. She mentioned that she hadn't felt the baby move in a couple of days.

"You know I used to have long periods of time when I didn't feel Ayler move in utero," I said. "He was so passive. Your baby is probably so huge and firmly engaged that he doesn't have any room to move." She thought that she was indeed in beginning labor, but it was too easy, so different, the pressure down there quite strong, yet the contractions weren't painful. I wondered if she was merely feeling Braxton Hicks contractions, those nice preliminary exercises.

We talked about my sister, Cia's baby, due so soon. They were supposedly going to give Cia an amniocentesis that afternoon, and if her baby's lungs were developed enough, they'd deliver the following day, either by inducing or Caesarian. Because my sister had diabetes, they had to keep a very close watch over her and the baby. I told Jill to just think of all my sister had to go through. One more little stress test just wasn't such an ordeal. And think, Jill and I had had babies together on the same day, a little over three years ago. Wouldn't it be uncanny and fantastic, if somehow this would also happen for my sister and Jill, again.

Jill wanted to know everthing that Dr. Incao had said to me, and I tried to remember, reading from my notes. He had given me an article that was printed in the American Medical Association News, discussing the case of a Philippine-American woman, who had become severely ill with lupus, and after taking large doses of cortisone, she returned to her native village in the islands, and a witch doctor removed a curse placed on her by a previous suitor. She returned to "normal" in all her tests. The commentary read:

> "It is unlikely that this patient's SLE "burned out." At the time of cessation of medication, histological changes were present on renal biopsy specimens, serum compliment levels were low, and ESR's—were very high...by what mechanism did the machinations of an Asian medicine man cure active lupus nephritis, change myxedema into euthyroidim, and allow precipitous withdrawal from corticosteroid treatment without symptoms of adrenal insufficiency?"

Perhaps more goes on in the spiritual world, concerning our health and well-being, than we truly care to admit, or could possibly understand with the rational mind.

My sister had written to me about going to a faith healer for her diabetes, and his response to her was unusual. "This very head-on-his-shoulders, apostle type of international renown man prayed that a curse be broken over me. I don't know much about curses," Cia wrote, "except that they do seem to get passed on the way blessings do, from generation to generation. You could pray that God would give you wisdom or revelation about it, in the event you needed something like that broken over your life. It's amazing how God will take big steps in arranging things on our behalf, for our benefit, when we take the smallest steps of faith towards Him."

We had made it back to Baldwin Hill, and I gave Jilly a squeeze for good luck, and we agreed that she would call before ten o'clock that night to let me know how the test went. I would have gladly accompanied her, but she thought it best if just she and Alex went alone.

As I got out of the car, a gust of wind slapped up, pre-torrential, beckoning, threatening, pushing and pulling. It felt like a night for transformation.

Walking inside, I realized no one was home. They had all gone out to eat. I felt slightly spooked. The wind was now blowing doors shut, and the house suddenly felt so large and dark. I turned on too many lights and began baking myself some fish, boiled potatoes, and a big heaping pile of grated carrots.

When Geoff, Jeanne and the boys returned, Geoff told me that my parents had called, and Cia was in labor! Just before they were to give

Cia the amniocentesis, her waters broke, all on her own, three weeks early, and she had gone into mild labor. She had been laboring now for most of the day. I was thrilled that it had all begun on its own, without interference. And Jill might be in labor now too. I was overjoyed at the prospects and could barely sit still, waiting as the minutes passed towards that ten o'clock phone call.

Then I realized that I had to go pick up the huge load of food I'd ordered from the Co-op. Jeanne said that she would come with me and help load it up—bless her always eager generosity and congenial helpfulness. We decided that we were both too tired to postpone the chore any longer, so at 9:45 we left for town.

It started to rain. What a night to be out in the elements, carrying vulnerable five pound bags of nuts and popcorn, oatmeal, rice, down a slippery lawn to load up. But we got the job done and slowly cruised on home.

As I walked into the kitchen, Geoff came out from his study, excited, saying that he had just talked to Mark, Cia's husband, and I was an aunt! I screamed with joy.

"What did she have?"

"A normal, seven pound, ten ounce, baby girl."

I clenched my hands and jumped, I was so thrilled. She ended up having a Caesarian, but she was doing fine, and the baby was beautiful.

Then I saw a curtain drop over his face, as if that very brief announcement was a preview, cancelled by a greater darkness.

"And Jill?" I asked. "Did Jill call?"

He looked down, and then said quietly, "Jill's baby is dead."

My hand made the gesture, stop—Stop It—"No. I can't believe it," hand to mouth, "I just can't believe it." My eyes felt wide with the shock of it, torn in two, the joy of one and the wreck of it, receiving life, returning it, given and taken away, at once, so simultaneous. The house could have been wrenched in half, and it would have been no more shocking. How would they ever survive this. Cia and her happiness were forgotten. The wind clapped and banged and blew. The rain whipped the windows from every direction. Hot and cold, dry and wet, here nor there, sleepless in a dizzying trance, it was a night for the primitive mind.

As I lay in the dark and tried to sleep, I was jolted with the clammy fear that death or something ominous was hovering close by, and I pictured my sister in trouble, shaking on the recovery table. Or would I have to pay. Was it my turn now. I tried to pray for both Cia and Jill, tried to keep my mind from inventing reasons for this. We can not use our human values in responding.

Cia's words came back to me, from her last letter, "God's value system is so much different than our own. Sometimes he gives the hardest trials to those who were meant to know more of Him."

It seemed true, that deep grief, great illness, suffering, loss, could work more of God's character into a person. But what a price, what a terrible privilege.

Wintering
November-January

After two weeks without Plaquenil, I began to feel something inside of me thawing, a soul ache. Dr. Incao had said how the Plaquenil and prednisone had simply frozen the arthritic process temporarily, and now the iceberg had begun to heave and flow. Sudden upheavals of tears seemed to be part of the process. Once Geoff found me sobbing over the dishes, and I thought, indeed, I could let it run like tap water.

Jill and I had certainly both had our time of tears during this thirty-third year of our lives. The loss and fear we'd faced, coming so differently to a similar place, where the physical life turns back and regards death, like a concave, convex mirror, and having this reflection, having each other helped.

As I said to her on leaving the hospital that night, when it was time to go, and her eyes widened, travelling over the room with its tiny flowered wallpaper, as if she were being forced to leave a place she loved very much, and would never see again, as her eyes began to fill with the first realization, I said it was good to cry, that there would be so many tears. She shook her head yes, but put her whole hand over her mouth, afraid that if she started, she would never stop, until she came to those tears one gives at the very bottom, that make you feel like something found when the snow turns into mud, ruined on rescue.

We were ready for a covering, where the external world was one in whiteness, imperfections all wiped out. Snow makes the outside world so silent, the internal, kindled, guarded.

The days so short and dark near Christmas, also darkened my mood some. I felt apprehensive about spending Christmas in this new place, without my extended family. Jill wanted to spend their Christmas alone, and I felt isolated.

Christmas day itself was peaceful and pleasant, with a long family walk, where we sang all the carols we knew. We then came home to a goose dinner, which we all found delicious, but there was still that effort to fill up the table with the sounds of celebration, and it was a little lonely. Is that one reason why folks gather to feast, to ward off loneliness at this time of darkness, to feel a greater unity of light. I longed for the simple past, for family, and childhood, and friends, wanting to extend beyond the nuclear, beyond the pain of the present tense.

Almost as a means of escaping this darkness, thoughts of a sunnier California tugged, letters beckoned. Soon the plum trees would be in bloom. The strength of that greater network seemed to catch my falling heart, trampoline it with lucky memories. I jumped, and decided to make a trip there alone, mid-February, and a new lightness caught me up.

Now I could thoroughly enjoy this cold, this suddenly buried climate; as the big bad blizzard we'd all been waiting for finally descended. I loved going out in it, dragging a toboggan over a fresh field, seeing the crystals as I'd never seen them before, textbook perfect on my dark brown coat. I walked the dream parcel, 20 acres down the road, going from the view pasture deep into the woods, where I lay down and made a big angel in the snow, wagging my arms and legs, like a kid, letting the flakes hit my lashes and nose, until the chill started to set in, and I had to keep going. When I got cold now, it seemed to stay deep inside me—as when you swallow an icecube whole, and the feeling remains in your stomach and throat. But as I walked along the border of the field, I realized how the silence and harmony of these days had been healing, no more adrenalin rush jarring the metabolism. In its place came vigor, and then the inexplicably relaxed feeling one's limbs have coming into the warmth after a stint out in the snow.

Almost every Sunday, Bunny Kirchner and I saddled up and rode the steaming horses over Baldwin Hill, field yielding to field, the freedom of farmland. Bunny was always willing to go wherever I wanted—"I'll follow you," as the black stallion pranced and skittered forward. He was a handful, and it fired me up to be on top of him, climbing hills, eating the wind that whipped up, putting a glow in my cheeks and light in my race-craving eyes.

But one Sunday, riding, a group of horses passed us in the other direction, and I felt a snap. Bunny pointed down and said, "Your girth's broke!" It had snapped in half, and there I was sitting on a saddle that wasn't even attached to my horse, like sitting on a chair on the wing of an airplane, ready to take off. Made me realize how precarious everything is, by what small means we're attached to a safe and healthy life.

When I went back to see Incao, he was pleased that I was doing so well, that I had a strong enough will to carry the shots and drops and everything through. "You may have to face a challenge sometime this winter," he added. I didn't think I was ready for that. It seemed that I'd regained a new strength, and peace of mind which I'd never had living in the city, and if I could still the apprehensions, I believed it wouldn't be so hard on me this time if I were challenged.

Dr. Incao also mentioned that he thought I might consider talking to a counsellor. He wanted me to work through emotional problems now, if they came up, not push them back, letting old, past problems resurface, then leaving them behind in peace. It wasn't enough to know, with my head, what these problems were. Perhaps it was a matter of unfreezing parts of my protective self. I took the name of the woman he recommended, but again felt apprehensive. Why did I always recoil from the suggestion of therapy. I was simply afraid of baring myself in this way.

Much easier to put myself in the hands of an anthroposophical masseuse, who I was to see for six sessions. I reasoned that I could only afford, money and time-wise, one extra curricular therapy at a time.

When I first went to see Elizabeth Schlieben in her tiny cottage in South Egremont, I had my period. She usually didn't do curative massage when the body was already in the menstrual struggle, enough was going on there, but when I told her that my periods were relatively light and easy, she went ahead and worked on me. I stripped down to my underpants and lay down on the massage table which nearly filled this grandmotherly-neat upstairs room. She had laid two blankets out on the table, and I wrapped myself up in the flannel and wool before she came up. I heard her warming her hands in running water. She was very calm and quiet, and the massage was extremely delicate, working with the etheric streams of energy. She said that she was especially working on the process of elimination and the kidneys with me. I had remarked, since following Dr. Incao's course, that my kidneys felt less sensitive. I wasn't so protective of that area, and my middle felt softer. Maybe I was just getting fat, or maybe I was getting less hard.

With apricot oil, Elizabeth massaged my stomach, my legs, feet, and turning over, my back and spinal column in particular. Then after she had massaged for about twenty minutes, she wrapped me up in the blankets, and added another heavy comforter, and I lay on my side and rested, actually falling asleep. When I woke, I could have been anywhere familiar, but I felt so comfortable and good, and the colors—soft green and yellow and tan, made me think I was in a little room at my grandmother's house.

This curative massage was supposed to loosen areas of denseness or tension and help bring about a balance of the forces that had become displaced in the body. I was amazed that such gentle work could have such profound affect. After the first session I felt extremely vague and foggy for the rest of the day, but that might have been partly due to my period. Then after future sessions, it seemed that I was extremely relaxed and refreshed. I continued to see Elisabeth for a while, and though sometimes I wondered whether the massage work would have long-lasting affects, I basically felt that allowing this time for myself, time for the healing process, was very important.

High Contrast

February, Berkeley

Gloria met me at the airport with a wand of flowering plum. It smelled glorious. Outside, the benign quality of air gushed up, warm and wet, enfolding, such a contrast to the freezing, blank whiteness I'd come from that morning, where the car's heat wouldn't reach my feet. Now this leap of late evening warmth, and the flowering perfume, sent a premature jump of sap flowing in the no-melt mind. Sprung into Spring. And entering back into the state of Berkeley was comfortable and easy, familiar and right. I knew where to turn without wondering where. Our house at 2016 Cedar looked remarkably the same. Same pale blossoms on same wet sidewalks, the gate to the cottage, just the same, with its jingle and slam, and Summer, there in her receiving room out flat on her back, was only altered by the torn ligaments she'd heard rip like a sheet that morning. "My Heidi," she moaned, and we laughed, her spirit the same, and her welcome as warm as it could have been. I felt at home, yet somewhat like a student come back from college, hovering over the curious, familiar past, knowing I didn't live here anymore.

On waking that first morning, I felt compelled to tackle my long list of errands—xerox, return books, yarn store, see Catherine, buy sour cream for enchiladas that night, asparagus, endive. But on the way from the Produce Center, back to Cedar Street, I stuffed my red wallet into one unzipped purse into one unzipped backpack, slung it over my shoulder, while carrying packages and raincoat, behind the blur of time travel, adjusting to the glut of speed, cars, intensity, and when I next looked, my wallet wasn't there. All travel cash gone. Plus credit card panic. I couldn't believe the stupidity of it all. Crazed and pressing as the traffic, I retraced my steps. No red wallet. I stood on the corner of our old block, waiting to cross, and could almost feel Ayler's presence by my side—walk, DON'T WALK, walk, DON'T WALK, and sensed the accumulation of all those strolls we'd taken here, facing this intersection, noise-color-movement demanding; Clovis too, during his young life's formation, had taken this in, and I wondered—had frantic little bumper cars entered their bloodstreams only to go crazy when someday called upon? Were their young malleable beings pounded hard on this pavement?

I thought of my last walk with Ayler, the morning before I left. It was below zero, but I wanted to get out, and so dressed Ay in layers of wool, red down parka, scarf over mouth, and we walked up the middle of the frozen mud road to Proctor's Farm on the corner, stomping and singing. Ay slid the heavy barn door open a crack, and we asked Rodney if we could come in, see the cows. He was cleaning out stalls, and it was warm with the wealth of livestock inside, cozy low ceilings, all whitewashed and worn. We slid the door shut behind us. Rodney was filling a wheelbarrow with a pitchfork. The cows beside him were gigantic with calf, soon to deliver. Ayler could watch Rodney filling barrows with manure until the cows came home, forever.

"Did you know I'm a farmer?" he said to me, turning up his perfectly serious, delicate blond face.

"And what do you farm?" I asked him.

"Farm cows," he said, turning back to business. He was surely at home here, and I was too, with the hay and animal odors. The littlest calves got our special attention. One newborn, pure black calf was a beauty, her coat luscious and shiny, sweet open eyes, thick coaxing tongue that grabbed a finger to suck. My favorite had the numeral 7 on her jersey brown brow, and another had a valentine on her forehead.

Now my valentine arrived in the form of one red returned wallet with all cash attached. Everyone was astonished that anonymous honesty still existed in Berkeley. But I also found a homemade heart in my suitcase from Geoff, and received a card from him picturing Lassie—he'd drawn a big red heart on her faithful chest. I had left three valentines at home, but I felt no impulse to call now, indulging in this restless freedom, the lack of responsibility, acting on impulse, grabbing up Joanna, my goddaughter, that little biscuit of bounty, in all her two year old firmness, taking her off to buy a pair of red French shoes. We also found a heart shaped helium balloon, and later that evening Summer pointed to her bed. Joanna was lying there clutching her red sock hobby-horse, and her red "loon" balloon, in her valentine outfit, utterly asleep.

But being back in Berkeley made me realize how good the country was for kids. I saw all that Clovis had dropped in the form of city guises, jive, anxiety and intensity, once he'd settled into country life, and a harmonious class at the Steiner school. He would always be a big physical presence and take up a lot of room, but he was no longer wrapped like a tight bud in green city cellophane. He had shed that covering, that costume, in order to fully bloom, and perhaps the country had opened all of us to a clarity of face, of eyes.

I was quickly losing that arrival freshness, whipped out into the whirl, flying from lunch to shop to dinner party, delighting in these small feasts with good friends, but slightly unsettled by the demands of my schedule, hardly able to sink into the present and enjoy it, as if I were reliving some old driven anxiety. I was grateful to sink into the hot tub with Judith late at night under the stars. Then up the next morning to make twelve fast phone calls, set up the next set, a great matinee, walk across campus to Telegraph Ave. to have a glass of wine at The Swallow cafe. I went through our heaped-high storage closet at 2016, stuffing three duffle bags full, and then showed a group of realtors through the house. I noticed that I was less emotionally attached to this "home" now, as they made their comments. Street level feeling—We have moved on.

Serenity of place had become a basic need. I pictured the Berkshires under snow, for a huge snow storm had dumped two feet the day I left, but that covering too seemed unreal now, as I lay in my afternoon tub, washing away the oil and funk and grime and smoke, trying to relax before that evening's activity. Snowbanks seemed so distant. Would it feel wrong on returning, all that space, open reach of whiteness, only the moonlight at night, waning and waxing, the tuck-in of night's complete silence.

I went out behind the house and picked three white callas in three early stages of unfolding. The calla was like a symbol of Berkeley— Exotic, erotic, neurotica. The excitement of the possible was palatable on these streets, the delectable morsel, the irresistible shoe. New age affluence, commercial dispersal, but I began to feel battered by this self-imposed pace, and knew if I had to live at this high boil for long, I'd be sick again.

I knew Summer had a different level of tolerance. There she was, flat on her back, entertaining a steady stream of visitors, phone in hand about half the time. She thrived on interaction, while I began to wither. Yet I could see the same happening to her, in isolation, cold, in the country. She was like an orchid, and I, like a bulb which needed the severity of freeze. Perhaps I was a creature of another climate. Perhaps we thrive best in our original birthstate, for I had arrived in Massachusetts with a Caesarian scream thirty-three years ago. Having grown up in Wisconsin, something in my blood was tempered for extremes. I had felt a youthfulness return with those crisp, clear seasons, as if that rhythm were as necessary as wakefulness and sleep.

Meanwhile, this warmer, westerly weather left my rhythms at an idle, and I enjoyed it, like delving into old temptations, doing the dazzle or smiling with darling and chuckles hilarious over bottles of California wine. It's easier to be *up* when you're alone and not responsible. I needed this week to be indulged.

One morning Gloria and I walked through her old neighborhood, near the hospital where Ayler was born, and Berkeley seemed so liveable, with its fecund remarkable gardens, dripping and shining, relaxed as a cat sunning on a windowsill—but suddenly we heard the tones of a pentatonic bell chime, the same set I'd given Geoff a year ago, and everything seemed like a brilliantly vivid postcard of a memory—lost to me, I had changed. The low haunting clang of those bell chimes was almost pleasantly painful, as if the past were a tooth growing back. Which couldn't grow back. I understood the transience of the present tense as physical, then the inevitable loss that grows where something solid once sat. Taken away though change. We lived here. We heard this music. We honored these friends. We left.

My bags were packed, I was full on conversation, the abundance of contact, and fine fine food, shops and the inevitable spending. I had had my dose of film and traffic and clear bay views. I was ready to turn back to winter, and wait for true spring in its turn, to return, to revive, delight and deliver—How would Baldwin Hill seem, breathing in flower. It was worth the wait, through shuddering rains and the long patchy melting, where snow was likened to old kleenex, and the ruts in the mud became a challenge.

So I sailed home on schedule, everything clicking like clockwork, and finally arrived to sight our house lights at 10:30 eastern time. The house was quiet and warm when I entered. Geoff's birthday flowers from nine days before were still in the centerpiece, but now dry and colorfully twisted under the low hung amber shade. A tempting stack of mail beside Ayler's message, written out by Geoffrey:

Dear Mom, I want to touch you on the summertime!

And I knew what he meant, the unconscious dreamy milk source, like summertime, soothing, where all is replenished, while winter was painfully conscious, the missing of Mama, a sharp separation.

I kissed them in their sleep.

Approaching Abundance
March, Egremont

Spring arrived gradually just as the snow withdrew, under the influence of rain and a sharper sun. For the first time in six months I felt the need to shield myself from the rising rays, but I also had cause to rejoice. On returning from California, I called Dr. Volastro, my rheumatologist, and he said that my last blood tests showed that I had returned to "normal." Complete remission. With that pronouncement, a magic ring of snowdrops sprang up around me with their little bowed heads, and I got down on my knees with the children, saw the leaf shoots of bulb plants working their way up. The rebirthing of spring was at work everywhere, and I felt the impulse to rejoice.

Mildly ecstatic on our first warm walk of the season, we went careening down the long dirt road to the cross-roads. The old farmhouse on the corner there had sap buckets hung on the maples, and Ayler let a little "honey water" drip on his fingers. A young toothy boy came out and showed us around, exhibiting the rabbits he bred in the big hay barn with its majestic hand hewn beams. The kids crawled around on the high piled bales. Then out back we saw their flock of maddened geese, and a cute cavorting goat who perched his front feet up on a rock to pose. They had calves and an old retired workhorse. One of the sisters was braiding its mane. She came and joined us, showed us one huge nervous pig that looked like it might stumble under its own enormous weight. What ears! It was all black, save for one white ring, like a lifesaver stuck around its middle. All the ducks ran about in the spring sunlight, and the chickens flapped up and down their plank, while Ayler picked up a little kitten, and the girls worried about how to move their turkey to a grassier pen. My boys seemed a bit dazed by it all, the active wonder of this place with its casual workings, the children all eagerly engaged in their chores, but also generous in humor and unaffected.

I spotted a big bush of forsythia, which would soon burst into flicks of yellow, and the lilac bush which looked so uninteresting before rendering those most succulent blooms. I wanted to picture the entire landscape in green chiffon, the light wear of first spring with its mist of blossoms. Poke by poke, it was already happening. Atea, Ayler's small friend from nextdoor, marched about showing us where the crocus leaves were already sprouting. "And then you'll have to stay to your path!" she announced, as she had been told last year, for soon this whole front yard would be a field of crocus flowers.

Down the road came Bunny Kirchner, with his saucy brown Shetland pulling a cart. Ay and I ran to meet him and jumped on behind. What a grand way to travel, over these quiet dirt roads, expanding into the expanse. I hopped off and walked alongside when we came to an incline. Surely we were halfway to heaven. I felt giddy, no longer so self-determined or guided by my own strong will. It was a subtle shift, this inner changing, but I felt directed by a Mighty Driver—*O try my heart and my reins*!

I had recently read a very simple, yet powerful document, *By a New and Living Way*, written by Mary Fullerson. In this slim volume she conveyed both reality and mystery in one breath, as spring does in each flower. Part of what she had come to understand conveyed a letting go, a dropping into acceptance.

> Make a conscious, mental and physical motion of dropping into My Presence. You know the centered area where I dwell! That is the Centre which must be fed at My Table. Then your spirit feeds directly upon My Spirit. Into the

essence of your being, My Being, My Body comes. Does it surprise you that it brings fullness and health to all parts? Does it surprise that once you have asked to be Mine you are weak and sickly without your natural spiritual food?...

Reading this book in the light of my afternoon work room, I felt something flood up in me as I dropped into the truth of it. I'd been like a colicky infant, struggling in her mother's arms, who finally knew relief and could appreciate nourishment, the milk of kindness. How long I had struggled against that kindness, rejecting peace for direction, self-driven all the way, but now I felt something give, as if an old rotten rope had finally lost its last grip on the pier's post, and I was released into a greater lake, a wider gentleness.

> I yearn over your body. I would be consciously in dominion in each cell—if you would call Me into them. But you will not realize the miracle of this. I wait....
>
> Honour, *respect* My Life in each cell of your body. Bow before the mystery of life and allow no tension to betray its full expression. Let each atom of your being BE in perfect peace, in perfect rest in Me....
>
> You have the living words you need, the living words within. 'Hear' them constantly in each cell of your body. Worship in bodily tissue until strength flows to you. Pray in body, rather than in mind or spirit. Pray with a consciousness of Light in every part of bodily being. It will accomplish the needed healing within....

It was a quiet, almost secretive, illumination, and I was careful of this delicate thankfulness, while also wanting to burst into praising delight—over the littlest things—for the steam and sight of that chicken pot pie on the red and white checked tablecloth, for the delicious hyacinth, for the colors on the clothesline and the ascending curves of this landscape, for the seven on the jersey cow's brow, for my own yellow room where I could write, for family and good friends, for rejuvenated hope, end of darkness and grieving, joyful planet, spring's rubber ice, pussy willows looking like rain stuck to stems, gladness for neighbors with open doors and ready laughter, joy for the woodchuck in the field—stunned by light, and the birds in abundance, making the trees shake with song, for the farewell to snow and the slow seepage, the comfort of rain and the pushing through, for this season of willow wands and resurrection—for loving kindness is apparent and waving high, as the light returns to help all earth things—up onto our knees, to our feet, for song and circle—Open to rejoicing—and so we sang—

> *Now the green blade riseth, from the buried grain;*
> *Wheat that in dark earth, many days has lain;*
> *Love lives again, that with the dead has been:*
> *Love is come again, Like wheat that springeth green.*

Yet I am slightly wary. I do not trust myself. I doubt if it will last. I do not take my health for granted. I carry it in my most precious cup, but I anticipate the inevitable spill, knowing it could be dashed tomorrow. But now, today, it seems to run and run over, and this little waterfall of words makes a pond upon a place where I would love to stay. The ripples of a new and gentle air pass over, and hope does not disappoint us.

Making Room
March-May

No one said that it shouldn't snow in March, but when the blizzard came, it was like a physical relapse. Unfair! We weren't prepared for it. We didn't want to have to go through all that again. But here in the Berkshires you have to be ready for anything.

When I went back to Harlemville to see Incao, I took both boys. Clovis had had a bad cough and laryngitis, and Ayler, an earache. With remedies, both of their problems were subsiding, but I was now tired from the extra mothering, and when it came my turn to see Dr. Incao, I felt cranky. He didn't seem as impressed that my blood tests had returned to normal, for as he said, "Well this is a disease of remissions and flare-ups." It was true. I wasn't exactly "cured." If I were to get a bad flu, and nothing were to happen, then I'd be more convinced. It seemed like the rest of the community was coming down with the flu, chickenpox or pneumonia, but so far, I hadn't been challenged.

He asked me if I'd called Penelope Young, a Psychosynthesis therapist who worked out of her home in Monterey, Massachusetts. He had suggested several times that I see her, and I replied, "Not yet. I can only do one thing at a time, and I was going to the masseuse," but he interrupted my weak defense.

"You sound like one of those people who say that they want to get well *first* and *then* get their lives together. But it doesn't work like that." He wanted me to work on all levels of healing. "Don't get me wrong," Dr. Incao said. "I feel like your life is quite together, but I think this might be important for you."

So I agreed in a half-hearted way, and acknowledged to myself that I shouldn't shove this approach to the back of the shelf once more. But I was feeling whiney, and had to add, "There's only so much time, you know. And I can only afford to give so much time to myself." As soon as that was out of my mouth, I heard it for what it was, a false justification. So much time, so little time....

> *So teach us to number our days, that we may apply our hearts unto wisdom.*

I was hungry for a greater wisdom, but I would have to make time, grab time, open the door. The Psalms were one door. And as I opened that door, other works came my way which influenced this emerging.

While reading Paul Tillich's essay, *The Meaning of Health*, these sections in particular struck me:

> This is the function of reconciliation, to make whole the man who struggles against himself. It reaches the center of personality, and unites man not only with his god and himself, but also with other men and with nature. Reconciliation in the center of personality results in a reconciliation in all directions, and he who is reconciled is able to love. Salvation is the healing of the cosmic disease, which prevents love.

> First, it is obvious that, as long as the idea of cosmic salvation or healing is accepted, bodily, mental, and spiritual healing are not separated. For all elements of reality belong to the cosmic wholeness.

> In the religious sphere, the classical expression for wholeness is "the peace of God" which, according to St. Paul, exceeds all *nous* (rational understanding) and which is able to safeguard the heart (the center of personality) and the *noemata* (acts of rational understanding). The "peace of God" (or "peace of Christ") is the exact opposite of "man against himself." It is "man reconciled."

Hiltner sums up the function of religious healing in the following description: "Real spiritual healing brings forgiveness... after the real guiltiness has been recognized... reorganization, after the powerful elements of disorganization have been investigated ... love, after one's capacities for hostility have been seen... security, after one's anxieties have been understood."

What did I discover from this? It helped me to acknowledge the fact that I was not reconciled. Not on any level. That the work had just begun. I could sense now what was meant by "the peace of God," but I never carried it with me for long. My spiritual yearning came and went like whims of weather. How could one sustain health? How was my stance against myself, against God. How could I recognize, reorganize. I had not thoroughly faced my capacity for hostility, and I didn't understand all of my anxieties. I was afraid of getting in there and stirring things up and causing a relapse. I didn't want to muddy the smooth lake waters. I didn't want to feel the power of my own hatred and anger. But I took the first step, I called Penelope Young, a Psychosynthesis therapist. She seemed genuinely nice on the phone, and after a long conversation, I almost looked forward to our first meeting, and what it might bring about.

Her house was visible in the Hupi Woods from the road. It was a dripping, cold end of March day. I went into the little backdoor, as she had instructed. A dark green carpet lay thick on the floor. I sat down on the chair in the hall and took out my knitting, as if anxious to sit unoccupied even for a moment.

But then Penelope walked in and we said hello, exchanging a jovial beginning. I followed her into the room where we would work together. The wall-to-wall carpet continued into this large windowed room as well. There was a floor mattress and pillowed area by the wall, and I sat down there while she faced me, also on the floor. Her face had a moonlike calmness, and her eyes were searching, though sympathetic and friendly. Penelope said that she liked to begin a session by a quiet meditative time. She felt that helped to let things rise. So we sat facing each other with our eyes closed. And yet I was almost holding my breath. I could hear her slow, deep breathing, and I felt panicked, suddenly hot. The tears rushed up in me, and stopped, eye level. I gulped them down. This was ridiculous. I had just met this woman. I couldn't start off this way. Why did I have to cry? What was wrong with me. Why was I being such a baby?

She came and sat beside me, put her arm around me. I liked that better, strangely enough, less confrontal. She encouraged me to cry, handing me kleenex. I visualized a silk scarf on water, such slight resistance. Hot in my face, tense in my body, I wanted to cry heavily, in downpour, a great need to cry and grieve. Silly and dumb, but o.k., why not? Maybe that's why I was there—The rigidity of false strength, and my great need to present a strong front constantly—strong jaw, strong will, but a weakness, a fragility, just under the surface, like a fake floor in a concrete building. Fear of being sick, incapacitated. I was *really sad*. Though I had this outer cheerfulness. I was afraid, though I barely admitted it. Afraid of being an invalid, of death, of being so cranky my children wouldn't like me. I couldn't be sick, couldn't allow myself to be sick.

Auto-immune disease. I was unable to accept some part of myself. Self against self, unresolved. Mother image territory returned. Sadness. Hurt. Penelope asked me how we were connected, my mother and I, and I pictured a uterus, a small shrunken uterus. Once it was large, full, throbbing with child, once we were one, now, a sharp separation. Penelope had me address my mother, eye to eye—"I need to be connected to you again."

I began to sense an old nightmare, the physical sensation of a well remembered childhood nightmare—a swirling of greys that pressed down with the weight of a tomb, crusty and yet simultaneously smooth, a heaviness swirling away, and then pressing back down on my head, sickening. I used to have this nightmare often as a child, but had never experienced it in a waking state or associated it with my mother before.

I pictured myself lying on my bed, my old canopy bed that was so high off the ground I needed a little step ladder to climb into it. I pictured my mother sitting on the edge of the bed. Penelope again asked me to look into my mother's eyes, but my mother had trouble looking at me, or I at her, trouble with touching. Tense on contact. I asked my mother to hold my hand, and this made my body especially tense. She felt hurt, looked sad, withdrawn into a hard, protective place. She didn't understand, but she *was* willing to be there, with me. She was afraid I would hurt her. I felt that many had hurt her. Her mother, my father, his mother, her children, all of them had hurt her, and I would hurt her again.

"Have you forgiven yourself for hurting her?"

But she was willing to stay there, with me, in the image. I asked her to accept me, to stay with me, that I needed her. How amazing. My rejection, a mirror reversal of this need to be with her, acceptance. I asked her, and she softened. She bowed her head, though her eyes were too agitated to focus on mine. They were too hard to look at.

Many tears, sobs, ripped out knitting, unkinking of pent up chest mesh, coming in yanked out rows, skeins of emotion, little girl sob, left alone on that bed to cry, sob swallowing sob. I needed my mother to hold me, but my whole body rejected that idea, and I had made it impossible for her. I identified with her sadness, her rejection, her difficulty at loving. Wanting to be loved, appearing rigid, hard, afraid. I wanted to be able to love her, and Penelope encouraged me to keep speaking to my mother, sharing my feelings, which I had never done. I said—"It hurt me when you were the brunt of jokes, when people called you M.M. for Mean Margaret. I want you to stay with me, to hold my hand." She was willing to stay there with me. Amazing. I felt more at peace. If I made room for love, I felt more at peace. Soothed in my head and chest, though still tense in my limbs. A greater easiness of breath, not gasping, constricted.

We closed with that affirmation—If I make room for love, I feel a greater peacefulness with you. When I make room for love, I feel a greater peacefulness within me.

○

Geoff and I had decided to sell our Berkeley home. We wrote the woman who was living in our house, and Geoff called Summer who was in our cottage. This decision came as a shock to both of them. I wrote Summer a letter explaining why we wanted to make this move now, sympathizing with her difficult situation, while not accepting guilt for our desire to consolidate our lives. Still, the decision to literally end our commitment to California, by selling our first home, leaving a phase of our lives behind, and making the east coast our future, brought great relief, and much additional anxiety.

When I returned to Penelope's two weeks later, I felt fragile, tired. Throughout March I had begun to notice slight arthritic symptoms in my joints, especially in my hands, and I wanted to shake off that rheumatic devil dance that was starting up. It weakened me, both physically and emotionally. I could feel myself slowly squeaking down, slipping down that same helpless slide.

It was April 11th, two days before my birthday, and irrationally I already felt cheated, hurt beforehand. I pictured myself giving and giving, and now I was afraid that it wouldn't come back. I knew that pure generosity wouldn't be resentful, exhausted, for true generosity would be regenerating, but perhaps I gave out of some baser need. I was angry with Summer, who had always represented a good, loving, all-embracing mother image for me, but now that I was withdrawing my support, by selling our house and the cottage where she lived, I was afraid that she wouldn't have time for me, as her short note back indicated—no time for a real response.

I was angry with my birthday. Angry with my thirty-third year. How dare you break me like this! I hated everyone who was normal and healthy. No presents came in the mail. *Nobody loves me. Nobody loves me! I'm going to the garden to eat worms.*

But I didn't really get angry. Instead, I was quiet, as I sat there with Penelope. I turned the anger back against myself and was hurt. Unexpressed, misdirected anger equalled hurt. Why was I so angry, anyway. Why did I feel cheated, and why did I have these great expectations and needs from my women friends, when I resented expectations myself?

No, I couldn't pound the huge turquoise pillow Penelope placed in front of me. She read the twitching of my upper jaw muscles moving down, then stopping. She saw something block. I couldn't release on a cellular level.

"You don't want to get angry with Summer, do you."

True, I would rather feel hurt, feel sad.

"This is a long shot," she said, "but perhaps you don't want to get angry, because you think you're better than she is." *Yes.*

"I was just thinking—I don't want to get angry, because I don't want to come down to her level."

Spiritual pride. She congratulated me for recognizing my own spiritual pride. Where did it come from? Recognizing it, hopefully, was the first step in doing away with it. Insidious thing, pride, to assume you are better, know better, deserve more... condescending while trying to control, just like my own mother's method of defense, putting down others in order to feel secure, better than, more righteous, but what a fragile security we had built for ourselves, out of sticks and straw, like the first and second little pigs.

o

Then our commitment to the Berkshires became a reality. Almost on a whim, we went to see a small Colonial house on the edge of Alford, a wonderfully quiet gravel road, and we fell totally in love with the place. The horseshoe shaped driveway was lined with hemlock and birch trees. The house was set sideways like a gem, catching light, amidst stone outcroppings, daffodils and magnolias, five acres of the most various, intimate land, little dips and hills, stone benches placed amongst flowers, and every kind of tree and plant imaginable, dogwood, pear, apple trees and maple, a big patch of raspberries, and established grapes, flower gardens spilling down rocky edges and stone walls—a stream ran down into a spring fed pond, and a red wooden bridge crossed over where a little waterfall fell. You could hear it from the downstairs master bedroom with its balcony overlooking the pond and forest beyond. A beautiful warm-blue sitting room was also part of this southern expanse, and there was a sunny dining room with Carl Larsen type details, built-in cupboards and a tiny pantry, while the kitchen felt like Normandy with a cathedral ceiling, baskets and pots hanging from the beams, odd little windows up high. Upstairs there was a playroom space and three intimately angled bedrooms, all with those marvellous old wide plank floors, and then there was the barn, with an insulated office-studio for Geoff, space for two cars with a hayloft above, a stall for a horse with a small connecting pasture. If we had listed all that we could have wanted and asked for the fulfillment of our dream, this would have been the place. It almost seemed uncanny. Too good to be. We made a bid. They made a counter bid. We made another and they accepted. An enormous step, but it was decided, and now the pressure was really on to sell the Berkeley house and make our multiple moves.

○

When I went to back to see Penelope, I could tell her that my birthday hadn't been a disaster. Jill had cooked up an incredible feast, a real birthday dinner bash, which was almost flooring, but I lapped it up. I basked in it. I hadn't heard from any of my Berkeley friends, and that bit into me some, but presents arrived later in the week.

I wrote Summer another long letter, saying how I realized she was facing difficult life changes on many levels, and how that involved pain, but how I also had to come back to my own life as well, and take care of that too. Generosity and sensitivity had to work both ways in a friendship. I needed to affirm my own needs in my own life to a woman friend, not to deny self, but to stick up for myself, and I was possibly taking that first step with Summer, almost as practice for the step I had to also make towards my mother.

When I talked to Penelope about this self-affirmation, she wanted to celebrate it, to deepen it. She wanted me to shine with all that was good in my life. She wanted me to take the time to experience, in the most immediate sense, all that was good about myself, and that seemed amusing to me.

"Why are you smiling?" she asked, smiling herself.

"Because I don't like to do that. I know I've done a lot of good things, but I'd rather not think about it, go on to the next project. I enjoy the process more than the result."

But she wasn't asking for results.

"I have trouble resting back, seeing that my work is well done. Almost as if there were a fear, a fear that I couldn't stop for long, and be judged."

I wondered aloud again about that nightmare dream. I had described it as a great pressure circling and pushing down on me, and it felt smooth and crusty at the same time, and I thought maybe it had something to do with birth, or death. But then, I thought that maybe it had something to do with shit. Why shit. And then I realized that shit was merely a metaphor for all that negativity I had had to swallow my entire life, sitting there taking it in, swallowing lectures whole, helpless against it, and it oppressed me still, that dark negativity. I didn't want it on my life anymore. I could walk away from it. But I hadn't yet. I began to feel the same sensations of that nightmare pressure coming down on me, and it was odd to feel it physically and consciously. Penelope had me bend low, head to feet, knees out, feeling it press down, nauseating me. I pictured a toilet overflowing, ruining the carpet and the furniture we weren't allowed to sit on, which was too important for real life. Penelope had me make vomiting motions and noises. She led me by making them herself. Just to get it back out.

Then she had me sit on another pillow, facing where I had been. I was to be my mother. I was my mother as a little girl. How did I feel?

I am Margaret, a thin, dark haired girl, very pretty—My father loved me and my mother was mean, a big bear. She was angry with me. I sat on my father's lap and had fun, but it was also uncomfortable in a way, because I loved my father, and my mother was angry. She thought I was wicked. I felt sensual bouncing on my father's knee, *a bushel and a peck and a hug around the neck*, but my mother thought I was a bad girl. It made everything sensual, loving, life-giving, bad, outside of me. I had to put it outside of me. I could fool people into thinking that I was good but if they didn't believe that I was good, then they were on my list. Even when I got married, I couldn't be the real me, my past hushed up. I was not approved of, and so, in defense, I learned to put people down, and I had a whip full of words to cancel my debt. I was terribly angry, only because I needed love and was never accepted. Would God accept me? Yes. But what if He wouldn't. I thought with my head—God would accept me, and I was cradled, protected for a moment, but that wasn't enough.

My oldest daughter, Laura, was hard and hateful toward me. She rejected me early on, but I was still proud of her, proud of her accomplishments, her beauty and her children. I admired her, for she was like me, and I was like my mother in punishing her, because she was the bad sister, the wrong daughter, and she wanted to exclude me too.

I heard Penelope ask me, how I would feel if my daughter, Laura, stopped swallowing the penalty for my life, stopped absorbing the negativity I had had to give her all these years. How would I feel if Laura stopped swallowing the shit I had had to get out of myself, and I said, from the deepest part of my soul, "I would be glad."

"Why would you be glad."

"I would be glad if she stopped accepting it, if she stopped taking it in, because then she would break the chain."

Be glad.

I changed positions and was myself again, facing my mother. I felt a crack of light opening in me, in response to my mother. I couldn't let it open too wide yet. I needed a distant light right now, not an embracing, merging love, but I did want to be understanding, and I did want to feel compassion, and I could step back. I didn't have to swallow any of it, and I wouldn't be sick. And we would be glad.

○

During each of the four Mondays that I'd visited Penelope, it had been overcast and drizzly. Good weather for bad tears, or bad weather for good tears. But today, despite the rain, I was in a fine mood driving out to Monterey. As I drove I popped in Geoff's tapedeck, and Handel's *Messiah* came on, and I let the sound fill, letting my own voice add to the fullness. I felt that rippling energy exciting my spine. Penelope noticed it when I came in and sat down. She wanted me to talk more about that, and I told her how singing certain songs, like *Jubilate Deo*, affected me. She wanted to concentrate on deepening this good feeling, and as we closed our eyes, she asked me how my spine felt now, and I noted a kind of after-energy. She asked me to describe my soul body, and with my eyes closed, I tried to describe what I saw—a light filled body, not exactly human shaped, but rounded and glowing. She asked me what I believed, in terms of that body, and I said that I believed my spirit would live on after my death, after the death of this physical body, and that my spirit would have certain experiences after death which would help enlighten this life, that it would pass through subsequent lifetimes, hopefully on an upward spiral, hopefully learning so that I could grow. I saw this spiritual body connected with the light source of God. She asked me to describe that light.

"The Light Source is shining, shimmering, flaming, red and yellow, wavery, like a fiery flower that showers warmth and comfort in a yellow glowing rain, and it is an endless source of energy, pulsing with heat. I am connected to that Source of Light by a fragile thread."

"Fragile?" she asked.

I tested the thread by travelling up and away on it, far far away from myself and out into space. It was a fine, thin thread, but it was amazingly strong, extending into cool, dark space, much further than I was willing to go, but I could see how very very far away I was, and yet still connected. Its firmness assured me. I felt like I had flown an amazing distance in a moment, that I could keep on soaring further and further away from the earth and my own vacant physical body, but something stopped me, as if that golden thread had felt a tug, *not yet,* and then suddenly I was back. When I opened my eyes, it was as if I'd woken from a deep, uncanny dream. The coolness of space stayed with me, but I was grateful to be at home in my own warm, flesh-and-blood body.

I told Penelope how far away I had been travelling out there, but how I felt connected to that thread, and I wondered if one didn't receive a kind of sustenance through their own personal thread, like an umbilical cord, spiritual sustenance. I told her that it hadn't seemed fragile, but how I wished it were more of a connection, not such a thin shining.

I knew that I hadn't tried to strengthen it, by opening myself up. I ignored my spiritual food. Though sometimes I could hold that special peacefulness, sureness, calm, for almost a week, soon I found myself becoming more critical, angry, outwardly active—Losing the thread.

I pictured this hard dark area inside me, which felt like a big lump of coal, but as I got up closer, I saw it was like a black fetus, rolling and falling and tumbling over and over and over, as if it could find no rest, no peace. Agitated. And then I also saw a shining white baby, which was securely held, swaddled from the chest down to a firm board, and its arms were wide open and head raised and it was filled with Light. It held its arms out and light streamed off of it in four directions. Then I saw the white baby stand right behind the black baby, so that the white seemed to support, or encompass it. I saw the light wrap this hard black area up, anthracite in a web of shining golden fibers, until it was completely covered and held securely. I believed that the light would help melt it. I said, "It feels like a dead fetus, a stone baby that I'm giving up, and I don't really want to give it up completely. Giving it away makes me sad." But then I also felt this gigantic relief as I released it, and saw that hard, dark lump travelling away on the light thread upward in an arc, carried away, and I knew that I had been relieved of a great burden. I felt a greater light and warmth entering me from my head, down through my body, down to my abdomen where it faded away, and I felt that funnel of light, which had been a thread, enlarged to a very strong solid pathway of light which was coming down to fill me, and I traced its pathway with my arms, from above to my forehead down around my face and into my torso, my stomach, and it *was* comforting, like hands gently rubbing downward on my hair and shoulders, a heavy shower of light now, which then also made me very sad, because I read it as love and forgiveness, and somehow I didn't feel worthy, not ready to fully accept it.

Penelope asked me what it would be like if I could completely open to that love and forgiveness, and I pictured a woman in a gauzy gown, with rounded shoulders and pulled back hair, modest and lovely, head slightly bowed. She seemed eternally feminine. She didn't seem to be myself at all, and yet I knew she was. But then I saw my other self beside her, in pants, more angular, boyish, masculine, and I knew these were both parts of myself. The two women joined hands and did a little walking—turning dance, up and down, but I felt cool towards this, almost jealous, and that slight nauseous pressure came back. I was having difficulty reconciling the feminine and masculine aspects of myself.

A Closing
June

o

As I sat there with Penelope, I didn't feel in the mood for a session. This was the first time I'd come to see her in the morning, and it was a beautiful day for a change, and I was fighting the inward process, when I wanted to move outward. I felt heavy in my body, when I wanted to be happy and light. "I want to be carefree," I said. She asked me to say that again. "I wish I wasn't here, but out in the park with the children. I don't want to have to deal with all this. I'm afraid to deal with this, because of the darkness, because I'm afraid I'm not a very nice person. I'm afraid that people will leave me."

I felt the false cheerfulness I'd entered with, dissolving into tearfulness, always, always, a return to that same tearfulness, and she encouraged it, saying, "Good. Allow it." She wanted me to begin to feel my immediate experience, rather than mentally trying to control it.

I said, "I feel heavy and tired, dragged down by my physical body." And then a little voice jumped in telling me that I shouldn't feel that way. I should be glad, because remember how sick I was a year ago, how I could hardly move, and now I could jump out of bed and take three hour horseback rides. I had no right to feel sorry for myself, to complain, to feel heavy and sluggish and dull. But I did.

I wanted to feel expanded, the way I did when walking on Baldwin Hill, with the big sky and huge landscape sweeping up into the distance, and I could feel myself, like springtime, reaching towards that distance, with flower health, a spectacle of color, dazzling in rain rinsed sunlight, as the air warmed up and sweetened. The lilacs were hanging in delicious clumps while mustard was filling the back field with yellow and even the birds seemed to be freshly dipped—a cardinal stroke in the purple bush—an oriole bursting like a lozenge of brilliance, *orange* in the air just above, while the asparagus pushed up through the loam, and the lilies of the valley dangled their little white bells from crisp slender stems, an adolescent aroma, tiny vases of them set in each bedroom, and the children learned how to suck the sweetness from the tips of columbine, as we sat on the big gracious porch, just rocking and talking, Jill and I. She was now pregnant again, and this son, Alden, would become my godson. The cherry and apple and pear trees were in bloom, and the children ran through the yard picking this and that, bringing back their prizes, a tulip, Johnny-jump-ups, a stem of bleeding hearts, while the clusters of viburnum smelled like sugar candy.

So why did I feel dragged down now, resistant to working through this heaviness.

"We haven't talked much about what you feel your higher purpose is," Penelope indicated.

I said that I thought my writing was part of my purpose in life, that writing about lupus would hopefully help others not to feel so alone.

"To help others," she repeated, as if from a distance.

"And I think having lupus has helped me to come closer to God," I added.

"Are you angry at God?"

"No, I don't think I'm angry at God," I said softly.

"Can you repeat what you said?" she asked.

I had trouble repeating, trouble saying it, phrasing. My mind was reluctant. I was fighting this today. "I said, that I believe having lupus, has helped me to know God."

"How do you feel when you say that?"

"I feel a tension in my arms."

"Say it again."

I did. "I feel a tension in my legs," I remarked. "I picture a tiny infant, in a crib, kicking and beating its feet against the headboard."

Very quickly, so that I wouldn't lose the impulse, she had me lie down on the long floor mattress, going with the experience, rather than suppressing it. "Do you want to do this?"

Yes, I went with it, and so I kicked and beat with my fists for a very long time, and kept kicking and beating, and then she yelled, "Nooo," and so I screamed, "NOoooo," and as she screamed louder, to help me reach that level, I tried to follow, from my gut, out, "NOOOOOO," Until I was too tired, arms and legs both very tired, and I lay quietly then, calmly on the bed, not wanting to talk, as she rubbed my forehead, and smoothed my hair. The physical contact made communication difficult, my responses even more distant. I did feel more peaceful now, but I wondered—Why do I have so much anger and hatred stored up in my body and soul. What is my potential for rage and for violence. Why do I want to embrace the world and reject its influence on me. Why am I made of such extremes.

During my next session I related a dream which seemed to exemplify these extremes. I was violently stabbing a long dark haired woman, who was lying on her back, arms up, head to the side. I didn't recognize her, but it was clear that my violence wasn't affecting her in the least, and then when I looked up in the dream, as if into a mirror, I saw that the sockets that held my eyes were pools of blood.

Both of these women seemed to be the passive and aggressive extremes I encompassed, and yet I was also struck by the Oedipal imagery, putting one's eyes out, hurting myself for the blind mistakes of my own inevitable destiny.

Penelope asked me to ask this image what it had to say to me, and as I called it back up again, it took on an even more hag-like appearance, and the image said, "I am your death. I can see your death. You are killing yourself." These statements were made clearly, with no overtones, but then I had to ask again, and the hag became more of a witch, cackling at me, insulting my ignorance, a faceless demon that became hunched and claw-like. Penelope asked me to try and enter into that aspect of myself, but I could get no further than a pale imitation of that spiteful intensity, and she suggested that perhaps my will was not aligned with choosing to fully experience that part of myself.

My belief system was often vague, but I did have this fear that if I opened myself up to this dark force, that it would gain greater control. I pictured myself and each human being as having a good and a bad part, an area of darkness and light, but I also imagined, that in the spiritual realm, there were these beings who were either aligned with God-like or Satanic forces, and I worried that during times of soul weakness, these darker agents could slip in and gain control. I felt I had to keep the lid on, keep my sword forever on guard, because I had a penchant for the dark side, and that made it even harder for me to act into my own darker aspects, to fully experience them, because I had always snuck into that realm, as if to tease myself with the taste of it.

Penelope felt that one had to enter into that acknowledgment of personal darkness in a more complete way in order to diminish that aspect's power. It had been her experience that the less conscious one was of one's own dark forces, the more they were projected out onto others, the more negative power they had in the world. Acknowledging that darkness inside, actually had the opposite affect of creating more room for Light. Becoming totally at one with that hag-like negative image might even help release that negativity on a cellular level, and she seemed to feel that was necessary since I was having physical symptoms. Seeing and understanding was not enough for me, and I basically agreed with her, but I couldn't quite deny my fears either, as if I were afraid of diving off a high board. And I was also embarrassed about acting out these aspects of myself, to feel their extreme power within myself. I knew it was possible, if I could only click into the decision. But I was reluctant. Thirty-four years of reluctance supported me in this.

I could see how some higher force of goodness could embrace that darkness, that hag-like being, and I pictured an angelic being who encircled that darkness in a wonderfully loving, understanding way, but then when I tried to let that same gauzy presence embrace me, I felt myself reject it, turning a cold shoulder, and I became like a pillar, an extremely old grey pillar, which was still strong, despite the acne-like erosion on its surface. It appeared Greek, perhaps tying in with the Oedipal imagery, and I asked the pillar what it had to tell me, and it shed no light on the matter for a good long while, grey and silent as stone, but then it came to me. "I'm not a pillar, I'm a person."

Perhaps in my eagerness for some dramatic culmination to my last session, I produced another startling eye dream, which I described in detail to Penelope. In the dream I gave my Left Eye, to the Right Church. And I gave my Right Eye, to the Left Church. Gave it as a gift, like a donation. Anyway, the Left Church seemed to accept my gift— all was quiet and in harmony there, while the Right Church was disturbed. Out of that church, a sinister, almost cartoon-like-sinister, man came running out, all bent over, carrying a gross blob of flesh, like a fetus, but it was *my eye,* and he ran out into the night, I was witnessing all this, and he quickly dumped the mess into my boot.

"You're smiling, you know," Penelope beamed, and I realized that I was.

"But anyway, in the dream, after I'd given my eyes away, I had these crinkly, sunken sockets, and my hair was cut very short, which gave me a certain freedom, and I appeared to be very wise, peaceful and happy." I paused.

"Maybe I'd rather not see. I'd rather not see something, my situation. I'd rather be blind and happy." I had been trying to figure this dream out all day, wondering if this image of physical blindness helped to give me inner sight. Were the two churches my parents, or my right and left brain? My conscious, unconscious. "It is a pretty crazy dream isn't it?" I laughed.

"Don't try to figure it out. Stay with your experience and maybe you can penetrate the gift which is the dream. It's very hard to do that if you just use your analytic mind. You *are* amused by it, aren't you."

I had to admit that I did think it was funny for some reason.

"Was it a prank? Do you like to be mischievous? Shocking?"

"I do like to be shocking. I like to be disgusting."

"Yes," she cheered, and we both laughed together.

"I feel like my writing has often been shocking. Maybe it's a form of rebellion. But lately, I've found myself conforming more and more to a community's idea of what is appropriate and good for children, for my life too, for our family at large, and that's been a bit of a struggle with Geoff at times, even with certain friends, and it is such hard work, fighting back the world's hardening influences, fighting back the destructive forces of the culture, removing the T V. It makes me feel a bit like The Censor sometimes, and then I feel less liked, the disciplinarian, which reminds me of my own mother who always felt forced into that role, while my Dad remained the easy-going good guy, and how that's really not fair. And it would be so much easier just to let things BE, but I really do basically agree with anthroposophy, and its indications for children, protective, nurturing, rhythmical, artistic, not high-tech, and yet sometimes, part of me would like to rebel."

As I sensed a shifting between these polarities, Penelope had me sit on another pillow, facing the conforming self.

"I feel rebellious at times. Sometimes, I don't want a community to instruct me in how to raise my children, even if it is just a subtle pressure. At times, I simply want to be different. I *am* different. I'll take what I want and leave the rest. I don't have to swallow anything whole. I don't want to live by anyone else's book, and I don't want to be judged."

Ah-HA. That was a big part of it, not wanting to be judged. Wanting to rebel, to be unique, but not wanting to be rejected or judged, afraid of being judged. I could feel an age-old upset rising, feelings of resentment that went way way back, and with eyes tight shut, Penelope guided my voice deep down, into even deeper gut levels, and she encouraged me to make sounds, animal sounds of howling growling aching anger, and then I had to say it, firmly, crying out from my gut—*"I'm tired of you judging me! I wish you would just stay out of my life, out of my house."* I beat on the pillow before me, hesitatingly at first, then harder as she encouraged me, *"and keep you negative shit off me! I wish you would die,"* I groaned. *"I hate your darkness. It oppresses me, and I can't stand it in my life anymore."*

"Good," Penelope said, though the fire had gone out as if a bucket of water had suddenly splashed down on it. I wasn't seeing the whole picture, and she wanted me now to see the other aspect of this experience, and so she had me move over to the facing position, back over to my conforming side, and she asked me how I could be a conforming daughter. I said, "I want my mother to accept me, to see me as a responsible, human adult, who is doing a good job with her life. I want her to appreciate, not criticize the new house we just bought."

Penelope pointed out that she was reading anger in this supposedly conforming side, and she also noted a pleading quality in my rebellious side, as if, here too, there was a crossover. She indicated that I might consider allowing my angry side to be clear and firm, definite, not pleading, like a whiney child, and to allow my acceptance and sympathy to be truly heart-felt, clean of the anger which belonged elsewhere.

That all sounded so true. Rebellion, conformity. It did seem to relate to rejection and acceptance, to anger and love. On some primal level I sensed that I still continued to have this unsatisfied need, and I looked to her—my mother, but with my back, rejecting out of a fear of non-acceptance.

What did I see? I pictured myself in a crib.

Penelope had me lie down, and I raised my arms, straining to be picked up. I wanted my mother to pick me up. I wanted to suck. I wanted to be held. I was yearning with my whole body, and my mother did come and she held me and fed me, but it wasn't enough! I wanted more, MORE. I couldn't seem to get satisfied, and when she did put me back down in this crib place, this cage, I was deeply resentful, Angry! I was so terribly alone, and lost, but I swallowed this realization of aloneness with a stiff upper lip. Stiff, STIFF. But I didn't want to be alone. I wanted to be held!

I realized that it was very hard to be a perfect mother, any mother, hard to mother a daughter, and that I had not ever been easy to mother either. Penelope had me picture my mother again, eye to eye, and I told her that the book I had just written, this book, had been a hard one, and I knew it would be a terribly hard one for her to read and to understand, and I was afraid that it would hurt her, and yet I also had this hope that it was worth it, and that she would understand, that I was trying to work for a greater good, and I pictured her understanding this. Her eyes were full of tears, but she opened her arms and embraced me, despite all the hurt, the hateful scenes, so seemingly unfair, one-sided, but she understood. Remarkable! And she picked me up and held me, carried me along, and I was in a white nightgown, like a six year old, and terribly distorted, arms all twisted, and my head was bent around so that it was facing the wrong way, and I seemed so grotesque, but still my mother was willing to carry me, even at my most ugly worst—She still wanted to love me, to hold onto me, and I wanted to be held, carried by her. No matter how awful, how hideous I really was, she would still love me, just as we both were loved, bathed in a Greater Love, and suddenly I felt so lucky—What a gift! Perhaps totally undeserved, but nonetheless I was thankful, for I was Accepted and Loved. I might be sick and angry sometimes, hateful or hurt and bitter, sarcastic, grotesque and disgusting, but I was accepted and loved. I knew that at the core of my being, as I lay there peacefully wrung out, while Penelope rubbed my forehead and smoothed my hair. So very tired, but at rest.

The next day we closed on our house. The morning was hot and bright, and we were both nervous and excited during those two hours of closing, but it all sailed through, and we sealed the deal with a kiss. It was June 21st, the summer solstice, and in our urge to make this paper transaction real, Clovis and I drove out to Alford, and put in a small summer garden on the rise above our new house, turning over the earth by hand, planting tomato seedlings, zucchini, three kinds of peppers, cilantro, basil, dill, lima beans and string beans, four short rows of corn. I was amazed at how good it felt, digging, planting, watering, sweating, drinking cold water from the hose. This little plot felt like a hope garden, a wish for well—More than a garden of metaphors. I splashed the hose over my head, pulled my large straw hat way down.

That night we went to a big community solstice party, down the road from our new place, to feast and dance and celebrate—Now that the tiny insects were floating on the bouyant light of summer, as the strength of the sun began to fade, and darkness kept its vow, now as the lightning bugs appeared in their own sporadic dance, their phosphorescent glimmer in the moon-lit depths, as the bonfire light was rising, high up higher with twelve foot flames that reared into the darkness, sparks flying in a teepee of warmth, all golden, consciences kindled like white roses fed to flame. And I did feel this age old longing, like a perfect mixture of happiness and sadness, which could almost be deciphered as heavenly pain, embracing all coming and passing, for as we grow older, the world really does seem more painful, and yet more profound in the shape of each beauty, just as the brilliance of the sunglow, just before sinking, makes us want to stop, connect and hold, and how each human being carries a part of that sun and darkness, both flower and ash, and how at different moments in each cycle of a life, the past streams forward, and we relive whole histories, the weight of joy—Just to be alive, and to sing again.

Go Round

The longest day will drive a crack—til Jubilaté windows in. Three parts that braid begin to fly—that something singing overlapping. White roses on the fire lit. The stick once put begins to curl. A wheel is rolling sparks for ten. She feels it here—but far away. High golden hills remind the day of St.-John's-wort. One yellow cup upon each end. Asha found three little bowls. The tones are gliding through the light. Mountains can appear we wave—and roll in dust and dark til then. Because the small ones can not stop. We find a way to circle so. We close into a fire pop. Open also leaves have room. And grow with pushes following through. We sing to leap the last of it. The nuts are gathered in a cup. The arc is scent, the curve a boat. To row and row the blinding stream. We hope to cast a shadow yet. A firm trail makes me follow up. We turn and run descend upon. To beat a beat upon the rim. A kiss in light before a name. The same few rise. Until she flew. The angel woke to be a bird. And never once the same again. The turquoise chamber turning parts. Lemon mint upon the flame. Old treasure sack. The tones do chime. And nut hats six can climb sky high. We wave we wheel around the bend. Though amber changed the wending way. Sinking deep in lion's mane. Go round she say to sign your flame. Seven stars are shining bright. The round is fine. Just out of sight. We see it dry to golden sheets. Though wet was once all flick and stain. Today will not remain again. Go round she say go round to me. And let the lifting bird come through. The gate is raised the sun can too. Go round go round. Today is different not the same. A new a new. Goodbye in waves for sinking down. Often time to see and bend. Around she say. Once more again. So ashes breathe—Around me now.

The Embrace

Alford & Wood's Hole, August, 1984

Geoff had stayed home for the three weeks we were in Wisconsin, and on returning I was ready for some resentment, but I wasn't prepared for a house filled with fleas and creeping mildew, *everywhere*. I swirled into a panic of cleaning, pushing myself until exhausted. But I was also mad for other more personal reasons.

While I'd been off, taking care of the children, he had gone out night after night. He told me how he had met up with this girl, who I knew he had had a crush on, and how she'd invited him to her dance performance, and how he'd gone out drinking with her afterwards. I was pissed. Why should I trust that the evening stopped there. I was jealous. I wasn't enough for him. He didn't really love me. I was just a mother of convenience. I was tired of this repeating in our marriage, mistrust, tired of feeling rejected. My mind seemed bent on a downward plummet, and so I rejected him, fierce in my hostility, but when I drove off alone, my eyes filled up with tears. Driving, anywhere, to get away from the ugly penetrating silence we'd erected like a barricade.

I was almost afraid to call Penelope, afraid to make that deep dive, down to the wound at the bottom of the water, but I knew I needed her again, needed her direction, and I realized that this turmoil was churning mainly in me, and if I could figure it out, then maybe my vision would clear, and love's true sight would be regained.

She greeted me with a hug, her clear blue eyes dazzling. I knew that I had a lot to get into this session. I had saved it up. I also knew, that it probably wouldn't end up being at all what I expected.

I started by voicing my resentments against Geoff, how he and my mother held this position, together, in my mind, and how I didn't really feel loved by either of them, how they both continually delivered these hard little jabs, and how I felt vulnerable to jabs of rejection.

Penelope had me address Geoff directly, and so I closed my eyes and spoke, "I'm angry at all the mess I came home to. You just act like you can ignore me and I'll go away. I'm pissed off that you went out to see that little chick. I'm tired of your caring for everybody else but me. I'm sick of your abrasive, too loud music." My voice got louder and madder, as Penelope pressed hard on my solar plexus, so that I would respond from that level, so that the verbalizations came from gut depth and were released. She had me move onto my knees, and pound the huge turquoise pillow. I had resisted doing that before, but now I was eager for it. She showed me, quickly, how to arch my back and raise both hands together, behind my head, slashing down with all my might, and I did—Beat and beat and beat that pillow as I voiced my resentments and hit and smashed, until I was tired of it, and sat there, more calm, but still hurt and helpless, and I continued to cry.

I admitted that I was afraid to stand alone, without husband, without parents, even without children, and yet something in me whispered—You are best alone.

"I won't exist unless you completely love me, without reservation," she said it for me, and I said it too, though I felt like that would never be forthcoming, that I could never ask for unconditional love, because, for one, I couldn't give it. Maybe no one but God could give it. Unconditional love.

"How do you picture yourself, standing alone?" she asked. I saw a tall, strong, statue-like woman, shining and golden like a trophy. But then I also saw this cartoon-type man figure who was fending off the evils of darkness. She had me stand up, and with eyes still closed, I made his moves, knees bent, arms out, swinging them back and forth, from side to side to ward off demons, illness, hatred, death. "Stay back," I warned, swooping from left to right. "Don't Come Near Me." But then this larger anger seemed to rise and spread, and again I beat on the pillow, harder and longer and harder, again and again, raising my arms, fiercely smashing with my hands locked together, with a powerful energy that was almost overwhelming, letting a deep gutteral, nonverbal rage come out to mark each stroke. I kept my eyes closed, for it helped to keep me in this unselfconscious world. Penelope kept encouraging me as I struck and lifted and lowered my blows. She knew I had a lot in me, that I could have gone on and on, but at last I stopped and just sat there.

She asked me how I felt.

More calm. But underneath this surface calm, I visualized this tiny peanut person, an angry, animated little peanut form, beating its little stick-like legs and arms. An angry, pitiful little thing, flailing and thrashing, and no one wanted it. No one wanted to pick it up, because it was ridiculous, and ugly, and a nuisance, and a baby, and a girl. Disgusting girl.

"How are you disgusting?" she asked.

"I want to suck, disgusting." I saw a breast before me. Just a giant breast. "Not like a son, but a girl, no good. I want to drink in the warmth of kindness from my mother's breast, but NO." This form of flesh, isolated in space, before me was too soft, too feminine, unattainable, never given to me. I was angry at that breast.

I flashed back to an earlier session, where I'd had nauseous feelings when it came to seeing the feminine side of myself. I remembered what Penelope had asked me. She had asked what I would be like in order to totally accept God's forgiveness and love, and I had pictured this feminine, lovely woman, in flowing gowns, almost Greek, long veils with hair pulled back, head tilted, bowed, humble and graceful, feminine, utterly feminine. Then I had pictured my more masculine side, and together, these parts of myself, moving, dancing together, had made me feel jealous and sick.

She asked me if I was ready to embrace this part of myself, to take this woman into me, and I said, clearly, "Yes." I really did want to admit her now. I conjured her image, and she swayed there before me, moving like a eurythmist with delicate, silken veils, and I said to her, "I need you." Penelope had me stand, and I copied her gestures, her calm and lilting dance, while I described all that she was. "She is soft, and flowing, embracing. Loving, humble, good and kind. She is knowing, yet quiet. Deep, pure, soft and round. Peaceful. She is very, very peaceful. She gathers with her arms. She embraces, and she flows."

I opened my arms to approach her, but then she seemed to retreat slightly, raising her veils to her mouth, and for an instant, her eyes became those of the hag-like creature, all that was her opposite. Perhaps this feminine creature, was part-hag, part-heaven, part fury and part grace, but I let that fleeting image go, and concentrated on her goodness.

"What do you have to do, in order for her to come and live inside you?" Penelope asked.

The answer occurred to me with instant clarity, and though it embarrassed me slightly, I said right away, "I have to go down on my knees. I have to ask God to bring her into me. To make me whole."

"Go down on your knees then," Penelope suggested, and I did, opening my arms, and asked God if he would allow me to embrace this woman in myself, this servant of His. I opened my arms wide, and slowly, gradually, she came to me, and I brought her to me, right into me, into my arms, which closed around myself, and I could feel her curling up inside of me, lying on my left side, with her head over my heart, with a pastel-rubbed, smooth vagueness, from my heart downward in a soft blue curve, and I likened her to an image of the Holy Mother, with her head and shoulders enveloped in a soft blue cloth, gentle and divine, and at last at peace within me. I lay down on the carpet in my own fetal position, and Penelope leaned over and patted my heart, and quietly whispered, "Welcome."

The next morning we packed the car and were off to The Cape, sailing along towards the ocean. In four short hours we were there, and how healing it felt, I'd forgotten, those sandy expanses and the warm water, legs lifted, body cradled. It was wonderful to be there with family, the easy laughter, catching up, the stories and shared secrets. Geoff's sister, Nicole, was like a sister to me too. She asked me about my lupus. "You look so strong and healthy," she said. "What do you think it was, that worked for you."

I had no absolute answer. There were so many different factors. Even the prednisone had come to my rescue at one point, but I believed that it was the homeopathic, anthroposophical medicine which had been most effective in keeping me in remission. I had reduced my shots from six a week to three, and I'd even had the flu several times and oral surgery without provoking a relapse. My red summer splotches spread across my cheekbones, but they too would eventually disappear altogether.

There would be future emotional challenges, and I'd be able to survive the upheavals with the help of Psychosynthesis therapy. I would even come to accept that wounded girl child inside myself, learn how to nurture and comfort her so that she could grow. Years would pass, and I would remain healthy, yet always on the alert, watching for symptoms, continuing my homeopathic remedies, growing stronger, less afraid, more relaxed.

Perhaps I was just one of the lucky ones. I knew there were many women whose struggle with SLE was much more devastating, but I still believed we had much in common, a lot worth talking about. "It's the same sun we stand under." Maybe someday we won't have to protect ourselves from the sun's intensity, but until that time, we'll continue to put on hats and sunblock, and try to lead our lives.

Here on the beach I used a sun umbrella to subdue the shock of light. I loved the relaxed warmth of this sandy expanse, the salty smell, the ease one felt, as if melted from the core, the lap lap lingering like a soothing touch massage on the back of the neckstem, and all the children playing in the sand, digging deep, burying each other, only to free themselves once more.

I decided to swim, ran out into the water, and swam way out, doing the breast stroke, my torso arching and pulling—up and down, up and down, until I was in the rhythm, and I felt like I really loved my own good body, with all its flaws. It cradled my spirit and soul, this time around, and I was thankful for it, grateful for the big embrace of the beach, for the stretch of time allotted, for the bonds of family, for this good salt water, which stung my eyes as I turned and swam out even further, confident, feeling my muscles pull and stretch, and it felt good and the sky was completely flawless, blue, one bird, one bobbing bunch of kelp moved by me. The water was that perfect temperature. I swam way out where I was sure no one would bump into me, then stretching my arms, I floated on my back, almost giddy with gladness and the realization that I could be held like this, lifted and carried so lovingly by the gentle, bouyant sea.

Afterword

When George Quasha called to say that Station Hill Press wanted to bring out a new edition of *Lupus Novice*, I was very pleased, but also somewhat distanced from my original condition and manuscript. Ever since I wrote *Lupus Novice* and recovered from my first and major flare-up with SLE, I have maintained a certain degree of amnesia concerning those painful places I once visited when I was thirty-three. Now I am forty-nine, and not significantly wiser. I had to reread my own book to remember the details of what I'd been through, and to bring the subsequent sixteen years back into focus—then a lot of little stepping stones along the path were suddenly beneath my feet again as I recalled the journey onward.

Luckily, throughout this period of recovery, I have had the help of a very gifted anthroposophical doctor, Jesse Stoff, who I began to see when he moved to Great Barrington in the eighties. He not only helped me maintain my stability in regards to lupus, but also helped me pull out of an exhausting bout with Epstein Barr disease. I was dragging around with a sore throat and swollen glands, and he was able to diagnose me and offer remedies that worked within months.

In the mid-eighties, I was going through a painful and yet liberating time, as I ended my seventeen year marriage. The woman on the beach in La Jolla had not been a figment of my imagination, but a reality that led to infidelities on both sides.

During the next seven years, I entered a rather wild phase, and took up with one exciting, emotionally abusive boyfriend after another. I also began smoking again. The two seemed to go hand in hand, gifts of self-punishment. I had originally started smoking when I was fourteen years old, though I managed to quit while I was pregnant, and when I was sick with lupus. I still feel that this addiction to cigarettes may have been one of the biggest threats to my immune system. Giving it up for good was also one of the hardest struggles I have ever undergone.

In 1987 I went to a series of talks that Thomas Moore was giving on the Greek gods, and after a particularly lucid lecture on Aphrodite, I thought—If I ever go back into therapy, I want to work with this man. Not long after that, I wrote to him and asked if he had time for me—he only worked with a handful of people, but he agreed, and soon I began intensive, weekly therapy. He was living and working in West

Stockbridge at the time, just twenty minutes from my home. He was also relatively unknown, as this era pre-dated his great success with *Care of the Soul* and *Soul Mates*.

I can remember our first therapy session well. I told him that I wanted to give up smoking, and I was surprised when he responded by suggesting that I *not* give up smoking right away—it would be too much of a heroic, suppressive battle. I relaxed a bit when he said this, thinking him an oddball. He often said the opposite of what one expected—"Of course, you should give up smoking immediately—you're killing yourself!" No, Tom suggested that I go ahead and keep smoking—"Enjoy yourself a bit," he said. At least for the time being.

I found myself amazed by his intelligent and sensitive range of references, as well as the quirky mode of his thinking, always turning things around, so that I saw the truth of the other side, the darker, unexpected side. I assured myself that I was not attracted to him—I had enough trouble with the men I *was* attracted to—but then, of course, I entered into a two-year therapeutic relationship that led to a full blown transference—a word I can still hardly begin to understand. All I know is that I surely must have tested him in every way possible, and he held his own, and allowed me to feel the golden wash of a very special love that led to a wonderful nourishing balm for my soul. I will always be grateful to him.

I think, in part, he helped me to find the inner fountain of self-love that I kept camouflaged beneath a blanket of smoke, a smoke screen that dulled my excess emotions and made them seem more tolerable. I was afraid if I quit something, I would feel some great inner emptiness that would swallow me up, but the deeper we went, the more sure-footed I became in this craggy decent. He urged me to take my writing further down into more difficult terrain, until I finally got into the coal pit where only gorilla girls go.

I gave up smoking and began smoking again with each new upsetting relationship. My weekly sessions with Tom continued, but I also tried other forms of therapy to help me break the habit, including hypnosis, meditation, fasting, foot reflexology and acupuncture. Acupuncture seemed to help quell the addictive craving. My acupuncturist, Lonny Jarrett of Stockbridge, told me that I was like a speeding car racing on empty, trying to get somewhere before the tank ran out. I found this an apt metaphor. He inserted needles all over my back for a cleansing treatment, which relaxed me to such an extent that I almost fell asleep sitting up.

Inserting tiny circular needles taped to the leafy portion of my upper ears (the same points used for heroin addiction), Lonny left these temporary acupuncture needles in for several weeks. Whenever I felt the craving, I could squeeze these points and the addictive craving would cease.

I went through this process about four times. Each time I would also go on a three-day fruit and juice fast, which helped dispel the craving. Usually, this method helped me quit in the short run, but as Mark Twain said, "It's easy to quit smoking, I've done it a thousand times."

I had been off of cigarettes for about a year when I dove into one more inappropriate romance, and this time with a chain-smoker who lit up in the morning before he left bed. Within hours of knowing this man, I was back into my own deep-seated addiction to nicotine, as well as my apparent need to look for love where it wasn't available.

But as the months went by and I continued to smoke, those old red discoid lupus spots on my cheeks appeared. I went through the motion of giving it up again. Within two weeks, the red spots were gone. But then we'd have another fight, and I'd start smoking, and the red spots would immediately reappear. I was obviously allergic to this toxin.

Even my acupuncturist was getting tired of trying to help me. After four or five attempts, he gave me an ultimatum. "This is the last time I'm going to do this," he said. I was a bit shocked, but I knew he was right. I had to give up smoking for good, and that meant giving up this unhealthy relationship. So that December, approaching forty, I surprised myself and kissed this good-for-nothing guy good-bye. Simultaneously, I made my farewell speech to all the cigarettes I'd ever known. Like a devoted Mama, I waved good-bye as their ship departed, and they waved back, smoking and ashing and slowly going out, the cigarette like life somehow.

A new phase of life commenced for me then. I was working like mad, raising my two wonderful boys, while maintaining a friendship with my ex-husband. I was happy to be living on my own, in my cozy old Colonial house. We kept a horse and a pony, and I had many good friends—life was full. Books came out, and I was in my stride. I was bringing my therapy with Tom Moore to a close. Looking back, it was one of the best times in my life.

Riding this high, I met my current husband, Mason Rose. It was rather odd getting involved with a truly decent human being, who fell immediately in love with me. I was happy, but a bit baffled—I was used to love being painful. I let him court me, and we took turns cooking wonderful, indulgent meals for each other. We were both rebuilding our kitchens, using the same inspired architect—his brother, Jonathan, who suggested we meet each other.

As we continued dating, I told Mason about my lupus, as well as other physical problems I had had, including occasional outbreaks of vaginal herpes, fairly dormant since my pregnancy with Ayler. They now only cropped up about once or twice a year when I was under unusual stress or pressure.

I realize now, that in my original manuscript of *Lupus Novice*, I had deleted the mention of herpes, because it embarrassed me, and because I didn't think there was any connection. But now I believe that there might be some connection. Many of the women who have called me about their problems with lupus have also had herpes. There also seems to be a similar pattern of emotional difficulty with the mother, unresolved anger there, and conflict with the internal feminine.

My health problems were a bit difficult for Mason to comprehend, since I always appeared so healthy. It was hard for him to understand why I got so nervous and creaky, slightly arthritic, when I had even the slightest brush with the flu. Emotionally I was also hyper-sensitive to the least symptom, exaggerated out of past fear.

Usually, I avoided a full-blown flu by fasting, or eating very lightly, doing garlic enemas—(which I believe may be the most effective means of scaring the willies out of the flu virus). *Blend three cloves of garlic in the Cuisinart with a cup of warm water, strain, and mix with more warm water.* Though a garlic enema can seem internally disturbing—it makes you feel as if you might explode or gag—the sensation passes quickly. I have learned that if you stop eating and administer the enema at the first sign of any symptom, you will usually feel fine in the morning. In conjunction with this regime, I also take Echinacea drops, Cinnabar Compound, Ferrum Phosphoricum. And Infludoron if I feel a viral cold or flu coming on.

Because of my compromised immune system, Dr. Stoff did not like me taking flu shots, and once or twice I did succumb to the flu. Then I administered to myself a two-week round of homeopathic shots (four fingers below my belly button) to help stimulate my immune system, and my lupus was never set-off. I always have ampules and syringes on hand: Echinacea/Argentum, Pulmo/Ferrum, and Meteoric Iron/Phosphorus/Quartz. I especially like the idea of ingesting the essence of meteor—I can imagine needing that antidote, as I race on—burning madly through my life.

The only other time I seriously worried about my health was while visiting Arizona with its intense Southwestern sun. As careful as I tried to be, I often took a midday swim without a cap, and the excess sun caused an allergic reaction. I found myself practically breaking out in hives and itching horribly around my neck and ears. At first I thought I was reacting to a round of shots I'd just taken, but when this same itchy reaction occurred the following year when I returned to Arizona, I realized it must be due to sun toxicity.

It can be very hard to remain as diligent as you need to be in relation to the sun. Dr. Stoff always told me that I should wear 45 sunblock on any exposed portion of my skin, and he was firm about this—"You have no choice." I chose to listen to his advice during the warm months of the year, but during the darker, winter months, from November through March, I was somewhat lax. Still, it is wise for all of us to use sunblock all of the time, even if it's only for vanity's sake.

It is sometimes tempting to think that I have outgrown my lupus. I've been basically healthy and lucky for so long. In fact, my overall general health is better that it's ever been. I am aware of my own body and my own psychic health in a way I never was before I encountered lupus.

But despite the many blessings I have received, I am always aware that another bout of lupus could return, that a series of events could mount up like an unsteady tower about to tumble, as they did in Berkeley years ago. I had almost forgotten how bad I felt, how immobilized I was, until I picked up my own book and read it again. Then I realized that this little number could still be in my cards, and that I had better not get too uppity, self-congratulatory or proud.

In the early nineties, I began to develop a rash of pimples on my forehead, and I lived with these blemishes for a while, covering them with make-up. Jesse Stoff had just moved to Tucson, and I continued to talk to him long-distance, seeing him in person once a year. When I came to his office, he always ordered extensive, (expensive!) blood work, but the Speciality Lab that he used in California gave very specific, sensitive readings, and told him more than a normal lab test would.

Looking closely at my condition, Jesse tried giving me supplements to help strengthen my over all sense of well-being, and I am still taking a variety of pills, including Vital Force, Maintenance Formula, Vitamins C and B, Super EPA 1200 (a natural fish oil concentrate), and Sof-gel EFA.

When I complained of moodiness, mild depression (which was not like me) and *post*-menstrual syndrome, (for I found myself becoming more testy, and likely to blow up at my mild-mannered husband right *after* my period), Jesse checked my blood for hormone levels, and saw that all of my hormones were at rock bottom level. He prescribed Pituitrophon which would help stimulate the adrenal glands to aid in the production of testosterone. I didn't even know that women had testosterone. I also began taking Estriol and Progesterone made from Mexican Wild Yam, which has none of the negative side effects of synthetic hormone pills. In fact, it is supposed to by anti-carcinogenic.

Most gynecologists won't prescribe hormone supplements until a woman's menstrual cycle stops altogether, but the supplements made a huge difference in the way I felt. I quickly left my blue period and had much more energy. I felt sexier too. Why, I wondered, shouldn't low hormone levels be treated like any other deficiency? Why should we have to wait for something to give out all together before treating it?

Although the pills I was taking made me feel better, stronger, the rash on my forehead continued to plague me. Sometimes it would be worse than at other times, but basically it was always lurking there. Finally, I decided to go to see a regular dermatologist. Dr. Kathy Anderson took one look at me, diagnosed the condition as rosacea, and said the only thing she could give me was a six-week round of antibiotics and two ointments I could alternate nightly.

I knew that Jesse wouldn't want me taking such drastic measures, but I was sick and tired of looking at myself, and I wanted to give this treatment a go and see if it might not kick some old bacteria out of my system once and for all. After a week on the little "hornets" as I called the yellow-and-black pills, all signs of the rosacea were gone, but guess who came to call instead? Those little red discoid lupus spots on my cheeks. I took the complete six-week cycle of pills and applied the two alternating creams to my forehead until I noticed, ever so slightly at first, that I was beginning to feel arthritis in my hands. I panicked! Called Jesse and explained what I'd done. Had I traded in my basically good health for a temporarily clear completion?

Instead of blaming me or lecturing me, Dr. Stoff helped me regain my physical balance, and the lupus symptoms retreated. Now, years later, the rosacea is back again. While I am hesitant to put my body through another round of antibiotics, I am also tired of this unsightly surface affliction. In preparation for my Christmas holiday to Venice and Switzerland, I decided to take a two-week round of Tetracycline 500mg, taking one capsule twice a day. Because I know that the pills make one sensitive to sunlight, I cut the six-week recommended dosage short, while continuing to use a small amount of Noritate cream on my forehead every morning. Six weeks later, I have had no negative response at all, and the rosacea has been effectively repressed without aggravating my lupus. Even here I have had to find my own individual path, swinging between allopathic and homeopathic remedies. I think for many lupus patients, this will be the case. It is hard for me to live life as a purist, while it might be the only path for someone else.

I think back to what Dr. Incao (an anthroposophical purist of the highest quality) once told me, that I had to approach my lupus, not like a dilettante, dabbling in one therapy at a time, but on all levels at once— physical, psychological, spiritual. (The Army, the Navy, the Air Force!) But I'm sure he was right. Any human being is a complex combination of seen and unseen bodies, which are continuously working on each other, tearing down the physical and building it back up. I am still most often in the *wear-it-out mode,* "a cross between Joan of Arc and Mighty Mouse," as Alice Howell, the astrologer, put it after looking at my chart, all fire and air— no earth or water anywhere. No wonder I had a predisposition for this fiery disease.

But in looking back, I believe I first found a real spiritual connection when I was slowed down during this first flare-up with SLE. It was the first time in my life since childhood that I had allowed for that quiet openness. I believe I was carried by so many prayers, and though I was truly a novice, it was a baby step toward a spiritual life for me. Of course, as soon as I suppressed my symptoms, jarred and jangled by prednisone, this aspect of inner peace slid away, swallowed up by the busyness (business) of everyday life, and I missed that communion, just as I missed the deep connection I had made with my dream life, once therapy came to an end.

One swims in and put of phases. Dreams seem to come back to me in swells. I have noticed, in my life as a writer, that different forms cycle back again too. Perhaps patterns repeat in our own life stories, and that is the reason why I believe another flare-up of SLE is possible. In the past year I have become a Catholic, which is a mystery I am not inclined to summarize here—that may be another book altogether. I am also just now concluding a book of non-fiction, *Holy Personal,* a pilgrimage to small private chapels and temples across the country. In many ways this book has a similar feel to *Lupus Novice,* perhaps because it is the story of a journey "charting the unknown as it becomes known to me."

I do believe in the possibility of miracles, but in my case so far, there is no simple, lightning bolt to report—it is more of an on-going process, remaining attentive to the present moment, remembering, imagining, getting it down. Meanwhile, I can only hope that each one of you is finding your own path—for that is what lupus is all about—coming to understand your own personal history, working with your temperament, dealing with hereditary gifts and weaknesses, your own individual symptoms, and moving with it—hopefully, moving beyond.

A Few Letters of Response

Dear Laura,

I only recently learned of your terrible illness or I would have written sooner to tell you how much I have thought of you ever since I first learned of your existence in New Mexico. As it is, I have worried away two weeks, wondering how to begin. But there is less time to waste, so that the life I have imagined for you—stern, urgent, pure—the life, which real or imagined, has kept me for some years now from writing you, this life must be enlarged.

I had heard so much about you before we met—things which, by comparison, made me feel somehow corrupted and impure—that when we did meet, I was tongue-tied. Last summer, I wanted to say this: I admire you. I admire the energy about your work. I wish we knew one another.

Now you are very sick with this strange disease, about which no one knows much, and I wonder why you. There must be some reason; disasters cannot be so randomly dealt. And I think maybe it's because you of all people will write about this. With all the energy left you, I know you will make sense of what is happening to you and so many other women.

I think of you first thing, every day, when I sit down to write, and I hope for your recovery. I very much want you to be well.

Affectionately,
Christine Schutt

Note: It was this letter that gave me the idea to write Lupus Novice. *After moving to the Berkshires, Christine and I, who grew up on rival lakes in Wisconsin, established a wonderful friendship which continues today. She is the author of a book of short stories,* Nightwork, *from Knopf.*

Dear Laura,

I have just finished reading your *Lupus Novice,* which almost fell from the shelf into my hands at a New Age bookstore nearby a few weeks ago. The title and flyleaf suggested that it might be helpful to a friend here in Connecticut who has recently been diagnosed as having lupus. Before sending it on to her, I decided to read it myself, and was so moved by your honest and beautiful sharing of this extraordinary experience in your spiritual journey that I must write to thank you with some commentary on the content.

First of all, we have the same birthday—April 13th! I've just celebrated my 80th and you must be 36 (figured by publishing date). I love the Berkshires, having spent many happy visits in Sheffield where I have a son, John Ingersoll. My two grandsons, who grew up in Sheffield, came to mind as you described Clovis and Ayler enjoying those glorious farm days as little boys.

But more than all that, to strike responsive chords—I have long been interested in spiritual healing and the process of inner growth. You mention Tillich, Thomas Merton and Psychosynthesis, all very meaningful to me. I have become more and more interested in homeopathy; in fact, have an appointment with a doctor in Massachusetts next week. My closest friend and I heard him speak at a *Course in Miracles* retreat in Amherst and were so impressed by his philosophy that we immediately made plans to consult him.

We have read some Steiner and are interested in the Waldorf Schools. Was also touched by your openness to various alternatives. I've recently had acupuncture to help me become more limber in the practice of Tai Chi. Your therapist in Monterey probably knows our good friend Alice Howell, a Jungian astrologer and author of several fascinating books. You can see why I feel very tuned in to your treasure chest of information on so many subjects, written with such sensitivity and beautiful prose.

I look forward to discovering your poetry besides the delightful bits in this book and hopefully, if that should be "in the cards," to meeting you one day. I'd like to explore the possibility of spending some time at Kripalu and also seeing other friends who live in the environs. October always beckons me to head in that direction so, who knows, we might plan a rendezvous if you have time and would care to meet.

Again, my thanks for a deeply rewarding time of entering into your life story at that juncture. I trust all goes well and that your health and being have continued to improve. With all blessings in your endeavors, whatever they may be.

> With much appreciation,
> Elmira Ingersoll

Dear Ms. Chester,

I recently finished *Lupus Novice* and feel very grateful to you—I would write more but it's difficult.

I'm recently having to deal with lupus myself and am also using traditional and alternative medicines together.

It would mean a lot to me to hear how you're doing. I am recently attending lupus support meetings. There are a good deal of resources here in New York.

Congratulations on your courage, inner and outer strength, perseverance and love.

I keep reminding myself that while all disease transforms our lives, maybe there is some inherent good if we could first learn to read the signals.

Sincerely,
Sally

Dear Laura,

Thank you for giving us the gift of *Lupus Novice*. I have read many books about lupus and yours has been the most enlightening. Your journey on your path through Lupus is much like mine. Although now my Red Wolf is very active awake and alive, I seek more than to "just accept it and live with it for the rest of your life." I seek true, whole deep and lasting healing. Your book is the only one I have found whose goals were the same as mine. I am currently using Chinese medicine, "Dreadnisone," (HA HA!) western herbs, acupuncture, prayer, meditation, chiropractic, Qi Gong and my next step is to have my toxic mercury fillings (which are numerous) removed. I believe that the mercury combined with bacteria, causing a deadly form of poison—methyl mercury—is causing the physical problems with my lupus.

I am anxious to start the process of removing the emotional stagnation which keeps this disease active. You are so lucky to have the many friends and healers around you during your difficult time. I was met by many people, including my friends and family and community, with apathy, resistance and *blame*. This made my illness much worse. I felt like I had no support system and no help. I felt totally alone. I also had to quit work and with a self-employed husband our financial situation was devastating. This also fed into the lupus. I almost died in December, and the experience actually brought welcome relief. At this time all my anger and bitterness was lifted from me. Now I can face my illness with a positive attitude. I have lived through the Dark Night of the Soul and have become kinder, more understanding, thankful and forgiving as a result. It is through people like you that I have been able to maintain and keep looking for and working on my goal of whole healing. Through you I have reached a greater acceptance of the journey itself.

Because of you, I continue the faith that God will answer my prayers. I thank you with all of my heart and soul.

Love Peace & Health,
Jennifer A. Shirley

dear Laura,

you gotta whey of making words, tasty as curds! I took a glad dive into your strawberry fold(er), was so engrossed and distended by the lucid/ account, the noxious fog that Lupita suspended(s) on the facets of your cutting, shaping, Daisywheel; the sense of abandonment on the backcourt, a few good lob-shots to stay calm, examine your gameplan, ask for Grace and wait for the ficus leaves to unfurl. As I read this morning (at Mayfair) "we must consider what is random, and what is important, and they may be the same thing"… it struck me as a nice edge on the quirkiness of truths and how we allow them to filter into our thoughts, our decisions, our FIELDS. I think the questions asked about our (collectively) drive mechanisms was strong… yours… push, control, etc. areas I exude in/ movement and results!(in my case) can be a rather narrowing wavelength; defensible intellectually, but nevertheless (and I know!) restrictive; better to have God's Big Tent in mind as a constant reminder of our myopic humanness; and as you nurtured yourself towards more humanness, toward self and family (mother) Geoff, it really touched me to see you write and clarify the spiritual response that grows so willingly once the water is applied/and a drip, a slow drip is as good as a fast gallop. I love you, I love you! Keep up the carbonated work. Flow further. Love, Bo*

Note: "Bo," whose full name is Robin Young, is the younger brother to my ex-husband, Geoff Young, and is married to the Michelle who helped me during my one severe lupus flare-up.

Dear Laura,

So good to have the privilege of reading your "Lupus Notes." The ms. informs me of much I didn't know about you these last two years. Can't encourage you enough to continue working on the book—it's an important memoir, both for yourself and others. You said you wanted to develop a more social side of yourself and the giving of this information to others is a real part of that. Your enormous energy and courage shines through the text. So keep on, no matter what!

I don't think that a writer who is conscious of her illness can write outside of it. O'Conner didn't write about it, but *from* it—it was part of her experience of the world, just as her biblical, religious background was. Once a condition is brought to conscious mind, a writer may write even more from that condition. Your writing will be informed by your experience though you may never write about it directly. Your spiritual needs may intensify by your experience, as perhaps O'Conner's did once she knew who she was and what condition of her body she had to accept. Wasn't all that concern with sin a metaphor for some feeling that she felt guilt for her illness? Maybe not, but whatever, we can't write outside of ourselves.

Love you,
Gloria Frym

Note: This letter was written in 1985, when I sent Gloria a manuscript version of Lupus Novice. *Gloria Frym is the author of* Distance No Object *(forthcoming from City Lights Books),* How I Learned *(Coffee House Press) and other books of poetry.*

Dear Laura,

It was such a pleasant and elevating also illuminating experience to unexpectedly get your letter and other news/views. Here's hoping the bent lap of your Eastern trek will go well. The mixture of peace and adventure, which you mention regarding the need for you to be in those beloved Berkshires of mine, is a very great paradoxical mixture to strive for. Good luck with this quest and (ad)venture!

The constant striving for creativity surging through your life and being "in spite of" the lupus *trying* "to claim" you—deserves my greatest respect! It was most thoughtful of you to send me the portion of your manuscript dealing with Curative Eurythmy and your exposure to it through me. Helpful, revealing and correct to do. You have a very alive and dynamic way of picking up things invisible yet palpable! Eurythmy is just that! Thanks for giving me credit for trying to bring this over. I never thought of myself actually as an artist (*even* in temperament!) but more as a movement researcher-scientist-people-helper (therapist is such a yucky "over-charged" word!). Because I am involved in Eurythmy as a healing mode one has to be transparent as well as centered (again a bit of a consciousness paradox—life is full of them!) to bring it across. Due to the fact that one is dealing with the images and dynamics behind it ("meaning-charged" movements, as you so astutely point out) one needs clarity of thought. The use of my actual name would probably enhance the text somewhat. If you think of what Veronica as a name means. "Ver" (True, Truth, as in *Veritas*) "Icon" a part of the rest of the name dealing with "Image." My whole life not just professional but personal strivings have been concerned with, and dedicated to the "True Image" of things— St. Veronica wiping the brow and face of Christ!!!

May I suggest two books which might help your inner processes to accompany the outer deeds and events of your new Berkshire life of peace and activity—creativity. Since all of us are in need of clarity, *movement*, and new modes to cope with the times we live in and move in and as women to keep our own femininity "in tact" and *in flo*, it is valuable to read, *"The Life of the Spirit in Women,"* a Jungian Approach, by Helen M. Luke, Pendle Hill Pamphlet #230, Pendle Hill pub. Wallingford, PA. 19086; as well as *"The I That is We,"* Richard Moss MD, Celestial Arts, Millbrae, CA.

This book is written by a physician who confronted an impasse in his professional and personal life resulting in his leaving traditional medicine. It is a revealing description of a personal quest for new modes and new consciousness to deal with life, love, healing, and survival. Very astute observations about our modern American culture both psychologically and spiritually. Do not be put off by his over use of the word "energy." Some of his insights, self derived, are similar to Steiner's, some of it is very original, quite challenging and soul expanding—very fluid! It deals with many aspects of the prevailing degenerative diseases claiming our culture, so it needs your attention! For once to read a man's work which deals with fluid states of consciousness—*anti-hardening in effect!* Finally, a man who himself has plunged into the watery waves and surges of his own femininity and plumbed the depths of his new Beingness the way women can more easily do—IF they have not been too hardened. We all have to soften up, dissolve and then regroup on a higher plane or level.

Wishing you all the best in those blessed beloved Berkshires hope they are a balsam to your Being!

Cordially,
"Verbal" Veronica (Reif)

Dear Laura,

ON STAYING OUT OF THE SUN

This, you see, is something I know something about. Fardels and fardels of radiotherapy having been shot into my poor mortal envelope, to the point where I felt like "Big Boy," the bomb that made shadows of Hiroshima, the whitecoats were very explicit on this score: *No sun.* Add more radiation to what I already was jellied with, and I could have gone into business as my own private nuclear power plant, initials no longer standing for Ross Feld, but for Raw Fusion. So, having no desire to be Oppenheimer-in-Brooklyn, I desisted, have done so for these lo six years. I became a creature of the shade.

Being a creature of The Shade.

It's got its points. As everyone turns like delicatessen-chickens under the Sun Our Mother, you are apart. Being roasted leads most people to a slow leak of the intelligence, so rarely are there any conversations worth hanging around much for on a beach, say. After all, as Renata Adler once wrote, if you've got a tan, what have you got?

Now, the being-apart part. This is where the real gestalt comes in. You suddenly have a much greater appreciation, nay even respect, for mushrooms, for instance. Mold no longer seems any uckier than cashmere. You find yourself manically and continually singing a certain Noel Coward song. Among your closest and dearest a new respect for your Victorian pallor develops. Out of a crowd, you'll always be the one a lost stranger asks for directions to Seattle.

Starts to sound good, right?

Also: those who are "in the know," who understand that your now umbrous proclivity has been other-dictated, give a lot more leash, in compensation, for other odd behaviors. People who stay out of the sun are given the same kind of edgy respect everyone always dreams about. God knows what they've been plotting, after all, under their bower.

You never liked Gauguin anyway, right?

And you learn the beauty of hats.

The Beauty of Hats

1) They hide.

2) When you are of a despairing bent (as I am always) a hat makes it easier to pull the world down around you. (spoken like the true Scorpio I am)

3) They hide.

4) You feel at least somewhat better protected in case, yes, the little chicken was right, and falling the vault of heaven actually seems to be.

5) One can go without washing one's hair for quite a spell.

6) They hide.

Henceforth therefore whatsoever betweentimes, you have my outline of anti-solar energy. Remember mildew will yet again have its day!

yours in the shadows,

Ross Feld

Ross Feld is the author of Only Shorter *and other novels.*

Dear Ms. Chester (Laura):

Thank you for your book, *Lupus Novice*. I was just diagnosed with SLE a couple of months ago. And, at this point, am bouncing around between allopathy, homeopathy, my doctor, my health food store owner, etc. etc. It was wonderful to read of someone else who went through a similar pattern/ followed a similar path. It was particularly helpful given that I live alone in a community, White-horse, which has limited resources, no live-in specialists and no organized support group. For these, and other reasons, I'm thinking of leaving my cabin in the woods (quite literally). All the reasons relate to healing. I'm finding it continually amazing that, at a time like this, there's such a sense of doors opening. Your book helped push a few a bit wide open. I identified strongly with a lot of what you went through, but I have not been able to read the last few entries. There's a block there which I think I'll have to respect for the moment. I'll have to take my time.

Thanks again for sharing your journey with me,

Lori

Dear Ms. Chester,

I read your book *Lupus Novice* about 18 months ago. I cried throughout the book from the realization that someone else felt the same and had experienced the same pain as I had. Your book was an incredibly positive experience for me because it gave me hope. My sister and mom had read the book first and debated for weeks whether to give it to me— they didn't want to upset me!

My lupus experience parallels your own in many ways, except my condition affected my ability to have any more children. (I am fortunate to have two wonderful kids). I was pregnant and developed blood clots in my lung and placenta. The baby died and I spent some time in the hospital. After that I began experiencing more of the classic lupus symptoms—joint soreness, facial rash, fever, and along with all of that, deep depression.

My internist finally diagnosed me with lupus and recommended a specialist who put me on Prednisone and Plaquenil. I have been on the medication for almost two years. My Prednisone dosage has been decreased to 5 mg. My goal was to eventually be medicine free. (I have also been on Coumadin since the blood clots). After I read your book, I was inspired to investigate the homeopathic treatments that you went through. I really believe in the power of the mind and alternative forms of treatment. Time slipped by though, and I was feeling pretty good. I wasn't depressed anymore and resumed most of my past activities. I did gain 20 pounds, which is disconcerting, but overall things were great.

In November, I decreased from 6 mg. to 5 mg. of Prednisone and started to notice small aches and pains returning. I thought that maybe it was the stress of the holidays and a new job. This morning I did not want to get out of bed. My wrists, fingers and feet hurt. I felt like crying (and surely did)! I felt scared as if the badness was back—naturally all rationality of thought escaped from my conscious mind.

I guess I have been denying the existence of this lupus and planned on it just disappearing without me thinking about it. I'm not sure that is going to happen now and I need to take action. I like my doctor but I don't know how receptive, interested, or educated about homeopathic alternatives he will be. I looked in the phone book for homeopathic doctors and there are many. I don't know where to begin and that is one of the purposes of this letter. Do you know of a way that I can find a homeopathic doctor and/or therapist to work with? I think that whatever stress in my life (my mind) that has invited this condition (lupus) to visit is still there. I thought that I had changed a lot but I need to do more. The questions and answers are not clear enough for me to do this alone or through books. I need the help of another human being.

I would appreciate it if you could direct me to an organization or doctor that would have information for this area of the country. Again, your book was wonderful—just looking at it again gives me strength.

Sincerely yours,
Susan Zacharikiw

Dear Laura Chester,

Hi. Hope this finds you well and staying warm this winter. My name is Gayle Crawford. I'm 39, soon to be 40. I just wanted to write you a short not to say "Thank you!"

Thank you for your book, *Lupus Novice*. I just finished it this evening. I found out a few months ago that I possibly have S.L.E., so I went to the library and checked out a whole stack of books, including yours. I believe God drew me to yours, as I read it first and am very glad I did! It made me feel as if I'm not "insane." You have helped me so much!

I hope to get a phone and a computer, to be able also to write of my experience with this extreme change of life. You are an inspiration to us all. I would like to know how your mother handled it, as we also have a lot in common on that score, you and me. Thank you again, and God Bless you.

Sincerely,
Gayle Crawford

December 18, 1985

Dear Laura,

Thank you for sending LUPUS NOVICE (which by confusion sat in the office 3 weeks before I discovered it). I have read it thoroughly and I think it's wonderful. Strange thing but I feel like you're an old friend now, a sudden new old friend. I was with you all the way, and I felt like you never let me/you/us down. I'm speaking on the level of writing and book-making, but in this curious and original sort of book there's no way of separating that from the human reality and the level of spirit-manifestation. I felt the actuality of the healing process coterminous with the writing; I sense how they got inside each other. I was proud of you—not exactly a very familiar feeling for me in the sense I mean it. It may have moved a mountain or two in me, or at least told those mountains not to get too set in their ways. I wouldn't have missed it for the world.

Beyond that I think you've done something important, which is to say, uniquely useful. I want to publish it.

Best,
George Quasha

Note: This is from George Quasha's letter of acceptance of Lupus Novice. *He is the publisher of Station Hill Press and Barrytown, Ltd., and, as poet, the author of* Ainu Dreams *and other books of poetry.*

A Short Glossary of Special Terms

[*Publisher's Note:* We have compiled this informal glossary to help the reader orient her/himself in what are intrinsically confusing medical issues. The author's experience testifies to the difficulty in "naming" the phenomenon of lupus, and by implication all general description of "disease" is called into question. A glossary will tend to reflect conventional medical opinion. Our sources for medical terms here are generally the most common ones: *Dorland's Illustrated Medical Dictionary*, 26th Edition, W.B. Sauders, Philadelphia, 1974; *Webster's Third*; and *The American Heritage Dictionary*. Note that we omit *lupus, SLE*, etc., in order not to compound the presumption of definition. For more technical descriptions see, under "Related Further Reading," *The Merck Manual* and the *Primer on the Rheumatic Diseases*, among others. —George Quasha]

ACUPUNCTURE: "a therapy used for the prevention of disease or for the maintenance of health. The practice consists of either stimulating or dispersing the flow of energy within the body by the insertion of needles into specific points on the surface of the skin, by applying heat (thermal therapy), by pressing, by massage, or by a combination of these. Acupuncture was developed by the Chinese, and its origins date back almost 6000 years." (Dr. S.T. Chang, *The Complete Book of Acupuncture*)

ACUTE: (when referring to a pathologic process) having a sudden onset, sharp rise, and short duration: e.g., an acute disease or inflammation.

ALBUMINURIA: the presence of albumin (protein) in the urine, usually a symptom of disease of the kidneys but sometimes a response to other diseases or physiologic disturbances of benign nature.

ALLOPATHIC MEDICINE: therapy with remedies that produce effects different from those of the disease treated—currently the predominant system of Western medicine. Samuel Hahnemann (1755-1843), founder of Homeopathy (see below), coined "allopathic" from Greek roots ("other than the disease") "because he felt [allopathic medicine] prescribed drugs on the basis of no consistent or logical relationship to symptoms." (See Andrew Weil, M.D., *Health and Healing*.) Allopaths organized the American Medical Association in 1846 to combat homeopathy, and, unable to get rid of the name "allopathy," perpetrated a false derivation from German roots meaning "all therapies."

ANALGESIC: a medication that reduces or eliminates pain.

ANTIBODIES: various proteins in the blood that are generated in reaction to foreign proteins or polysaccharides and, neutralizing them, produce immunity against specific microorganisms or their toxins.

ANTIGEN: a substance that when introduced into the body stimulates the production of antibodies.

ANTI-INFLAMMATORY: an agent that counteracts or suppresses the inflammatory process.

ANTIMALARIAL: an agent such as Plaquenil that is therapeutically effective against malaria; also regarded as helpful in treating lupus.

ANTINUCLEAR ANTIBODIES (ANA): proteins in the blood that react with and are destructive to the nuclei of cells.

ARTHRALGIA: neuralgic pain in a joint.

ANTHROPOSOPHY: ("the wisdom of man") the philosophic system articulated by the Austrian, Rudolf Steiner (1861-1922), including a wide range of highly developed ideas and practices whose origins are both traditionary and original to Steiner. He is credited with many innovations in diverse areas, such as education (the Waldorf Schools), agriculture (biodynamic gardening), art therapy (Eurythmy), sociology (the Threefold Social Order), medicine (anthroposophical homeopathy), and "spiritual science." Owen Barfield says that anthroposophy "is not a theoretical system but a collection of the results of direct observation.... Whereas the findings of natural science are derived from observations made through the senses, the findings of spiritual science, anthroposophy, are 'occult' inasmuch as they derive from direct observation of those elements in man and the universe which both generate and underlie the sense world but are not themselves phenomenal in it." Steiner, who learned much from Goethe, sought to awaken consciousness to the interface between the physical and the spiritual.

ANTHROPOSOPHICAL MEDICINE: a mild yet effective variation of homeopathic medicine developed by Rudolf Steiner, which takes into account the body, soul and spirit of the individual and offers special strategies in the use of microdose remedies to address the three aspects of human physical organization.

ARTHRITIS: rheumatism in which the inflammatory lesions are confined to the joints.

AUTOIMMUNE: directed against the body's own tissues; autoimmune disease refers to any group of disorders in which tissue injury is associated with humoral or cell-mediated responses to the body's own constituents; they may be systemic (e.g., SLE, systemic lupus erythematosus) or organ specific (e.g., autoimmune thyroiditis).

BACH FLOWER REMEDIES: a special mild form of homeopthic medicine involving remedies derived from the essences of wild flowers, developed by Edward Bach.

BIOPSY: the removal and examination, usually microscopic, of tissue from the living body, for the purpose of precise diagnosis.

BUTTERFLY RASH: a reddish facial eruption over the bridge of the nose and cheeks, resembling a butterfly in form.

CHRONIC: persisting over a long period of time, or with recurring flare-ups.

COLLAGEN: the main supportive protein substance of the white fibers (collagenous fibers) of the skin, tendon, bone, cartilage, and all other connective tissue.

COMPLEMENT: a complex series of enzymatic proteins in the blood which are consumed in antigen-antibody reactions.

CORTICOSTEROID: any of the steroids produced by the adrenal cortex (except the sex hormones of adrenal origin); also their synthetic equivalents.

CORTISONE: refers mainly to one of the early synthetic corticosteroids, also called steroids, including cortisone, hydrocortisone, prednisone, prednisolone, methylprednisone, triamcinolone, dexamethasone, paramethasone, betamethasone, and fluprednisolone.

CURATIVE EURYTHMY: a special use of Eurythmy (see below) that prescribes specific movements suited to a particular problem or disease, aiming to harmonize the processes of human anatomy and physiology and their relation to non-physical aspects of being.

DISCOID LE: lupus erythematosis affecting mainly the skin.

DNA (deoxyribonucleic acid): the protein material in all cells of the body that carries genetic information.

ERYTHEMATOSIS: redness of the skin produced by congestion of the capillaries.

EURYTHMY: an art form and a science developed by Rudolf Steiner, where precisely choreographed movements embody the formative power inherent in speech; a physical and spiritual practice in the context of Anthroposophy (see above) and an art therapy.

EXACERBATION: flare-up or reappearance of symptoms.

FALSE-POSITIVE SEROLOGIC TEST FOR SYPHILLIS: falsely diagnosed results of a standard test for syphillis, due to the presence of an antibody that shows up with that disease and coincidentally in many cases of SLE.

FANA TEST: fluorescent antinuclear antibody test. A method of demonstrating antibodies which might be directed toward the nuclear materials in a patient's own cells, in the blood. The test is positive in more that 90% of people having SLE, but also may be positive in other diseases as well as in normal people.

FLARE: reappearance of symptoms of a disease, exacerbation.

HOMEOPATHY: (meaning "like the disease," from Greek roots; cf. "Allopathic," above) a system of medical treatment based on the Law of Similars ("like cures like"): "A substance that produces a certain set of symptoms in a healthy person has the power to cure a sick person manifesting those same symptoms." It was developed by Samuel Hahnemann (1755-1843) around 1810 through a practice of "provings" (testing the effects of specific substances, initially on oneself), who produced a "materia medica" or body of known and tested substances that serve as remedies.

HEMOGLOBIN: the oxygen-bearing, iron-containing protein in red blood cells.

INFLAMMATION: localized heat, redness, swelling, and pain as a result of irritation, injury, or infection; a protective response to destruction of tissue.

INTERNIST: a physician who specializes in the diagnosis and medical (as opposed to surgical and obstetrical) treatment of diseases of adults.

LE CELL: a specific cell found in blood specimens in 60-90% of patients with SLE and much less often in patients with closely related diseases.

LUPUS VULGARIS: The most common and severe form of tuberculosis of the skin: not related to SLE.

MONOCLONAL: derived from a single cell; pertaining to a single clone.

ORTHO-BIONOMY: a system of bodywork developed by Dr. Arthur Pauls, which helps bring about a profound release of stress, tension and pain.

PLEURISY: inflammation of the lining of the cavity containing the lungs.

PREDNISONE: a synthetic corticosteroid (see Cortisone, above).

PROTEINURIA: the presence of an excess of serum proteins in the urine.

PSYCHOSYNTHESIS: a form of therapy, founded by the Italian psychiatrist Roberto Assagioli, which ultimately aims for a unitive experience in which all polarities and contradictions within the personality are resolved through the higher or transpersonal self.

REMISSION: the condition of being free from the symptoms of a disease but not necessarily being cured.

RHEUMATOID ARTHRITIS: a chronic systemic disease of the joints marked by inflammtory changes in the joint lining membranes which may have a positive LE cell and ANA tests; the cause is unknown but auto-immune mechanisms and virus infection have been postulated.

RHEUMATOLOGIST: an internist who specializes in rheumatic diseases.

SEDIMENTATION RATE: a test which measures the precipitation of red cells in a column of blood. A high rate usually correlates with disease activity. In SLE, however, it may be persistently elevated.

SERUM: clear liquid portion of the blood.

STEROIDS: usually a short term for corticosteroids (see above), anti-inflammatory hormones (natural or synthetic) derived from the adrenal cortex.

SYSTEMIC: pertaining to or affecting the body as a whole.

URINALYSIS: analysis of urine.

WBC: white blood cell count.

Related Further Reading

Aladjem, Henrietta, *The Sun Is My Enemy*, out of print, Scribners, New York, 1985.

_____ "Psychosocial Aspects of a Rheumatic Disease—A Patient Speaks," see below Rodnan, *Primer*.

Amren, D.P. Ed., *Lupus And You: A Guide for Patients*, St. Louis Park Medical Center Research Foundation, 5000 West 39th Street, St. Louis Park, MN 55426.

Assagioli, R.A., *Psychosynthesis: A Manual of Principles and Techniques*, Hobbs-Dorman, New York, 1965; Penguin, Baltimore, 1976.

Bach, Edward, *The Bach Flower Remedies*, Keats Publishing, New Canaan, CN, 1931.

Berkeley Holistic Health Center, *The Holistic Health Handbook*, And/Or Press, Berkeley, 1978.

Blau, Sheldon Paul, M.D., and Dodi Schultz, *Lupus: The Body Against Itself*, Doubleday and Company, Garden City, NY, 1977.

Bott, Victor, *Anthroposophical Medicine*, translated by F.L. Wheaton and G. Douch, Rudolf Steiner Press, London, 1978.

Buhler, Walther, *Living With Your Body*, Pharos Books, Rudolf Steiner Press, London, 1979.

Chang, Dr. Stephen Thomas, *The Complete Book of Acupuncture*, Celestial Arts, Berkeley, 1976.

Cousins, Norman, *Anatomy Of An Illness as Perceived by the Patient*, W.W. Norton, New York, 1979; Bantam, New York, 1981.

Coulter, Harris L., *Homeopathic Science and Modern Medicine: The Physics of Healing with Microdoses*, North Atlantic Books, Berkeley, 1980.

Crampton, Martha, *Psychosynthesis: Some Key Aspects of Theory and Practice*, Canadian Institute of Psychosynthesis, Inc., 3496 Marlowe Ave., Montreal, Quebec, Canada, H4A 317, 1977.

Dubois, E.L. Ed., *Information for Patients with Lupus Erythematosus*, American Lupus Society, 23751 Madison St., Torrance CA 90505.

_____*Lupus Erythematosus, A Review of the Current Status of Discoid and Systemic Lupus Erythematosus and Their Variants*, 2nd Ed., University of Southern California Press, Los Angeles, 1976.

Fullerson, Mary C., *By a New and Living Way*, Vincent Stuart Publishers, 45 Lower Belgrade Street, London SW1, England 1963.

Gerson, Max, M.D., *A Cancer Therapy: Results of Fifty Cases*, Totality Books, Del Mar, CA, Distributed by The Gerson Institute, 1977.

Grossinger, Richard, *Planet Medicine: from Stone Age Shamanism to Post-Industrial Healing*, North Atlantic Books, Berkeley, 1982/rev. 1987.

Hahnemann, Samuel, *The Chronic Disease, Their Peculiar Nature and Their Homeopathic Cure,* translated from the 2nd enlarged German edition of 1835 by Louis H. Tafel, Boericke & Tafel, Philadelphia, 1904.

Haserick, J.R., and R.E. Kellum,: *Primer on Lupus Erythematosus . . . for Patients,* Pinehurst Medical Center, Pinehurst, NC 28374, 1973.

Husemann, Friedrich, M.D., *The Image of Man as the Basis of the Art of Healing,* The Mercury Press, Spring Valley, NY. See Juhan on copy.

Kushner, Harold S., *When Bad Things Happen to Good People,* Shocken Books, New York, 1981.

Lievegood, B.C.J., M.D., "Rudolph Steiner's Medical Impulse," *Weleda News* Spring Valley, NY, Number 1, 1980.

Mann, Felix, *Acupuncture: The Ancient Chinese Art of Healing and How it Works Scientifically,* Random House, New York, 1973.

The Merck Manual of Diagnosis and Therapy, Merck Sharp & Dohme Research Laboratories, Rahway, NJ 1982.

O'Connor, Flannery, *The Habit Of Being: Letters of Flannery O'Connor,* Farrar, Straus & Giroux, New York, 1979.

———*Everything That Rises Must Converge,* Farrar, Straus & Giroux, New York, 1965.

———*A Good Man is Hard to Find,* Harcourt Brace, New York, 1955.

Rodnan, Gerald P., M.D., and H. Ralph Schumacher, M.D., Editors, *Primer on the Rheumatic Diseases,* Eighth Edition, The Arthritis Foundation, Atlanta, 1983.

Siegel, Bernie S., M.D., *Love, Medicine, & Miracles: Lessons Learned About Self-Healing from a Surgeon's Experience with Exceptional Patients,* Harper & Row, New York, 1986.

Sontag, Susan, *Illness as Metaphor,* Vintage Books, Random House, New York, 1977.

Steiner, Rudolf, *The Case for Anthroposophy,* translated, arranged and with an Introduction by Owen Barfield, Rudolf Steiner Press, London, 1970.

———*Spiritual Science and Medicine,* Rudolf Steiner Press, London, 1975.

——— *What Can the Art of Healing Gain Through Spiritual Science,* The Mercury Press, The Fellowship Community, 241 Hungry Hollow Road, Spring Valley, NY, 10977, 1924.

———and Ita Wegman, *Fundamentals of Therapy,* Rudolf Steiner Press, London, 1967.

Tillich, Paul, *The Meaning of Health: The Relation of Religion and Health,* North Atlantic Books, Berkeley, 1981.

Trager, Milton, M.D., and Cathy Guadagno, Ph.D., *Trager Mentastics: Movement as a Way to Agelessness,* Station Hill Press, Barrytown, NY, 1987.

Wallace, Amy & Bill Henkin, *The Psychic Healing Book*, Wingbow Press, Berkeley, 1978.

Weil, Andrew, M.D., *Health and Healing: Understanding Conventional and Alternative Medicine*, Houghton Mifflin, Boston, 1983.

Wolff, Otto, M.D., "The Threefold Nature of Man as the Basis for an Extended Art of Healing," *Weleda News*, Spring Valley, NY, Number 1, 1980.

_____*Anthroposophically Oriented Medicine and its Remedies*, The Mercury Press, Spring Valley, NY, Number 1, 1980.

Whitmont, Edward, *Psyche and Substance: Essays on Homeopathy in The Light of Jungian Psychology*, North Atlantic Books, Berkeley, 1979.

Further Sources of Information

ANTHROPOSOPHIC PRESS
3390 Rt. 9
Hudson, NY 12534

THE AMERICAN LUPUS SOCIETY
23751 Madison St.
Torrance, CA 90505

THE BERKSHIRE CENTER FOR
PSYCHOSYNTHESIS
P.O. Box 152
Monterey, MA 01245

THE GERSON INSTITUTE
P.O. Box 430
Bonita, CA 91910

HOMEOPATHIC EDUCATION SERVICES
2124 Kittredge St.
Berkeley, CA 94704

LONNY JARRETT, Acupuncturist
Stockbridge Health Center
P.O. Box 1093
Stockbridge, MA 01262
(413) 298 4221

THE LUPUS FOUNDATION OF AMERICA, INC.
11921A Olive Blvd.
St. Louis, MO 63141

LUPUS NEWS
Henrietta Aladjem, editor
111 Pleasant St., Apt. 27
Watertown, MA 02172

OHANA HEALTH CENTER
Zoee Cramer, Ortho-Bionomist
63-D Wailani St.
Wailuku, HI 26793

THE PSYCHOSYNTHESIS INSTITUTE
3352 Sacramento St.
San Francisco, CA 94117

VERONICA REIF, Curative Eurythmist
2923 Florence St., #303
Berkeley, CA 94705

ST. GEORGE'S PRESS
Box 225
Spring Valley, NY 10977

SAN RAFAEL PHARMACY
7957 California Ave.
Fair Oaks, California 95628
(916) 962 1099

SCHOOL OF EURYTHMY
285 Hungry Hollow Rd.
Spring Valley, NY 10977

SOLSTICE PHARMACY, an outlet for
vitamins and minerals
(800) 765 7842

DR. JESSE STOFF, M.D., SOLSTICE
2122 N. Craycroft Avenue
Tucson, Arizona 87512
(520) 290 4516

WELEDA PHARMACY
6 Red Schoolhouse Road
Spring Valley, N.Y. 10977
(914) 352 6165

PENELOPE YOUNG, L.C.S.W.
San Diego Center
for Psychosynthesis
(619) 576 9046

About the Author

LAURA CHESTER has been writing, editing and publishing numerous volumes of poetry, fiction and non-fiction for over twenty-five years. Her most recent books include a short story collection, *Bitches Ride Alone*, Black Sparrow Press; and a novel, *The Story of the Lake*, Faber & Faber. She has edited several important anthologies, *Deep Down, New Sensual Writing by Women*, Faber and Faber, and *The Unmade Bed, New Sensual Writing on Married Love*, HarperCollins. Recently she has been working on another non-fiction book with the photographer Donna DeMari: *Holy Personal, A pilgrimage to small private chapels in the United States*. Having grown up in Oconomowoc and Milwaukee, Wisconsin, she now lives with her husband, Mason Rose, in the Berkshires of Massachusetts.

Other Books by Laura Chester

Nightlatch, prose poems, The Tribal Press, 1974

Primagravida, nonfiction, Christopher's Books, 1975

Chunk Off & Float, poetry, Cold Mountain Press, 1978

Watermark, a novel, The Figures, 1978

Proud & Ashamed, poetry, Christopher's Books, 1978

My Pleasure, voice pieces, The Figures, 1980

Lupus Novice, nonfiction, Station Hill Press, 1987

Free Rein, prose poems, Burning Deck Press, 1988

In the Zone, selected writing, Black Sparrow Press, 1988

The Stone Baby, a novel, Black Sparrow Press, 1989

Bitches Ride Alone, short stories, Black Sparrow Press, 1991

The Story of the Lake, a novel, Faber & Faber, 1995

Kingdom Come, a novel, forthcoming

Rising Tides, 20th Century American Women Poets, Simon & Schuster, 1973

Deep Down, New Sensual Writing by Women, Faber & Faber, 1988

Cradle & All, Women Writers on Pregnancy and Birth, Faber & Faber, 1989

The Unmade Bed, Sensual Writing on Married Love, HarperCollins, 1992